PRAISE FOR
THE FAITH OF JESUS

"Nash make so many great connections between and among things—putting things together rather than breaking them apart. He offers a great blend of the scholarly and pastoral, the intellectual and personal, in his reflections, and I think it works wonderfully. The appendix is a helpful complement to the book as a whole.

"I can really see this book being used by individuals and communities who want to read along with their pastors and the liturgical year, for insight, spiritual edification, and faith development. What a great gift to the Christian community!"

—Dan Cowdin, Salve Regina University,
Chair of Religious and Theological Studies

"As a preacher and pastor, I see all kinds of potential uses for this book. It could be used for Bible study, for small group discussions, or for personal devotions. However, personally, I would use it as a resource for preaching. As he discusses the assigned biblical texts for each week, Jim [Nash] conversationally engages the reader with questions, personal stories, insights on the text from scholars, new ideas, church year connections, word study, and present-day illustrations. All of which is helpful as a preacher prepares their sermon. This will be a useful resource for any preacher as well as for others interested in what the Bible says for us today."

—Duane Paetznick, Pastor of twenty-seven years,
Evangelical Lutheran Church in America (ELCA)

"Reading the reflections from *The Faith of Jesus* helps to center my mind on the words of God and makes me excited to listen to what my parish priest has to say about the same verses. Now when I go to Mass, I experience the Gospel and my parish priest's homily much better. This is my new Sunday routine."

—Milena Kupczyk—Zielona Góra, Poland

The Faith of Jesus
Questions from the 21st Century
by James Nash

© Copyright 2023 James Nash

ISBN 978-1-64663-876-5

All rights reserved. No part of this publication may be reproduced, stored in a retrieval system, or transmitted in any form or by any means—electronic, mechanical, photocopy, recording, or any other—except for brief quotations in printed reviews, without the prior written permission of the author.

Published by

3705 Shore Drive
Virginia Beach, VA 23455
800-435-4811
www.koehlerbooks.com

the

FAITH

of

JESUS

Questions from the 21st Century

JAMES NASH

VIRGINIA BEACH
CAPE CHARLES

Dedicated to the guests of the Cathedral of
Saint Matthew's Monday Morning Program
For helping us all to live in the spirit of the beatitudes:
humble, joyful and merciful.

And to Paul Desjardins
Teacher, mentor, and friend,
who showed me the way when I was lost.

TABLE OF CONTENTS

Author's Note 1

Introduction 2

First Sunday of Advent 11

Second Sunday of Advent 17

Third Sunday of Advent 24

Fourth Sunday of Advent 29

Christmas Mass at Midnight 33

Feast of the Holy Family 37

Feast of the Epiphany 43

Baptism of the Lord 47

Second Sunday Ordinary Time 52

Third Sunday Ordinary Time 54

Fourth Sunday Ordinary Time 60

Fifth Sunday Ordinary Time 67

Sixth Sunday Ordinary Time 71

Seventh Sunday Ordinary Time 78

Ash Wednesday	87
First Sunday of Lent	94
Second Sunday of Lent	101
Third Sunday of Lent	104
Fourth Sunday of Lent	108
Fifth Sunday of Lent	110
Passion Sunday	115
Easter Sunday—Vigil	122
Second Sunday of Easter	127
Third Sunday of Easter	130
Fourth Sunday of Easter	136
Fifth Sunday of Easter	141
Sixth Sunday of Easter	145
Ascension Sunday	150
Pentecost	154
Trinity Sunday	158
Corpus Christi	163
Twelfth Sunday Ordinary Time	169

Thirteenth Sunday Ordinary Time ... 177

Fourteenth Sunday Ordinary Time ... 182

Fifteenth Sunday Ordinary Time ... 188

Sixteenth Sunday Ordinary Time ... 194

Seventeenth Sunday Ordinary Time ... 200

Eighteenth Sunday Ordinary Time ... 205

Nineteenth Sunday Ordinary Time ... 210

Twentieth Sunday Ordinary Time ... 216

Twenty-First Sunday Ordinary Time ... 220

Twenty-Second Sunday Ordinary Time ... 225

Twenty-Third Sunday Ordinary Time ... 229

Twenty-Fourth Sunday Ordinary Time ... 234

Twenty-Fifth Sunday Ordinary Time ... 240

Twenty-Sixth Sunday Ordinary Time ... 244

Twenty-Seventh Sunday Ordinary Time ... 247

Twenty-Eighth Sunday Ordinary Time ... 253

Twenty-Ninth Sunday Ordinary Time ... 258

Thirtieth Sunday Ordinary Time ... 264

All Saints ... 272

Thirty-Second Sunday Ordinary Time ... 273

Thirty-Third Sunday Ordinary Time ... 278

Christ the King ... 284

Abbreviations ... 291

Appendix A ... 292

Appendix B ... 305

Appendix C ... 312

Bibliography ... 322

Endnotes ... 322

AUTHOR'S NOTE

APPENDICES A. B. AND C are found at the end of this book. Appendixes D, E, and F have been placed on my website and can be found by going to: thefaithofjesusbook.com/appendices

INTRODUCTION

The Faith of Jesus: Meditations on the Lectionary
(Year A 2019–2020)

THIS BOOK GREW from two different yet connected life-changing experiences.

Most immediately, these reflections flow from discussions of the Sunday gospel reading I led for years at the Cathedral of St. Matthew the Apostle in Washington, DC. We have a Monday-morning program that serves breakfast and lunch and offers clothes to those in need. After everyone has eaten and received whatever else we have for them, anyone who wants to, both guests and volunteers, is invited to stay for an hour to discuss the gospel passage read at Mass the previous day.

I received a PhD in moral theology from the Catholic University of America in 1990, and as soon as I graduated, I taught there for a few years. In fact, I spent the first half of my life teaching in high schools and colleges; I later worked as a journalist. When I retired in 2012, I used my teaching experience and brought a degree of "scholarly apparatus" to the table at these Monday-morning programs. Of course, our discussions were quite different from the classes I taught at Catholic University—and I loved that!

I learned a lot from these gatherings through the years, both from our guests—many of whom are unhoused people of color from the US as well as immigrants—and our mostly White, middle-class volunteers. Because so many of our guests spoke only Spanish, and since I am bilingual, everything we said was translated into both languages.

We stopped serving our guests inside the cathedral in March 2020 because of the pandemic, and our discussions ended then too. Although we continued to offer food and clothes outside, we are an urban parish, and there was no quiet, safe place to hold the discussions outdoors.

One spiritual benefit of the pandemic was to reveal what matters most for us. The end of these weekly discussions was one of my most sorrowful losses. Yet, to paraphrase John Millbank, like an expert tennis player, God finds a way to return even the toughest shot, hit it back over the net, and keep the game going. Sometime in the summer of 2020, I finally heard the Spirit whisper in my ear, "You cannot discuss the gospel with your friends any longer. You have tons of time now to spend in your home. So why don't you try to write something similar in their absence? I will help you." So, with the Holy Spirit's help, I started writing.

The voices of my very diverse gospel-discussing friends inform everything you will read here. I do not quote anyone directly, and obviously the responsibility for what I have written belongs to me. But I hope I have remained faithful to the spirit of what I learned from them: their questions, their insights, their problems.

I am certain I have been faithful to the method we used to dig into the meaning of these texts as it relates to those of us who are living today in our nation's capital. Each week, I would begin the discussion with a little background on the gospel reading: often the meaning of a Greek word whose translation into English or Spanish I questioned; other times an issue of historical or theological context. The background was usually important to frame the real heart of our discussion: questions.

Every week, the gospel passage presented me with several questions I wanted to explore with our guests and volunteers. The same kinds of questions frame what I have written here about the Sunday readings. After a while, our guests and volunteers got the hang of it and began to ask their own questions, and we would try to answer theirs as well as mine.

I have come to believe that questions are sacred starting points in our lifelong quest for God and meaning. I have some solid support for this view. After all, St. Thomas Aquinas's entire *Summa Theologica* is a series of questions he proceeds to answer. Twentieth-century German philosopher Martin Heidegger wrote, "Questioning is the piety of thought."

The second source for these reflections lies at the beginning of my adult life when I was a student at Haverford College: my beloved, long-gone mentor Paul Desjardins. Paul was a philosophy professor who specialized in Plato and the pre-Socratics. He tried to live the life of a modern-day Socrates. Like Socrates, he questioned everyone, at any time. Paul was also a Catholic, and he invited undergraduates to join him Sunday mornings for Mass at a local parish and then to return to his house for coffee, bread, and a discussion of the readings for that Sunday.

Regular exposure to the way Paul's mind worked was a privilege that has fed my soul to this day. He changed the way I thought, the way I looked at the Bible, the way I related to other people, and the way I looked at the "things" of nature and culture. I can best explain by example.

Paul's favorite story from the gospels was the Visitation (Luke 1:39–56), Mary's visit to her cousin Elizabeth. He loved the notion that as soon as Elizabeth heard Mary's voice, Elizabeth's unborn child "leapt in joy." This was, in a way, Paul's goal with everyone he met—to have his words and voice make the "unborn child" or the unborn promise we all carry inside us "leap for joy."

He did this often by using his uncanny ability to perceive who you were and what you were going through—often better than you yourself could. He might say to one person that he was "appetitive," or to another that she had "a lot of character," maybe because she went to Exeter. Somehow his insights into people stayed with me. He helped me to discover who I was inside and to understand others. I came to see that we are all struggling with certain unresolved questions, or even contradictions. An important goal in relationships with others is to try to discern these inner tensions and shed light on them.

Paul had a sacramental imagination. He saw the beauty and truth in things and in nature. I cannot look at a barn without thinking of him. I remember him talking about how important the pitch of the barn's roof is: the angle must be neither too obtuse nor too acute for the size of the barn. Otherwise, the barn will be "lacking in character."

His sacramental imagination re-enchanted the world for me, restoring much of the luster it had lost when I grew up. Seeing the sacredness inherent in things, the way they reflect the "Author of Beauty," changed my life. But this new enchantment was now placed within a broader theological and philosophical canvas, deepening its meaning and expanding the connections.

Paul taught philosophy, so of course he paid attention to the way our minds work and "what is meant by thinking," to paraphrase Heidegger. I think we tend to overrate analysis when we try to make sense of things. Analysts are what we call those who tell us what political or economic developments are supposed to mean. These people break things down so we can understand them. The assumption seems to be that by separating what has happened into little pieces, we will better understand reality.

Analysis has its place, but I would argue that making connections—piecing things together, painting a coherent vision of what has happened—is more important, and more difficult, in understanding anything. Paul's mind worked synthetically, not analytically. He was brilliant at making connections and weaving a web of meaning among such disparate phenomena as the pre-Socratic philosophers, Plato, the Bible, current politics,

Confucius, a Japanese tea ceremony, or his life growing up on a farm in Upstate New York.

I came to Haverford as a rather literal-minded young man searching for God and a reason why I should do something with my life. I was searching for truth, and what I learned from Paul was that the truth is not found in abstract conceptual ideas or principles, where I had been looking. The obvious logical, conceptual, and historical contradictions in the gospels frustrated me. I began to see that for Socrates, as for Jesus, truth is personal, relational, contextual; and it is often discovered by finding or making surprising, revealing connections. Like poetry. Or parables. Apparent contradictions may point to a deeper harmony. I also took formal philosophy courses from Paul. Gradually, I learned how to think.

I had been raised a Presbyterian, but a few years after college, I was ready to join the Catholic Church, in part thanks to Sunday mornings with Paul and the other students who joined the discussion.

In what follows, I have been guided by what we did with Paul during our Sunday-morning discussions of the Scripture readings we had just heard in church. We also began with questions and focused on the gospel reading. Paul usually attempted to connect the first reading from the Old Testament with the gospel; the lectionary is put together with this in mind. It is usually harder to see the relationship to the second reading, the epistle, and so I have generally not made the effort to do so.

My hope is that the faith of Jesus will serve as a bridge connecting the insights of biblical theological scholarship with questions the thoughtful layperson carries about how to understand what she hears in church and how to live a life faithful to the gospel.

The book is by design episodic but I hope not incoherent. Now that I have finished it, I can see at least two recurring themes.

One of them is an emphasis on the full humanity of Christ. Let me say a word about this at the beginning.

The great twentieth-century theologian Karl Rahner wrote that while the typical mistake of those outside the Church is to ignore or minimize Jesus's divine nature, the faithful are prone to the opposite error: a denial of Jesus's full human nature. My emphasis on Jesus's humanity is justified in part because I expect the primary audience for this book will be those who go to Mass regularly—that is, "the faithful."

As I explored St. Matthew's Jesus this year, however, I discovered that in many ways there need not be a "trade-off" between Jesus's humanity and divinity, as if by stressing his humanity, his divinity must be diminished.

One example of this is my view that as a human being, Jesus did not have knowledge of the future. This means that what he freely chose to go through in his passion rested solely on his total trust and surrender to God's will. That kind of faith is truly divine! If you maintain that Jesus's divine nature meant he knew God would raise him on the third day, his passion is far less powerful. Both his divinity and his humanity are diminished.

In all four gospels, Jesus repeatedly stresses the importance of faith to fulfill the Great Commandment to love God and neighbor as yourself. But if Jesus knew exactly what would happen in the historical future, he would have no need for faith, no experience of it. In this case, he would literally not know what he is talking about! Such a Jesus would have little credibility for me when telling me I need to have faith and trust in God.

Perhaps the story of Jesus's baptism by John makes this point even more clearly. It is one of the few events recorded in some form by all four evangelists. It is almost certainly historical, as by the time the gospels were written, Jesus's sinlessness and divinity were established as articles of faith. No one would make this story up because Jesus's baptism was an embarrassment for the early Church. John's baptism was for repentance: why would the sinless God-man need to repent?

The question is, did Jesus know he would remain sinless throughout his life? I believe the answer must be no. Not only is it not human to know the future, but Jesus tells us it is humility and watchfulness that protects us from sin and temptation. "Knowing" I am incapable of sin would be the opposite of that. It also would make Jesus's baptism and later temptation in the desert a charade.

There is explicit scriptural support for the notion that Jesus lacked divine omniscience about the historical future and needed to figure things out little by little, just as we do, as suggested when Luke says, "And Jesus progressed in wisdom and age and favor before God and men" (Luke 2:52).

St. Paul's famous description of kenosis, or the self-emptying of Jesus before he took human form, adds further support to the idea that we should conceive of Jesus's mind, learning, and need for education as akin to our own: "Be of that mind in yourselves that was also in Christ Jesus, who, though he was in the form of God, did not count equality with God a thing to be grasped, *but emptied himself*, taking the form of a servant, being born in the likeness of men" (Philippians 2:5–7, emphasis added).

Most important of all, Jesus's humble desire to be baptized reveals the loving Holy Trinity, as God the Father calls him "beloved son" and the Holy Spirit descends on him like a dove. It is precisely when Jesus shows himself to be most humbly human, accepting John's baptism, that he is clearly embraced within the loving unity of the Holy Trinity. Rather than demonstrating tension between Jesus's full humanity and his full participation inside the Godhead, Jesus's humble human action seems to spark the Holy Trinity to begin firing on all cylinders! It is the clearest revelation of the Holy Trinity in the Bible.

In addition to the Passion and Resurrection and his extraordinary teaching, Jesus's miracles were, and are, powerful signs that he was the Son of God. As we will see, these signs depended upon his faith and the faith of those he healed. I believe, therefore, that Jesus's divinity is deeply intertwined with his extraordinary faith. This is one reason the book is entitled *The Faith of Jesus*.

Although in some ways I see myself as "a recovering moral theologian," allow me to put on my moral theologian's hat for a moment. As the God-man, Jesus is our maker's message to us humans: *This is what I created you to do, to be like.* To put it into crudely consumerist terms, we could see Jesus as an analog to an "owner's manual," a way of showing us how to use the purchased product. If we want to be in harmony with the nature the Creator has given us, we need to look to God's Son, Jesus. This is another way to see how Jesus's full humanity and full divinity are both necessary for our salvation, and not in conflict.

Another unifying theme in these weekly reflections is Jesus's consistent revelation of both what it means to live a life that is truly open to the present reality and a transcendent way of living in this present.

What I learned from my Monday-morning friends is that we all are hungry for meaning. Yet we cannot explain the ultimate meaning and purpose of our life in this world from within the confines of this world. This world can be understood and explained only by means of a perspective that both exists inside it and transcends it. This is what Jesus, the God-man, does for us.

I hope that in what follows, the Jesus of St. Matthew will come alive to shed his light on your life and your search for its meaning.

Finally, I want to offer an apology and a bit of advice to readers. What follows is all "positive," or cataphatic, theology. It assumes we can know God by means of words, the use of our minds, and ends with propositions about God. Well and good; this is almost required if we are to take Scripture seriously. Jesus commands us, after all, "to love God with all our mind."

But by itself, this way of trying to know and love God is unbalanced and doomed to failure. Why? The unknown author of *The Cloud of Unknowing* tells us, "Because God may well be loved, but not thought. By love he can be caught and held, but by thinking never."[1]

The anonymous author of this fourteenth-century mystical classic is a firm believer in apophatic, or "negative," theology: God is unknowable mystery. We can only come close to God by forgetting everything we know; the way we can reach God is through the centering prayer of wordless, longing love.

I see no reason why we need to choose between positive or negative theology. Both have value. Because this book is so heavily tilted toward the cataphatic way, however, I strongly recommend you read appendix C, the final appendix article in this book. Ideally, you would read it as soon as you finish this introduction! It will serve to balance and make real everything that lies in between.

In this article I try to explain how to do the kind of regular, centering prayer *The Cloud of Unknowing* believes is essential if we are to love God and experience God's love for us. Without this concrete experience, I fear that the reflections in this book will end up as "more words, mere words." After completing arguably the greatest work of positive theology ever written, *Summa Theologica*, St. Thomas Aquinas had a mystical experience. Afterwards, he reportedly called everything he had written "straw" in comparison to what he had experienced.

Loving and knowing God aright is a chord, and if we are to do well the job we are created for, we must strive to strike all the notes of that chord. One of those notes, I am convinced, flows from the wordless-longing love prayer so beautifully described in *The Cloud of Unknowing*, and which I attempt to summarize and urge upon you in appendix C.

FIRST SUNDAY OF ADVENT

Isaiah 2:1–5
Romans 13:11–14
Matthew 24:37–44

WHAT DOES JESUS mean by "stay awake" or "watch"? Obviously, he cannot mean we should never go to sleep. The Greek word St. Matthew uses here is *grēgoreīte*. It can be translated as "stay awake, alert, and vigilant," or "to watch, to be awake."[2] It also has a metaphorical connotation: to be alive.

We can read this as a warning. We need to be watchful to prepare for a danger we cannot now perceive: the thief in verse 43 who will come in the night when we least expect it. If we are watchful, we will not let our houses be broken into.

The connection between "to watch" and "to be ready" is confirmed in verse 44 when Matthew uses *hetoimoi*, which David Bentley Hart translates as "to be ready."[3] We are to stay awake and vigilant, and to be ready for an unseen, unknown danger that will come at an unknown time. What is this danger?

One danger is that we "sleep-walk" through life, unaware of the spiritual possibilities—and temptations—that surround us. The biggest danger I fear is death and God's judgment of me. Am I prepared for that? This is the time of year to think and pray about it as Jesus and the season of Advent ask us to prepare for this scary but unavoidable reality. We know we will die, but like the thief in the night, we don't know when it will come upon us. Because we don't like to think about this unpleasant truth, it can be easy to forget about it.

The New Jerusalem Bible Commentary[4] says watchfulness means "eschatological alertness to the will of God." I like the idea of trying harder during Advent to be attuned to the will of God. What is distracting us? This time of year, in addition to all the parties and holiday "stuff," we have the long nights of seasonal depression, self-pity that we aren't as happy as we are "supposed" to be, thinking things should be a certain way when they are not, anxiety. For this reason, I embrace the secular substitution for "Christmas": I use the word "holiday" to mean the commercial-cultural residue left over when the spiritual meaning of Christmas has been eliminated. Advent is inviting us to let go of all that junk so we can focus on preparing to meet the Savior of the world. What a relief!

How do we prepare for death and judgment? I think the last reading of this Church year, in which Jesus describes the Last Judgment, sheds light on this, the first reading.

We won't get to it until the end of November, but in Matthew 25:31–46, Jesus describes the Last Judgment when the Son of Man returns in power and glory. This passage comes almost right after the one we read this week; both have to do with the end time. The Son of Man tells the sheep on his right hand, "Come, you who are blessed by my Father, inherit the kingdom prepared for you from the foundation of the world." And what did the blessed do to deserve this joyous blessing? They clothed the naked, fed the hungry; they cared for the needy, and in doing so, Jesus tells them, they cared for him! The goats on his left hand did nothing for the poor, and they are promised a punishing future.

All too often, Advent is seen only as a time of preparation for Christmas. I learned from Thomas Merton that St. Bernard of Clairvaux believed this may keep us too focused on our current lives in the flesh. Bernard speaks of three Advents. The first is the birth of Jesus, the Savior of the world, which we celebrate at Christmas. The second is the presence of Christ in our lives right now, and one example of this would be that passage from Matthew 25:313–46: our recognition of Christ in the needs of the poor and meeting those needs now. The third Advent is when he comes again in power and glory to judge us and everyone at the end of time.

The three Advents are connected. I am suggesting we prepare for the third Advent of judgment by serving now the Jesus present in the needy. Clearing space and time in our souls so we are ready to meet the birth of Jesus at Christmas will make it easier to recognize the Christ already present inside of ourselves and others.

Staying alert and being prepared means watching for all three Advents. It also means paying attention to those habits of mind and body that distract us from them. Like "Christmas" parties. I put Christmas in quotes because these parties are usually celebrated during Advent and have little to do with Christmas.

We sometimes hear in the mainstream media about a supposed "war on Christmas." I would say the war on Christmas was lost by Christmas long ago: the commercial takeover happened well before I was born. I do, however, believe there is currently a war on Advent! Advent is not a time for frivolity, presents, and drinking bouts. We have too much to watch out for. That said, it is a cold and dark time of year; our spirits do long for some fun as well. How to navigate this perilous and often depressing season?

One way for Christians to resist the commercial exploitation of Christmas while preserving its spiritual values is to keep watch all through Advent and then let go with some fun and frivolity during the twelve days when it really is Christmas. True, we will have to pass on some holiday parties. Recall that in our reading this week, Jesus points out that people were "eating and drinking" in the days just before the flood killed them. Declining the party invitations can be a respectful way to be a witness to our faith. We can say, "I'm sorry, but I don't go out much during Advent. Let's get together when it's Christmas."

I write this during the pandemic year of 2020. We are being told by the secular authorities to stay home and avoid all large gatherings. That is a beautiful message for Advent.

If we slow down and embrace the silent darkness to make time and space for Jesus during Advent, he will help to fill the emptiness we are tempted to fill with parties, presents, and all the other excesses of the commercial Christmas. I have a book for Advent with daily prayers and short readings from the Bible and Thomas Merton.[5] I love it, but there are plenty of other books available. I also have a four-candle Advent holder, and I look forward every day to the moment when I turn off all the lights and light the candle(s) in my dark living room. Then I pray, read, sing, and play Advent hymns on my piano. Each week, we get to light another candle as we approach Christmas. Personal household rituals like this help fill the dark emptiness of the season, bringing a joy deeper than mere happiness. I now look forward to Advent.

One of the most depressing aspects of the secular "holiday season" for me is the obligation to feel a kind of mindless happiness. In fact, a sorrowfulness is built into our celebration of Christmas. We know that the baby whose birth we celebrate grew up to die a horrible, unjust death, tortured by the authorities, betrayed and abandoned by his friends, misunderstood by everyone.

The gospel that begins our church year has the same message as the one Jesus gave to his favorite three disciples near the end of his life when he was praying in agony at Gethsemane: watch! But they fell asleep on him. The candle I light does not eliminate the shadows; it sharpens them.

Many of us also have personal and emotional reasons for sadness this time of year. We might grieve anew for someone we loved who is no longer with us to celebrate the holidays. Is it just me, or does the Advent-Christmas season seem to invite us to tally up our many losses? Those of us who are old may recall with sadness the innocent joy bubbling inside us at Christmas as children. No matter our age, if we have some beautiful memories of past Christmases, we may mourn how distant that time now feels. It can be tempting to think that other people's families are far happier than ours. If we are lonely, Christmas will heighten it. And it's dark all the time.

For all these reasons, this time of year makes me so grateful for my faith in the Lord! God normally speaks to me, as he did to Elijah, in a "still small voice" (1 Kings 19:12). But it is as if God is now shouting at me, "This world is passing away! Focus on the eternal, you idiot!"

Culturally, Christmas seems to be all about kids and our lost childhood, but more importantly, in a spiritual sense, Advent-Christmas invites us to become childlike. In Advent we prepare to celebrate the birth of a child. Jesus said, "Truly, I say to you, unless you turn and become like children, you will never enter the kingdom of God" (Matthew 18:3).

What does it mean to be childlike? Jesus certainly meant we need to be humble, and that is a central motif of this season. The King of Kings is born as a little baby in a stable!

Another characteristic of children is that they are looking ahead with joyful anticipation rather than looking back in sorrow. Remember how as children we could not wait for Christmas to arrive? For an adult Christian, looking ahead means a joyful anticipation of meeting Jesus, whether at his second coming or when we die.

The first reading from Isaiah paints a beautiful picture of this future kingdom. I can't wait to see swords beaten into plowshares! Won't it be wonderful when wars are a thing of the past? It is easy to become depressed at the gap between the promises of the Christ we celebrate at Christmas and the sad reality of our fallen world.

However, we tend to be blind to the many ways our world is far, far better now than it was before Jesus was born, and blind also to the role the Holy Spirit of Jesus played in creating these improvements. To mention just a few advances: the status of women, children, slaves, and outcasts of all sorts, and the end of crucifixion and gladiatorial games where people paid to see wild beasts devour live human beings.

Still, we live in the "in-between time," between the promise and its complete fulfillment. That can depress us, but if we are truly confident in the third Advent, that Jesus will come again in glory, we have so much to look forward to that we can be like children awaiting Christmas, striving to be worthy of the gifts promised us.

I am not saying this is easy or that it comes naturally. We need God's help to feel it, to believe it, and to act on it. But this spiritual goal may be the greatest Christmas gift of all.

SECOND SUNDAY OF ADVENT

Isaiah 11:1–10
Romans 15:4–9
Matthew 3:1–12

WHAT IS REPENTANCE? Our gospel reading this week tells us to repent, but what does that mean? And why should we do it? Repentance doesn't sound like "good news" but rather some unpleasant duty.

This is one reason I prefer David Bentley Hart's translation of the New Testament. He translates verse 2 as "Change your hearts; for the Kingdom of the heavens has drawn near." Changing our heart is something we can all relate to because we see it happening to us and around us all the time. Sometimes it happens suddenly, and sometimes over a period of time. For example, I have had a gradual change of heart over my responsibility for global warming and the health of the environment. So now I compost leaves and kitchen waste, have installed solar panels, and ride my bike whenever I can rather than driving my car. Pope Francis has spoken of the necessity for an "ecological conversion."

We discover that repenting is not an unpleasant duty at all but a sign of growth, of living in the Spirit, once we understand the meaning of the Greek word we translate as "repent," *metanoeîte*. It is actually a compound of two words, *noéō*—to think, to have insight, to understand—and *meta*—afterwards, or later. To repent, then, is to have an insight when we consider our past. To change our minds about our past behavior is a sign of growth, even liberation from being stuck in destructive habits. In fact, I would say that not altering our understanding regularly about our behavior is a sign of being dead. This reminds me of what Soren Kierkegaard once wrote, paraphrased here: "Life is lived forward . . . but understood backward."

Changing our minds about our past behavior is the first step toward genuine repentance, but it is not enough, as the Baptist tells us in verse 8 of this passage in Matthew: "Bear fruit worthy of a change of heart." New insight about past actions is worthless if it does not lead to different behavior now.

The joy of repenting is that it shows we have faith that with God's help, we can change to live richer, more rewarding lives. It is the religious version of the secular New Year's resolution. I've always hated NYRs because of the assumption that we can and should fulfill these promises through sheer willpower; this never worked for me, and I ended up feeling worse than before. Based on what I hear about the many unused gym memberships starting in early January, I am not alone!

Repentance, on the other hand, is relational. It means we are allowing ourselves to be guided by the Holy Spirit of Jesus. If we learn how to listen, the Spirit will show us how we need to change our thinking and give us the strength to alter our behavior. We end up closer to God so that it is easier to listen, repent, and change in the future.

I've made the case for the joy of repentance. Still, it's not as much "fun" as walking in the park or having a drink with friends. Why would we feel called, or even compelled, to repent?

Because we are suffering. I am not referring to just any kind of suffering. I wouldn't see the need to repent if I were suffering from a serious illness, or from injustice. No! Jesus came in part to dispel the idea that God uses illness or misfortune to punish us (John 9:1–4).

The danger now lies elsewhere. We have reversed the

dynamic; rather than believing God is punishing us, now we blame and punish God when we suffer. This raises the question: where is God in our suffering? God can seem totally absent, indifferent, doing nothing to ease our pain. Therefore, either God does not exist, or if God does exist, God is not loving but cruel. And life itself is a cruel, meaningless joke.

I mentioned Soren Kierkegaard above, and he wrote an excellent essay on this subject: "The Joy in the Thought that in Relation to God a Man Always Suffers as Being Guilty."[6] I am convinced guilt has gotten a bad rap. So long as we know we will be forgiven, guilt is the engine of change in our lives and a sign of hope, not despair. Kierkegaard's essay reveals this.

If we are suffering spiritually, if we are in despair about the meaning of our lives or the value of life in general—and if we are honest, we all will feel this from time to time—we have two choices. We can conclude our hopelessness is appropriate: the universe is cold and indifferent to our predicament, and there is no such thing as a loving God who has counted the hairs on our heads (Matthew 10:30). Or we can conclude that we are wrong to be in such despair. We, not God, are the reason we are suffering spiritually—not physically. We are in the wrong to doubt that God is love. This guilt is joyful because now we realize there is an answer to our suffering! As Soren Kierkegaard writes in *The Gospel of Suffering*:

> IF, ACCORDING TO the assumption of the discourse, it is true that a man in relation to God always suffers as guilty, then this constitutes the joy: that the fault consequently lies in the man; that, as result of this, there must constantly be something to do, there must be tasks and yet also human task and along with the tasks the hope that everything can and will become better, when he becomes better, more industrious, more prayerful, more

obedient, more humble, more devoted, more sincere in his love, more ardent in spirit.[7]

I do not see how this shift from suffering despair to hope can happen without faith and repentance, and this is why Jesus so often talks about how important it is. Objectively, there are plenty of reasons to conclude there is no purpose to life as we know it. Especially this time of year! Check out the brilliant song by the rock band the Godfathers, "Birth, School, Work, Death." Everyone we have loved, everything we have done, will soon be dead and forgotten. What's the point of trying? If we go along with the dominant secular assumptions, we may feel trapped in the iron cage of this (immanent) world.

The only answer I know to the built-in futility of our natural life is one that transcends it. The Christian tradition holds that we would not have the longing for something that transcends this world unless God, who is transcendent, placed it there. As St. Augustine famously wrote, "Our hearts were made for you, O Lord, and they are ever restless until they rest in You."

I can suggest one more pathway to feel this joyful guilt: the example of Jesus. Excruciating suffering will come to all of us at one point or another. I have no doubt that it will not be greater than what Jesus endured: betrayal and abandonment by his best friends, public humiliation, torture, a long, agonizing death for a totally innocent, sinless man. Jesus endured this without cursing God! He did not even have the Kierkegaardian joy that comes from knowing that in relation to God, he suffers as one who is guilty. But that is because his suffering was primarily emotional-physical.

Jesus also faced spiritual temptation. He was tempted to renounce his mission and the suffering it entailed in the Garden of Gethsemane, but his faith survived the trial. If we are tempted to doubt God's love when we suffer less, and with more justification, than Jesus, that is another path toward joyful guilt.

Because Jesus could endure so much more than we will ever have to, without losing his faith, he points us to the easier route we can and must follow.

Still, it is not easy to remain faithful when great pain comes. I have seen more than one person lose her faith when this happens. I have been on the brink of it myself, although I probably have so far been spared the over-the-top kind of suffering I have witnessed others endure.

Spiritual temptation is a transcendent experience. The only real answer to it is a transcendent one: faith in a loving God. God did not answer Jesus's Gethsemane prayer for deliverance (Matthew 26:39) in this life. So why should we expect God to do so for us? God's answer, Jesus's resurrection, transcended this world. That is the basis for our hope that also transcends this world. We can get there by reconsidering our past, gaining insight, and changing our behavior. In other words, repentance.

Our passage raises another question that has long puzzled me. Why do we need John the Baptist when we have Jesus? John supposedly prepares us for the advent of Jesus, the Messiah. Matthew quotes Isaiah: "Prepare the way of the Lord, make straight his path." John says, "The one who is coming after me is mightier than I."

Why do we need John to prepare us for Jesus? Two thousand years after his birth, we are so used to Jesus that we have lost sight of what a shocking revolution he presented to everyone who knew him: *Love your enemies. Forgive everyone for everything. Embrace all "losers," especially the poor and sinners. Challenge all secular and religious authority, accept their punishment for doing so, but never resort to violence, even to defend yourself. Forget about money and status in this world. Lead by serving. Above all, trust in God.*

These commands are now familiar to us, but two thousand years later we still find it hard to follow them. Imagine how hard it was for people hearing this message for the first time! John the Baptist was necessary. But not sufficient.

Why does John say he is "unworthy to carry [Jesus's] sandals"? Why does Jesus say, as we will read next week in Matthew 11:11, "Truly, I say to you, among those born of woman there has risen no one greater than John the Baptist; yet he who is least in the kingdom of heaven is greater than he"?

Matthew's John preaches repentance, but he differs from the versions in the other gospels because Matthew's John does not connect repentance with forgiveness. This is one way John's message is inferior to Jesus's, but it's limited to Matthew. Like Jesus, John challenged religious authority, attacked injustice, and his popularity with the people alarmed the leaders. They eventually killed him, just as they did Jesus. John had no "home," just like Jesus, and when the people flocked to the wilderness to be baptized by John, they voted with their feet and rejected the Jerusalem Temple and all it stood for. Again, just like Jesus.

Another challenge John posed to the status quo was his universalism (Matthew 3:9). The prophets always understood God chose the Hebrews to be a light to the Gentiles, to all nations. God did not choose the Jews as a privileged, exclusive sect but rather to serve God's purposes. The history of salvation is one of ever-expanding growth. The Jewish leaders of Jesus's time had lost sight of this prophetic universalism; they tended to see the Law and Temple worship as their possession.

We see this prophetic universalism in our first reading at Isaiah 11:10. John reveals the Jewish leaders' blindness to this in verse 9: "And do not presume to say to yourselves, 'We have Abraham as our father,' for I tell you, God is able from these stones to raise up children from Abraham." This is a huge shift: religious faith is no longer tied to ethnicity.

What's missing in John's harsh, "Old Testament-ish" justice message, I believe, is Jesus's emphasis on mercy and love, as well as forgiveness. John can be seen as the last of the Old Testament prophets. His is an angry voice that speaks of judgment with threats of "unquenchable fire" and "the coming wrath."

I am not convinced the Bible definitively reveals there is a hell of eternal punishment (see appendix A). However, John the Baptist sometimes talks like he is certain many people are doomed to go there. This may be another reason why he is unworthy to carry Jesus's sandals.

Our passage from Isaiah is so beautiful that I want to close with it. Edward Hicks, a Quaker minister and artist, painted sixty-two pictures based on Isaiah 11:6. They are also beautiful—look them up.

The brutality of nature is another challenge to our faith in a loving, all-powerful God. Yes, nature is also a thrilling revelation of the Author of Beauty. My soul is fed by my daily bicycle rides through Rock Creek Park. I fear it would have dried up long ago without it.

But the peaceful beauty of nature can conceal its predatory violence. Black widow spiders eat their mates! There is something wrong here. Like us, nature is beautiful yet flawed. The prophet gets it. This too is something we believe God will transform when Jesus comes again.

For now, we must be content to relish the poetry of the prophet and to allow it to deepen our sense of the mysterious peace promised us by a helpless baby lying in a manger, the Savior of the world.

THIRD SUNDAY OF ADVENT

Isaiah 35:1–6a, 10
James 5:7–10
Matthew 11:2–11

TODAY'S GOSPEL READING asks us to compare John the Baptist with Jesus, as we began to do last week. Doing so will help us prepare for Christmas, the Feast of the Incarnation, because it will deepen our love and appreciation for the gifts Jesus, and he alone, continues to give us. John was the very best the ancient Hebrew tradition of Law and Prophets had to offer. To see how Jesus transcends even this powerful legacy is to understand why he is, truly, the Savior of the world. And our savior started out life just as we all do: as a drooling, mewling, pooping, helpless baby!

I love how our reading begins, with John sending his disciples to ask Jesus if he is "the one to come." I love it because I believe this is almost certainly historically accurate, and it helps us to correct for the hindsight fallacy, a constant problem whenever we are doing history. And anytime we read the gospel, whether we like it or not, we are "doing history" because we are reading about events that happened long ago.

The hindsight fallacy we must always be aware of is this: when we read about people in history, we have to remember a huge difference between them and us, viz. we know how things turned out, while they did not. We believe Jesus is "the one to come," but John did not. By comparing how Matthew tells the story with the parallel in Luke 7:18ff, we can see that Matthew may have already fallen into the hindsight trap because Matthew, unlike Luke, starts off by writing, "When John the Baptist heard in prison of the works of the Christ . . ." Luke does not yet refer to Jesus as the Christ, but Matthew, looking back, cannot restrain himself from confessing what he so firmly believes, God bless him. Still, come on, Matthew; the whole question here for John is whether Jesus is the Christ or not!

We might ask, "What does it take to convince you, John, that Jesus is the one to come? Restoring sight to the blind, curing the lame, the deaf and lepers, raising the dead, and comforting the poor is not good enough?!"

This problem is, however, another example of the hindsight fallacy. We now understand that healing the sick, raising the dead, and serving the poor were all essential to Jesus's messianic mission. But the people of Jesus's time had very different messianic expectations.

They expected the Messiah would be a political-military leader, like King David. The NJBC[8] tells us the term "Christ" means "anointed" in Greek ("messiah" in Hebrew) and it refers to "the anointed king of the Davidic dynasty who would establish in the world the definitive reign of Yahweh." Yes, the Messiah would be religious just as King David was, but people wanted deliverance from Roman oppression and the corruption and complicity of their Jewish leaders. Healing the sick and serving the poor was not going to get that done.

Jesus had a problem with these erroneous expectations, and that explains why he says something that is also, on its face, puzzling. After listing his many mighty deeds, Jesus adds, "And blessed is the one who takes no offense at me." Why would anyone be offended at his restoring sight to the blind? Because that is not what messiahs are supposed to do! They are supposed to win battles and establish the just reign of Yahweh through military force.

The word we translate as "offense" is *skandalisthēi*. It is connected to our word "scandalize," and it originally meant a snare or stumbling block; it also means "to stumble." It appears in the passive voice here, and *Abbott-Smith's Manual Greek Lexicon of the New Testament* tells us that in this case, it is always a metaphor for that which hinders right conduct or thought. In his *A Greek-English Lexicon of the New Testament*, Walter Bauer reports it means to be repelled by someone, as a result of refusing to believe a person falls into sin.

I suggest there is another, more modern sense in which Jesus's mighty deeds are "scandalous." We don't really like miracles—they are an embarrassment for most modern believers. They offend the dominant modern Western model of reality that is based on empirical scientific methods. Miracles are, by definition, events that are not in accord with the laws of nature. Therefore, miracles are difficult for us to believe because our vision of reality is defined (dare I say limited?) by scientific plausibility. Miracles were also an embarrassment to the early Church. In those days, there were charlatans and mountebanks who worked wonders by means of tricks in order to hoodwink people.

More recently, however, science itself has stepped away from such a rigid conception of reality. Quantum physics has revealed that randomness—or mystery!—is built into the way nature works. Genuine novelty is a real possibility in our universe. In the words of Shakespeare, "There are more things in heaven and earth, Horatio, than are dreamt of in your philosophy" (*Hamlet*, 1.5.166).

Still, even if miracles cannot be ruled out by the latest laws of physics, it does not follow that we can or should believe in all the miracles in the Bible. Interpreting Jesus's miracles has become so fraught for us that I have devoted an appendix article to it (see appendix D on my website).

When Jesus listed his mighty deeds, he may have wanted John to think of our first reading from Isaiah, verses 5–6. Although

Jesus was not fulfilling the Davidic messianic prophecies, he was fulfilling Isaiah's prophecy of the restoration of Israel. Jesus added cleansing lepers, raising the dead, and preaching the Good News to the poor. He was guided by Isaiah, but not restricted by him.

Isaiah is more poetic here than Jesus, as our text reads not that the lame walk but that "they will leap like a stag." The beauty of the passage is a reminder that today is Gaudete Sunday, the third Sunday of Advent, a time of rose-colored vestments and beautiful music in the liturgy. In the midst of this dark time of year and the penitential time of Advent, today is a day to rejoice and give thanks to the Author of Beauty.

In our gospel passage, Jesus is making two points in his answer to the question from John's disciples. First, in asking people why they went out to the wilderness to listen to John, Jesus is trying to build on the people's love of John. The same hunger that drove people out to the desert, away from the Jerusalem temple, to be baptized by John would also lead them to follow Jesus. John was the last prophet in the Old Testament tradition, the best that tradition could offer.

Jesus was a prophet, yet he was "more than a prophet." His second point is to distinguish his mission from John's. Did John cleanse lepers, raise the dead, heal the lame, the deaf, and the blind? No, but John offered judgment and hope for a better future.

In these reflections on the gospels, I will often refer to a wonderful collection of ancient Christian commentaries on Matthew, *Ancient Christian Commentary on Scripture*.[9] G. K. Chesterton wrote that tradition is "the democracy of the dead." I think it is important for us to read the Bible in the company of those who came before us.

Hilary of Poitiers (c. 315–67) believes John symbolizes the Law and that "he thoroughly accomplished all the work that belonged to the law."[10] Hilary goes on to say,

THEREFORE, WHEN THE law (i.e., John) was inactive, oppressed as it was by the sins of the common people and held in chains by the vicious habits of the nation, so that Christ could not be perceived, the law (John) was confined by chains and in prison. But the law (John) sent others to behold the good news. In this way, unbelief would be confronted with accomplished truth of what had been prophesied. By this means, the part of the law that had been chained by the misdeeds of sinners would now be freed through the understanding of the good news freely expressed.

The religious tradition of Israel is often referred to as "the Law and the Prophets." John represented both the culmination of the Law and the Prophets and the transition to something that transcends this tradition: the gospel of Jesus Christ. And because John is the transition to Jesus's kingdom, he is also "more than a prophet." No prophet before John was so close to the arrival of God's kingdom. Yet because he was killed just as the Kingdom was arriving, Jesus adds the words of verse 11: "but a lesser man, in the Kingdom of the heavens, is greater than he."

Jesus offered mercy and healing to the lost children of Israel and fulfilled the hope John foretold. Jesus followed the tradition of the Law and the Prophets—and transcended it.

Jesus got similar questions from Pharisees and Jewish leaders, but here he answers forcefully without getting offended. He did have to prove himself. He did so, in part, with miraculous healings—and blessing the needy and the "lost children of Israel," helping them, and serving them, not judging as John did. As prophets did.

FOURTH SUNDAY OF ADVENT

"Stay true to the dreams of your youth."
—Herman Melville

Isaiah 7:10–14
Romans 1:1–7
Matthew 1:18–24

TODAY'S GOSPEL READING, unique to Matthew, raises many questions. What shines out, however, like the Star of Bethlehem, is the faith of St. Joseph. I thank God we have four gospels! Luke's gospel highlights the faith of Mary, while Matthew directs our attention to Joseph.

If I were St. Joseph, I would be hurt, or angry, or depressed, or maybe some toxic combination of all three if I discovered that Mary, my betrothed, probably a young teenage girl, was pregnant before I ever slept with her. Maybe Joseph was, but Matthew makes no mention of it. Instead, Joseph takes the sober, kindhearted, mature, even "wise" approach of planning to divorce her quietly.

Joseph's initial plan adheres to Jewish Law, but his compassion leads him to avoid exacting upon Mary the full penalty. Mary should be stoned to death according to Deuteronomy 22:20–21. This reality underscores the tremendous faith-based courage of Mary in her agreeing to become the mother of God by the Holy Spirit. She risked her life and the life of her child by her decision. But Matthew's account is about Joseph.

Jesus's mission will transcend the Law and the Prophets, the beautiful and sacred tradition of Israel. How perfectly appropriate that even before he is born, he is challenging his parents to do the same!

This complicated, even ambivalent relationship with Israel's history is revealed in the genealogy that immediately precedes our verses. In fact, Matthew calls his gospel "the book of the genealogy of Jesus Christ, the son of David, the son of Abraham." As if the book is only about genealogy! Matthew traces Jesus's ancestry all the way back to Abraham and through King David to St. Joseph.

One problem with this genealogy: Joseph was not Jesus's father. Matthew is very clear on this point in our reading today. Hilary of Poitiers resolves this issue by pointing out that Mary and Joseph belonged to the same kinship line.[11] If this is so, the focus on Joseph's bloodline rather than Mary's is an example of ancient patriarchy. Perhaps Matthew is also telling us that Jesus is both deeply connected to his Jewish ancestors and essentially cut off from them.

Joseph hears the call to go beyond his compassionate mollifying of the Law. He takes the pregnant girl into his home and marries her. This astounding act of generosity and love would be remarkable at any time or place. It would have been almost unheard of in first-century Palestine. Does not Joseph's love and faith here contradict the Law of Deuteronomy?

Matthew tells us Joseph heard this message from an angel in a dream. I wonder how Matthew, writing many decades later, would know such a thing? It might be his best guess, inspired by the Holy Spirit. Assuming Joseph did have such a dream, it is still not so clear to me why he would allow a mere dream to lead him to make such a life-altering decision. Would you?

When St. Joseph had this dream, he must have still been a relatively young man, about to start a family. He must have thought long and hard about that dream in the cold light of morning. He was not risking his life, as Mary had, but he was risking his reputation as a law-abiding Jew, his future happiness, and his heart. That's a lot. I believe the dream must have been confirmed by many long hours of prayer and discernment. Joseph's decision to stick with Mary is so out of the ordinary that it can be seen as a miracle. Matthew clearly sees it this way, and that's why he explains the decision as the result of an angel's message in a dream. In the end, St. Joseph followed his dream, and his life changed forever.

The angel in Matthew tells Joseph the same thing he told Mary: "Do not fear." Faith casts out fear. But the angel's reasoning is one that could provoke still more fear, at least to my mind: "for that which is conceived in her is of the Holy Spirit." *What?!* he probably thought. *What kind of girl am I marrying who is carrying a Holy Ghost child?* Of course, we cannot know everything going through St. Joseph's mind as he made his fateful decision. What we know and believe is a) he was not the father of the unborn Jesus; and b) he took Mary into his house anyway.

It is easy this week to connect the first reading with the gospel because the gospel quotes it as a prophecy that was fulfilled. But was it? When Isaiah predicts that "a virgin" shall conceive and bear a son, the word he uses means "young woman"; it is not the technical term for a virgin.[12] Even if we read it as "virgin," however, Isaiah is not suggesting the virgin will remain a virgin after she conceives.

Even more striking is that the prophecy says the child shall be named Emmanuel ("God is with us"), but Joseph obeys the angel's command to name the child Jesus ("savior"). This prophecy—"They shall declare his name to be Emmanuel"—from Isaiah is repeated by the angel in today's gospel reading. What is going on here?

St. John Chrysostom (c. 347–407) offers an answer that makes sense to me.

WHY THEN DO they not call him Emmanuel instead of Jesus Christ? Because the text says not "you shall call" but "his name shall be called." This means that the multitude and the outcome of the events themselves will cause him to be called Emmanuel. For here he puts the event as a name. This is customary in Scripture, to substitute names for the actual events. Therefore to say "they shall call him 'Emmanuel'" means nothing else than that they shall see God among us.[13]

This is an ingenious way to resolve the dilemma. I have another one. We have already seen Joseph's connection to and break from the Law. By not naming him Emmanuel, Joseph follows this up by aligning with—yet breaking from—the Prophets as well! This is an example of how the Bible's inconsistencies point us to a deeper truth. In addition, both names are necessary for the truth of each. Jesus is our savior because he is God with us, the Incarnation of God.

The Gospel of St. Matthew ends with one of my favorite passages in Scripture, a reference to how the gospel begins; Emmanuel, the name Jesus, is not given but lived out: "I am with you every day until the consummation of the age."

CHRISTMAS MASS AT MIDNIGHT

The Feast of the Incarnation

Isaiah 9:1–6
2 Timothy 2:11–14
Luke 2:1–14

THE READINGS FOR this Mass are quite familiar to anyone with even a little exposure to Christianity. Luke is a masterful storyteller, and his gifts never shine more brightly than in the portrait he paints of Jesus's birth. Maybe he is too good, so good that we can be distracted by the details—the baby Jesus lying in a manger, the shepherds—and lose sight of the central mystery of this feast: the Incarnation.

Before examining this mystery, however, I do want to spend a little time thinking about verses 8–14. God puts on quite a show for these shepherds! First an angel appears, announcing the birth of Jesus, then "a throng of the heavenly army, praising God and saying, 'Glory to God in the highest places and peace on earth among men of good will.'"

Wouldn't you have loved to see this heavenly army? This extraordinary revelation of God's glory does not happen every day. What I find most extraordinary about it is that God chose to reveal it to shepherds. Shepherds, in Jesus's time as well as our own, are close to the bottom of the social-economic-religious-educational hierarchy. You do not have to go to school to learn how to be a shepherd. It is not going to make you rich. You spend lots of time sleeping outside with animals.

Why did God choose to reveal God's glory to shepherds? If you go to all this trouble with angels and the heavenly army, would you not want it to have the maximum impact? That would mean showing this display to people in a large city. Who is going to believe the reports of a few low-class shepherds? People will say they were dreaming or hallucinating after spending too much time outside with the sheep.

Yet that is precisely in line with all the other details of Jesus's birth. The glory is covered—and magnified—by humility. Jesus's birth resembles his death in this way; the transcendent power of the event is heightened, not lessened, by human vulnerability and lowliness.

The majority of Scripture scholars are dubious about the details of Jesus's infancy narratives. It is precisely because Jesus was born to a simple, humble family that we do not know very much about his birth. If he had been born an earthly king, we would know far more.

What we do know is really all we need to know. Jesus, the Son of God, the Incarnation of the Word, the second person of the Trinity, was born in humble circumstances to Mary and her husband, Joseph. This is the mystery of Christmas. I prefer to call it the Feast of the Incarnation because Christmas has become so wrapped up in cultural, even commercial, phenomena that obscure this fundamental truth.

This is one reason why the Christmas season lasts more than two weeks for Catholics, from Christmas Day to the Feast of the Baptism of the Lord. We need at least that much time to enter into this mystery. I do not believe a lifetime is long enough to come to grips with it!

As I mentioned in my introduction, I think most Christians struggle to believe Jesus is both fully human and fully divine. If we conceive of Jesus's humanity and divinity as always somehow at odds with one another—as if the more human he is, the less divine he is—we will not get very far in grappling with this mystery. Logically, rationally, there is a conflict between the two, but the mystery of the Incarnation transcends logic. It points to a deeper truth about the nature of both humanity and divinity.

Medieval theologians asked why God waited so long after Adam's Fall to send us the Redeemer. The first reading from Isaiah offers one answer. The Old Testament prophets gave voice to the deep longing in the human heart for a savior, for someone who will redeem us from the apparent futility and pointlessness of human life: birth, school, work, death. Perhaps it took us a while to understand that we cannot make sense of this life and this world unless someone who utterly transcends it comes to help us. This is another reason why Jesus needs to be both fully human and fully divine.

The reading is apt because it is so dark this time of year in the northern hemisphere. It is now easy to be in touch with the lonely emptiness of our death-doomed lives. One exercise I do during Advent is to imagine what my life would be like if I knew nothing of Jesus. Bleak despair, especially this time of year. So, thank God for the Feast of the Incarnation! But it is not easy to swallow.

Christians are asked to believe quite a number of things that "strain credulity," as my sister likes to say. The virgin birth, Jesus's many miracles, like walking on water, the Resurrection. Still, the hardest doctrine of all has got to be the Incarnation. If we can believe Jesus is true God and true man, everything else is easy to believe.

What we believe is important. Jesus repeatedly emphasized the importance of having faith. However, the power of God's truth does not depend solely on what we believe or think we believe. And this makes me hope that we all may believe in the truth of the Incarnation after all.

I am referring to the gradual growth, since the time of Jesus, in our recognition of the dignity, the transcendent value, of every human being. This was not a common view in Jesus's time: the Romans enjoyed watching wild beasts devour human beings; slaves were often not regarded as fully human; the practice of crucifixion existed; and so on.

The belief that God took human form, and especially such a humble one, means that all humans have a certain dignity. Our culture and our economy do not always honor this dignity. Some cultures do better at this than others. We clearly have a long, long way to go in respecting the dignity of all human persons. But it seems to me that when someone's human dignity is violated—by sexual abuse, violence, a violation of human rights—in the twenty-first century, it bothers us. It gives us a guilty conscience. We know something is wrong.

I do not believe this was true before Jesus. I do believe it is one of the truths of the mystery of the Incarnation that is going to affect us whether we like it or not, whether we believe it or not. Thank God!

A second truth of the Incarnation is that Jesus is God's Word for us. If God took human form, it must mean God is telling us something about how our Creator intends for us to live. When you buy a product, the maker of it will send you an owner's manual telling you how to operate and care for it.

Since God created us and then took on our human flesh, it must mean that God is telling us, "This is what I made you for. This is how you are to live to fulfill your human nature." Jesus came, in other words, partly to show us how to live, think, and feel. Sometimes the teaching is clear, especially in St. Matthew, God bless him! We get to spend a lot of time with him because it is Year A. But often Jesus's message is more complicated or indirect and requires digging to uncover.

In the meditations on the lectionary that follow, I will be trying to discern the message implicit in the Incarnation: God is telling us how to live the life God has so lovingly given us.

FEAST OF THE HOLY FAMILY

Sirach 3:2–6, 12–14
Colossians 3:12–21 or 12–17
Matthew 2:13–15, 19–23

WE SEE IN today's readings St. Matthew, and the Church, emphasizing the continuity between Jesus and the Jewish prophetic religious tradition. By choosing the Sirach reading, the Church stresses another theme in Matthew: how Jesus's very survival depended on the faith and obedience of his family. The book of Sirach, like Proverbs, is part of Israel's Wisdom tradition. Unlike Proverbs, however, it is in the Apocrypha and was written much later—only two centuries before Jesus's birth.

In last week's reading, Matthew tied Jesus to King David, and in his genealogy just before this, Jesus's ancestry is traced back to Abraham—two crucial figures in the Hebrew tradition. Today's reading connects Jesus to the third great figure in this tradition: Moses.

Moses also survived the slaughter of male babies, ordered by the Egyptian king (the massacre of the Holy Innocents recounted in Matthew 2:16–18 is omitted in today's reading). Like Jesus, Moses also returned to Israel from Egypt. As the NJBC puts it, Matthew sees Jesus as leading his people in a new Exodus, out of the slavery of sin to liberation.[14]

Matthew goes one step further by referring to an unknown prophecy in verse 23: "He shall be called a Nazarene." The NJBC explains this is probably a reference to a nazir "consecrated" in Hebrew. This would connect Jesus to Samson, a heroic strongman who fought and killed the enemy Philistines (cf. Judges 13–16) soon after the Israelites returned to the promised land from Egypt.

Jesus the Samson figure! That's a stretch, to me at least. Jesus was always committed to basing his kingdom on nonviolence. For this reason, tying him to King David, the great military leader, is also inappropriate. Jesus himself shrank from the messiah title because of its Davidic connection. No messiah in the King David tradition would ever be crucified by the enemy occupiers.

It seems as though Matthew is "throwing the kitchen sink" at the problem of Jesus's ties to Israel, trying to connect him to all the big names in Jewish history, no matter how preposterous, in order to root Jesus firmly into the religious history of Israel. Apart from Matthew, we have no other account of the flight to Egypt or the slaughter of the Holy Innocents. The NJBC tells us we cannot be certain about this or any of the other details concerning Jesus of Nazareth's origins, except that he was born around 4 BC, his mother was Mary, and his legal father was Joseph. The consensus among most Scripture scholars is that we cannot know whether the flight to Egypt and the killing of the Holy Innocents happened. I would say these two events may tell us more about St. Matthew than they do about Jesus.

The "historical Jesus" is not the same as Matthew's Jesus, and we must remember it is Matthew's Jesus who we are exploring this year. The interrelationships between the gospels, the Jesus of history, and the Jesus we believe in are complicated, and I explore these issues in depth in appendix D.

Matthew wants very much for us to see Jesus as the complete fulfillment of Hebrew prophecy and as a figure in complete continuity with the religious traditions of Israel. New Testament scholars believe this is because Matthew's community was made up Jews who had become Christians and who fervently wanted no separation between Judaism and Christianity. God bless them! If only they had succeeded. Alas, Judaism and Christianity, once joined at the hip, eventually went their separate ways. I believe both traditions are the poorer for it. I respect Matthew's noble efforts to keep them together. However, his devotion to this cause has some (unintended?) consequences that we need to be aware of.

Why do we have four gospels rather than only one? Because each one helps us to see part of the mysterious truth of Jesus. We have to be careful when reading Matthew to remember this preoccupation with the relationship between Jesus and the Jewish tradition. It does shed light on who Jesus is, but at other times Matthew's vision of the Jesus–Jewish connection seems at odds with the Jesus we see in the other gospels—and even in Matthew.

The many ingenious efforts of Matthew to embed Jesus in the Jewish tradition paradoxically reveal the ways in which Jesus also breaks with that tradition. I have already mentioned his nonviolence versus King David's militarism. We will see many other examples of how Jesus creatively challenges Jewish religious traditions as we read through St. Matthew. I believe it is important to do justice to both the continuity and the discontinuity between Jesus and his tradition, not only to understand Jesus better but also so that we can understand better why so many devout, upright, God-fearing Jews could not—and cannot—in good conscience follow his teachings. This will help Christian believers today to maintain our respect and reverence for the Jewish religious tradition.

This interpretive key to reading Matthew will also help us understand better the problematic chapter 23, in which Matthew's Jesus incongruously attacks the scribes and Pharisees as "hypocrites," "fools and blind men," and repeatedly threatens them with "Woe to you!" It is incongruous because Matthew's Jesus told us earlier, in 5:22, "I say to you that everyone who is angry with his brother shall be liable to judgment; whoever insults his brother shall be liable to the council, and whoever says, 'You fool!' shall be liable to the hell of fire."

At the shallowest level, we could read chapter 23 as a plain contradiction of chapter 5 and Matthew's effort to embed Jesus in the Jewish tradition. If we dig a little deeper, however, I would argue that Matthew's over-the-top chapter-23 Jesus reveals the dangers of trying "too hard" to bind Jesus too tightly to a tradition to which he was both deeply faithful yet also transcended.

Our first reading sheds further light on Jesus's transcendence of his tradition—if, that is, we read just one verse beyond where the Church interrupts Sirach. In speaking about how a son should treat his parents, verse 3:7 of Sirach reads as follows: "he will serve his parents as his masters."

Yet Jesus repeatedly undermines family ties, as he was creating a kingdom based on a community that transcends family ties, which is demonstrated in Matthew 12:50 when he declares that "whoever does the will of my Father in heaven is my brother, and sister, and mother." He even prohibits a potential follower from burying his father (Matthew 8:21–22). He promises he will cause family conflict (Luke 12:49–53) and emphasizes this when he says, "He who loves father or mother more than me is not worthy of me" (Matthew 10:34–39).

I do not see how any of this is at all compatible with serving our parents as our "masters." I go into more detail in appendix E regarding how a careful reading of the Wisdom tradition, and especially Sirach (a book written less than two hundred years before Jesus's birth), reveals many of the ways in which Jesus broke with the Jewish Wisdom tradition.

Jesus no doubt wants us to be kind and loving to our parents, and that is what our reading today (without verse 7) advises. Jesus commands us to love everybody, after all. As you will see in my appendix article E, parts of Sirach are problematic. Because our reading today omits verse 7, it is not contradicting the gospel message. Still, with its emphasis on "family values," I would say the first reading is more alongside than inside the Good News.

Let's return to Matthew and the insights of John Chrysostom before wrapping up this week's reflection. Chrysostom points out that the holy family were exiles, refugees, and fugitives through no fault of their own.[15] Fortunately, the ancient world had not "progressed" enough to require visas and passports for those wishing to flee for safety to other countries. We Christians today need to remember this story in the gospel and show compassion for the many refugees and immigrants who are fleeing to our nation for safety and economic security.

Finally, one crucial dimension of Jewish prophecy is that one day "all the nations" would recognize Yahweh as the true Lord of the universe. As NJBC tells us, Israel realizes during and after their exile in Babylon that "the universal lordship of Yahweh cannot be vindicated unless he is recognized as Yahweh by all peoples."[16] The prophets frequently wrote about how "all the nations" would come to Jerusalem and know the Lord; many psalms also pick up this theme. We can see it in Isaiah 45:18ff as well as in next week's readings for the Feast of Epiphany: Isaiah 60:1–6 and Psalm 72.

This is a prophecy that Jesus clearly does fulfill. And as John Chrysostom informs us, Matthew was right on this. The Magi came from Persia or Babylon, while the holy family fled to Egypt. We can quibble with whether Matthew's account of the infancy narrative is historically accurate. But it was prophetically true: Jesus's message was universal and eventually spread throughout the world.

Chrysostom asks: why was the Christ child sent to Egypt? From that point onward, we see that the hope of salvation would be proclaimed to the whole world; Babylon and Egypt represent the whole world. Even when they were engulfed in ungodliness,

God signified that he intended to correct and amend Babylon and Egypt. God wanted humanity to expect his bounteous gifts the world over. So he called from Babylon the wise men and sent to Egypt the holy family.[17]

The universalism that is symbolic at the start of Matthew's gospel becomes explicit at the end. This is important: Matthew ends his gospel at 28:19–20 as he begins it—with the call to spread Jesus's message throughout the world. This passage is so beautiful that, in closing, I am going to quote it in full. I remember as a boy being struck with how comforting those final words are: "I am with you always."

> GO THEREFORE. INSTRUCT all the nations, baptizing them in the name of the Father and the Son and the Holy Spirit, teaching them to observe everything that I have commanded you; and see: I am with you every day until the consummation of the age. (Matthew 28:19–20)

FEAST OF THE EPIPHANY

Isaiah 60:1–6
Ephesians 3:2–3a, 5–6
Matthew 2:1–12

LET'S START OUT by stating we have no way of knowing whether the three Magi saw a star, spoke with King Herod, or visited Jesus and Mary. We don't "need" to believe this happened either, because the saving truth of Jesus's life and message do not depend on this story. What we can learn from today's reading is something about Matthew's Jesus as well as the prophetic vision of the Christ.

Placing the first reading alongside the gospel is a reminder of Matthew's concern that Jesus fulfill the predictions of the prophetic tradition: "And nations shall come to your light." Check. "They shall bring gold and frankincense and shall proclaim the praise of the Lord." Check.

What are magi? The Greek word is *mágoi*; it means a wizard, sorcerer, or a Magian—a member of an originally Median sacred caste who conformed to the Persian religion of the time while retaining some of their old beliefs.[18] They were seen as experts in astrology, science, the interpretation of dreams, and other secret arts; in other words, magicians, according to Bauer.

The New American Bible translation[19] says the Magi have come to Jesus "to do him homage." The Revised Standard Version[20] says they have come to "worship him"; David Bentley Hart uses the word "obeisance." The word translated here is *proskunēsai.* It can mean the homage one pays to a human superior; for Persians and many from the East, this involves prostration.[21] But the word can also mean the worship given to polytheistic idols or to God, according to Bauer.

The ambiguity of the word means we cannot be certain whether the Magi see Jesus as (only) an extraordinary human being or divine. Matthew uses this same Greek word when describing the disciples' worship of Jesus once they fully recognize him to be the divine Son of God at the end of this gospel in 28:17.

Why do the Magi come to worship Jesus? I see them as representing the pinnacle of ancient Gentile sacred wisdom. Their worship of Jesus shows that he transcends the deepest thinkers, the most profound insights the world had to offer.

Why do the Magi follow a star? St. Gregory tells us the shepherds listened to the preaching of angels while a star guided the Magi because the shepherds, though uneducated, were Jews and therefore capable of using their reason.[22] As a "Gentile" myself, I now take for granted that I am a Jew by adoption, thanks to Jesus. But I should not take this for granted. Another reason to be grateful for the Incarnation, and for St. Paul's mission to the Gentiles, is that now I am just as able and worthy to hear the Word as Jews have been for thousands of years.

It is fitting the Magi arrive well after the shepherds and the birth of Jesus. All the first Christians were Jews! We Gentiles arrived late to the party, just like the Magi. Although Judaism and Christianity are now, unfortunately, separated, we should never forget our Jewish heritage in Jesus Christ, the disciples, and the apostles.

John Chrysostom offers another reason the Magi needed the star. There was nothing extraordinary about the place where Jesus was; as Chrysostom puts it, "The inn was ordinary. The mother was not celebrated or notable. The star was needed to manifest and illumine the lowly place."[23]

The NJBC tells us that ancient people could feel oppressed, imprisoned by a fate they were powerless to alter, by the claims of astrology. The star's alignment with Jesus's birthplace as well as the worship of the Magi establish that the Christ's birth liberates us from the trap of fatalism.

Why was King Herod and all Jerusalem troubled by the Magis' question: where is the newborn king of the Jews? Herod was afraid of losing his power. Matthew is telling us that "all Jerusalem" was afraid of this as well. In other words, Jerusalem was quite comfortable with the status quo. Jewish religious and political leaders were complicit with Roman rule and the oppression of Jews. A new king might mean a risk to the wealth and power they enjoyed. Maybe the new king would want to rule from some other city or prefer new counselors and officials. I live in Washington, DC, so I understand very well how an entire city profits from the political status quo. Chrysostom writes of Jerusalem that while God was offering them new freedom, they were once again mindful only of the fleshpots of bondage in Egypt.[24]

When Matthew writes that Herod assembles the chief priests and scribes to help him understand where the Christ will be born—so he can kill him—we can see it as a dress rehearsal for Jesus's trial by the Sanhedrin at the end of the gospel. Jerusalem was against Jesus of Nazareth right from the start.

Notice that in Matthew the Magi find Jesus in a house or inn rather than a stable, as in Luke. And where is Joseph? Presumably the holy family moved out of the barn once they found room in a more comfortable place. Of course, we cannot be sure the details of the infancy narrative are historically accurate. Reading that Jesus is now in a house, however, helps me appreciate the beauty of him lying in a manger, surrounded by animals.

I love Gregory the Great's spiritual interpretation of the Magi returning to their home "by another path." Gregory writes that our true home is paradise and we have been expelled from it by sin. Christ invites us to return to this home, but we need to go there by a different road from the one we took to get where we are.[25] We need to repent, change our hearts, and follow him.

BAPTISM OF THE LORD

Isaiah 42:1–4, 6–7
Acts 10:34–38
Matthew 3:13–17

UNLIKE THE INFANCY narratives, we can be confident the event in today's gospel reading is historical. All four evangelists write about it, each in his own way. The first gospel to be written, Mark, gives us a version (1:9–11) that is straightforward and unabashed. With Matthew and Luke, we start to see some embarrassment in the treatment of Jesus's baptism; below I will explain this in more detail. By the time we get to the last gospel to be written, John's, we find no mention of the actual baptism at all (1:29–34). Instead, the Baptist hails Jesus as the Lamb of God, and the gospel recounts the descent of the dove onto Jesus and how Jesus will baptize with the Holy Spirit.

The growing discomfort in the early Church with Jesus's baptism, reflected in our four gospels, is further proof that Jesus was indeed baptized by John. I love that despite their difficulties with Jesus's baptism, our evangelists tell us this story anyway.

The test of true leadership is telling your followers what they need to hear but do not want to accept. I am especially aware of this because only a few days ago, and only a few miles from where I live, a mob attacked and entered the US Capitol. These people did this primarily because their leaders refused to tell them the truth they did not want to hear: that their favored candidate lost the presidential election of 2020. Matthew, Mark, and Luke are, like

Jesus himself, true leaders because they are courageous enough to tell us an inconvenient truth: Jesus was baptized by John.

Why should John's baptism of Jesus be problematic for the early Church—and for us as well? Mark tells us that John preached a "baptism of repentance for the forgiveness of sins" (1:4). But Jesus was like us in all ways, except he was without sin. If he never sinned, why did he need to be baptized? Why would he consent to it?

The central question posed to me by today's gospel is this: did Jesus know he was sinless? My answer to this question is rooted in two ideas: the kenosis as well as the hindsight fallacy, which I explained in the third Sunday of Advent. We easily fall into this fallacy whenever we read history because we, unlike the people we are reading about, know how things will turn out. To preserve our own humility, and the proper respect for those who came before us, we must never forget this built-in advantage we have over them and this unbridgeable chasm between "us" and "them."

Kenosis is a Greek word that means "self-emptying." St. Paul writes in Philippians 2:6–7 that Jesus, "though he was in the form of God, did not count equality with God a thing to be grasped, but emptied himself, taking the form of a servant, being born in the likeness of men." This means that the historical Jesus, though divine, emptied himself of divine attributes while on earth to be fully human.

I explore the meaning of this crucial idea in more depth in appendix B. For now, I want to suggest that to be human is not to know what will happen in the future. I would go further and assert that if you do know what will happen in the future, you are no longer fully human.

Jesus was baptized before his temptation in the desert. He was baptized long before his agony in the Garden of Gethsemane, when he sweat blood and prayed God to deliver him from the torture of crucifixion. Yes, we know how these, and many other temptations which we are unaware of, turned out. But did Jesus? I believe the answer of the kenosis may well be that he did not. Who knows—perhaps Jesus may have wondered if he had sinned in the past. Was his failure to return home with his parents in Luke 2:41–51 on his conscience? This is pure speculation, of course.

However, for every human being I have known, genuine humility protects against sin. Is true humility compatible with the certain conviction that you never have *and never will sin*? By emphasizing the fragility of Jesus's sinlessness, am I at risk of denying his divinity? I don't think so. Affirming Jesus's full humanity and his full divinity is always going to be difficult. We must not forget that Jesus is "one who in every respect has been tempted as we are, yet without sinning" (Hebrews 4:15).

The moral cost of robbing Jesus of his full humanity is high because it lets us off the hook. I have heard people who are regular churchgoers say, "You can't expect me to be like Jesus—I'm only human." No, Jesus *was* fully human as well! His sinlessness makes him more human, not less. If you met him, he would not have a halo over his head. And he would probably smell bad.

The fact that Jesus was baptized by John and no one thought much of it at the time tells us that no one realized he was the sinless one until later. We cannot know if Jesus realized he was sinless. I suspect he hoped and prayed he would be faithful to God through all the trials he knew he would face. Yet faith is not the same as knowledge. In the end, the extraordinary faith of Jesus is precisely what reveals him to be divine. If we give Jesus divine foreknowledge, we belittle the power of his faith.

Let's shift gears for a moment and imagine Jesus had refused to be baptized by John. What would that look like? First, would not that mean he rejected John's teaching? That would have provoked a division between Jesus and John's followers that might have hindered the coming of the Kingdom of God. John's gospel (1:37–41) tells us that some of John's followers ended up becoming Jesus's disciples. Acts 19:1–7 confirms that followers of John the Baptist later were received into full communion with the Church and baptized with the Holy Spirit by Paul.

Let's imagine Jesus had said, "I will not be baptized by John because I don't need to. I'm sinless now and I always will be." That statement would have been technically accurate, but how would it have gone over? Baptism is the sacrament that makes us part of the Christian community. Becoming a Christian means to follow and imitate Jesus. How can we do this if Jesus was not himself baptized? Jesus's baptism expresses his solidarity with us, and ours with him.

What is the meaning of baptism? Exploring this question will give us yet another way to come to grips with the "scandal" of Jesus's baptism. We have already touched on its two principal elements. First, baptism remits both original and actual sin and their punishment.[26] Second, baptism unites one with Christ in the life of the Holy Spirit. While John spoke of a baptism of repentance for the forgiveness of sins, a full understanding of the participation with the Holy Spirit developed later. This meaning of baptism is one the New Testament authors affirmed: "For by one Spirit we were all baptized into one body—Jews or Greeks, slaves or free—and all were made to drink of one Spirit" (1 Corinthians 12:12–13).

We see this dimension of baptism clearly in our passage this week, as Jesus had an intense experience of participation with the Holy Spirit: "the heavens were opened and he saw the Spirit of God descending like a dove and alighting on him" (Matthew 3:16). In the following verse we have a revelation of the Holy Trinity, as a voice from heaven proclaims, "This is my beloved Son, with whom I am well pleased."

Another way to affirm Jesus's full humanity is to recognize that his participation with the Holy Spirit grew over time. How could it not? Surely his faith and understanding of God was not the same when he was six as it was when he was thirty years old. Luke 2:52 calls attention to Jesus's growth "in wisdom and age and favor before God and men."

Jesus's baptism is a way of marking the progress he has made in coming to know God and God's Holy Spirit. Prior to his baptism, Jesus was presumably working, making a living like everyone else. How long was he praying and asking whether he was ready to be baptized? Possibly for many years. His baptism is a critical turning point in his life. Only now is his connection with the Holy Spirit strong and deep enough to send him on his mission.

In Matthew, right after his baptism, the Spirit will lead Jesus out to the wilderness to be tempted by the devil. We might see Jesus's baptism and temptation as two essential steps he needs to take to prepare for his mission.

The first reading is yet another reminder that God established a covenant with Israel not for Israel's sake alone but so that Israel would bring God's light and justice to the entire world. In his words, "I am the LORD, I have called you in righteousness. I have taken you by the hand and kept you; I have given you as a covenant to the people, a light to the nations" (Isaiah 42:6). Jesus's baptism into full participation with the Holy Spirit is connected to this universal mission. After Jesus's death and resurrection, the Holy Spirit takes over in guiding the Church to fulfill this mission.

In the first verse of this chapter, Isaiah also speaks of God's servant, who has a special role to play in this mission: "Behold my servant, whom I uphold, my chosen, in whom my soul delights; I have put my Spirit upon him, he will bring forth justice to the nations." "The nations" means the entire Gentile world.

This is one Old Testament prophecy that has clearly been fulfilled by Jesus Christ.

SECOND SUNDAY ORDINARY TIME

Isaiah 49:3, 5–6
1 Corinthians 1:1–3
John 1:29–34

ALL FOUR GOSPELS refer in some way to Jesus's baptism and depict the Holy Spirit descending upon Jesus as a dove, although they differ on some of the details. Last week we read Matthew's version of this event; this week we read St. John's far more oblique account. As I mentioned last week, Jesus's baptism was an embarrassment to the early Church because it suggests Jesus might have needed to repent from sins. John's gospel, the last to be written, omits any explicit reference to Jesus's baptism.

The Baptist here emphasizes Jesus's full participation with the Holy Spirit, contrasting his baptism with water with Jesus's baptism with the Holy Spirit. What does this mean? We read in today's final verse that one meaning—for the Baptist, at least—is that "Jesus is the Son of God." It means Jesus's participation with the Spirit, the indwelling Spirit, helps to account for Jesus's divinity. Jesus then dispenses this Spirit to others, something John the Baptist could not do. Baptizing with the Holy Spirit, rather than mere water, was one important difference between Jesus's ministry and John the Baptist's, as today's gospel reading makes clear.

As we participate with the Spirit through our following of Jesus, we also participate in divinity. How? Anytime we are able to forgive those who have hurt us. Anytime we follow the beatitudes. Anytime we are able to love our enemies. Anytime we work for justice and show mercy. This is our participation in the Spirit of Jesus, which is the Spirit of God, the Holy Spirit. The Baptist is here calling attention to this phenomenon, which is new in history. He is the first to see it and call it out.

What does he mean when he says Jesus is the Lamb of God who is taking away the sin of the cosmos? And how does the Lamb of God do that?

Taking away the sin of the cosmos does not mean there is objectively no more sin in the world, although it could perhaps lead to less sin in the world, gradually, over time. John the Baptist says "sin," not "sins." There is a difference.

Sin can be a never-ending cycle that traps us, like a net. I hurt you, then you hurt me, and so on. Taking away the sin of the world could mean Jesus offers us the chance to interrupt the hold sin has on the world by loving enemies, not responding to violence with more violence, and forgiveness. Jesus shows this by his life, and even more by his nonviolent, loving, forgiving acceptance of an unjust death.

Sin can also stem from a guilty conscience. *What I have done is unforgivable, therefore I am in despair, and I might as well keep on sinning.* I have heard convicted criminals say these very words. John the Baptist's statement could also mean Jesus takes away the guilt we all have individually for the sins we commit, by offering us forgiveness and love—by showing that even when we do the worst possible thing, killing God's sinless son, we are forgiven.

Today's OT passage is yet another reminder from the prophetic tradition that Israel's selection by God to be his chosen people was not about them but rather about their God-given mission to spread God's word to "the nations"—that is, to the entire world. Jewish Law was unable to achieve this, but Jesus's new law of love was.

THIRD SUNDAY ORDINARY TIME

Isaiah 8:23–9:3
1 Corinthians 1:10–13, 17
Matthew 4:12–23

IN TODAY'S GOSPEL reading, Jesus begins his public ministry in Capernaum. Matthew tells us that three events preceded this important new phase in Jesus's life: baptism by John, temptation in the desert, and the imprisonment of John.

We have already read about Jesus's baptism. Jesus's temptation in the desert comes just before today's reading in Matthew, and we will encounter this passage on the first Sunday of Lent. The first question that presents itself to us this week is this: why did John the Baptist's imprisonment lead Jesus to withdraw into Galilee, leave Nazareth for Capernaum, and begin to call his disciples?

By waiting until after John was imprisoned to begin his public ministry, Jesus fulfills the Baptist's prediction in 3:11: "he who is coming after me is mightier than I." Had Jesus begun his mission prior to John's imprisonment, he would not have come "after" John; he might have run the risk of appearing to compete with the Baptist. Their messages were similar in many ways, yet distinct. I suspect that Jesus may have waited for a while between the end of his trials in the desert and John's imprisonment, although Matthew does not explicitly tell us this. He places today's reading immediately after the temptations without commenting on how much time has elapsed.

John's imprisonment may have been the sign Jesus needed to begin; it also reveals Jesus's courage. John was later executed, and everyone at the time must have known this was a possible, or likely, outcome as John had threatened the political and religious authorities with his preaching. Jesus surely realized he would face the same dangers.

Jesus showed courage, but he was not foolhardy. By moving out of Nazareth to Capernaum, he distanced himself from the government center at Sepphoris, not far from Nazareth. Capernaum was near the border of the province and on the shore of the Sea of Galilee; if necessary, Jesus could easily escape to the Decapolis or some other political jurisdiction. As the NJBC points out, he could even have slipped away by boat at night.

It is worth noting that Hart translates *katóikēsen* in verse 13 as "took up his dwelling," while the NAB has that he "went to live in" Capernaum. According to Bauer and AS, the Greek word carries another connotation that surprised me: "to settle (down)." I had thought of Jesus as homeless, itinerant. In 8:20 Jesus says, "The Son of man has nowhere to lay his head." It may be that Jesus did originally intend to settle down in Capernaum because of its strategic location, but with time he realized he had to travel to spread his message beyond that little town. Obviously, this was before the kind of communication systems we have today, so for large numbers of people to hear the gospel and experience his healing presence, he would have to be personally present.

These considerations reveal that Jesus gave a good deal of thought into when and where to begin his mission. Yet what we read about the calling of his first and closest disciples is so cryptic and enigmatic!

I agree with NJBC[27] that the call of the disciples "may have undergone extreme compression." In other words, it seems quite possible that Jesus and these men got to know each other and there was some time for mutual attraction to grow. It strains credulity that people would leave their family and their livelihood for someone they scarcely knew.

On the other hand, we know from elsewhere in Matthew (8:21–2) that Jesus did demand prompt obedience from his followers. An essential part of Jesus's message to everyone was *The Kingdom of God is arriving now! There is no time to delay. You must decide now to follow me and enter the Kingdom.* Jesus makes this very clear in verse 17 of today's readings—"Repent, for the kingdom of heaven is at hand"—and in the following passages from Matthew: 3:2; 6:33–34; 10:7ff; 16:26–28; 22:1–10; 25:1–13. Luke 12:13–21 is another powerful passage illustrating the urgency of repenting now.

Jesus insisted on an immediate response, I believe, for several reasons. First, because he knew his mission was time sensitive. God was now intervening in history to bring about the culmination of salvation history. What started with the call to Abraham was now fulfilled in Jesus's call to Israel and ultimately the entire world. Jesus may not have known precisely how or when God would act, but he believed something definitive would happen soon. And he was right: Jesus's resurrection was followed by the outpouring of the Holy Spirit at Pentecost and the expansion of the Church.

Jesus was in a hurry for another reason: he surely realized that he didn't have a lot of time. His explosive message would probably upset the political and religious authorities. Jesus already knew John was imprisoned and faced execution; he had no reason to believe he would fare any better.

Finally, Jesus demanded an immediate response because he understood human nature. If we put off making an important decision, it often means we remain stuck in our current situation and will continue with business as usual. Jesus's gospel message either cuts through business as usual or falls on barren ground.

I conclude, then, that the call of the disciples may have taken a bit longer than our passage suggests. But for the reasons we have explored, it is quite likely the decision was swift.

Why did Jesus call fishermen? Of course, he had disciples from other walks of life as well, but the first four were fishers, and his inner circle of intimates, Peter, James, and John, were all fishermen. I don't know; no one can. But that will not stop me from proposing a theory!

One reason he may have chosen fishers is because that's what existed in Capernaum. He settled there for practical reasons, as we have seen, and practical considerations may have led him to choose fishermen for disciples.

Curiously, Matthew leaves out one detail in our passage that we see in Mark. James and John left their father, Zebedee, as well as "the hired servants" to follow Jesus in Mark 1:20. The hired servants suggest they were fairly well off, unlike Simon and Andrew. Matthew is working from Mark, but Matthew leaves out the bit about the hired servants.

I don't even have a theory for this one. However, assuming Mark is correct about the hired servants, it sheds some light on the incident later (20:20ff) when James and John (and their mother) ask Jesus if the two men could sit at Jesus's right and left hand in his kingdom. This incident shows utter incomprehension about the nature of Jesus's kingdom as well as the form of servant leadership Jesus models and demands from his followers. But if these two clueless disciples came from a wealthy background, it might make sense that they, and their mother, would be looking to advance in the world. It suggests that the motives for many of these disciples may have been more complicated than following Jesus because of his charisma and fascinating message.

James and John may have exited the prosperous family business because they thought it was a savvy career move, a chance to improve their status. At the same time, let's give them credit. By following Jesus, they were giving up more than the others. Maybe that's why they expected more later.

Fishing was, and still is, a hard and dangerous way to make a living. Following Jesus was even more dangerous. Fishers would have to be brave, strong, and capable men. They would have some practical expertise in a range of skills that doubtless came in handy during Jesus's ministry.

Finally, fishers were not likely to be well educated. They would not be considered "wise" with respect to Jewish religious tradition (see appendix E). The learned did not generally buy Jesus's message. He fought openly with the scribes and the Pharisees, who were learned in the Law and the Prophets. At one point (11:25–26) Jesus even thanks God that God "has hidden these things from the wise and understanding and revealed them to babes." As the four gospels make very clear, it's not as though these disciples were always such smart, courageous, or charismatic people. Maybe their ordinariness is the point, as it reveals the transforming power of the gospel when they go on to face martyrdom and lead a movement that changes the world.

I am chastened by this because I am an educated man, with some letters after my name. Education can make us arrogant, status-conscious, and it can turn us into conformists. All three of these traits are inimical to following Jesus.

On the other hand, Matthew's Jesus also commands us (22:37) to love God "with all your heart, and with all your soul, and with all your *mind*." I added the emphasis, of course. But I have enough experience in academia to know that using one's mind to love God is not always the same as "becoming educated."

In Isaiah's time, Zebulun and Naphtali had been conquered by the Assyrians in 734 BC. As a result, Gentiles came to live there and began to outnumber Jews. Isaiah prophesied their liberation from "the darkness and death" he associated with the political and religious oppression of Gentile domination.

According to NJBC, Matthew includes these passages here

because he believes Jesus's ministry fulfills this prophecy and in order to justify the location of Jesus's work in northern Galilee rather than the religious capital of Jerusalem. I would add that these two passages are good examples of the way Jesus fulfills and transcends the prophetic tradition. Jesus does not liberate Galilee in any political or military sense. But his ministry is all about how "light overshadows death."

FOURTH SUNDAY ORDINARY TIME

Zephaniah 2:3; 3:12–13
1 Corinthians 1:26–31
Matthew 5:1–12a

"THE SERMON ON the Mount is St. Matthew's masterpiece": so says NJBC,[28] and I agree. I would add that the beatitudes, which we read this week, are the best part of this masterpiece.

Between last week's reading and this, we skipped Matthew 4:24–25. These verses note that people brought to Jesus "all those who were very sick, suffering from complicated illnesses and enduring torments, demoniacs and lunatics and paralytics, and he healed them." Matthew adds that large crowds began to follow Jesus, people not only from Galilee but from down south in Jerusalem and across to the eastern side of the Jordan River.

Jesus healed people for various reasons. It certainly made him popular, and he took advantage of the crowds by teaching people about the Kingdom of God. While God takes the initiative in the arrival of the Kingdom, the Sermon on the Mount reveals how we are to respond to this new reality: it is about our response-ability.

"Blessed" is the standard translation of the Greek word *makarios*. While there is nothing wrong with this translation, it needs to be filled out a bit. Hart translates it as "blissful," and I think that is superior. What do you feel when you hear the word "blessed"? It suggests a combination of good fortune ("She was blessed with a sharp mind"), but it also has a slightly stuffy, "churchy" odor for me.

There are several steps in the Church's process for declaring a person is a saint. The final step before sainthood is to be beatified, and these people are called "blessed." We will later read the beatitudes on All Saints' Day because these verses show us the way toward sainthood. And one meaning of "blessed" is that a person is on their way.

Makarios means "happy" as well as "fortunate." It can have a religious connotation: "the privileged recipient of divine favor" (Bauer); but the Greek word was also used without any religious meaning at all. Abbot-Smith tells us it could mean "congratulations!" I suggest you reread the beatitudes and replace "blessed" with "congratulations," "fortunate," or "happy." None of these words is quite right, either, but using them helps fill out the picture. The NJBC tells us that in form a beatitude is "an exclamation of congratulations that recognizes an existing state of happiness."[29]

Are the beatitudes telling us who is happy now or who will be happy later? Pay attention to the tenses of the verbs and you will notice they "vibrate" between present and future. The first one, in verse 3, is entirely in the present: "How blissful the destitute, abject in spirit, for theirs is the Kingdom of the heavens." Hart points out that the Greek word *ptochos* "is a poor man or beggar, but with the connotation of one who is abject: cowering or cringing."[30] The word connotes both material poverty and the spiritual humility it often provokes.

Here is where it is unfortunate that Matthew calls it the "Kingdom of the heavens" rather than the "Kingdom of God," as the other evangelists do, because it suggests the Kingdom is not here, not now. Remember, just last week in 4:17 Jesus announced that "the Kingdom of the heavens is at hand." As a pious Jew, Matthew shrank from using God's name, so he often prefers "Kingdom of the heavens." For this reason, we shouldn't let Matthew's preference for "Kingdom of the heavens" lead us to believe he's talking about the Kingdom only in the hereafter. The fact that he uses the present tense—"Theirs is the Kingdom of the heavens"—underscores this point.

More important is Matthew's addition of "abject in spirit." Luke has only "Blessed are you poor" (of course, it is equally possible Luke subtracted "in spirit"). What does it mean to be "abject in spirit"? At first, it might not sound good. Being abject in spirit could mean an impoverished spiritual life, someone who has little spirit. Spirit is cognate with life. But I don't think that's what Matthew, or Jesus, intends here. The abject in spirit are those who, whether they have money or not, are as humble, as generous, and as aware of their need for God as the poor so often are.

By adding "in spirit" to "abject," Matthew has shifted the emphasis away from social-economic poverty to the spiritual dimension of being poor. Bauer says the meaning of this verse "is difficult to determine with certainty." But he suggests it refers to those who are poor in their inner life because they lack the spiritual pride of the Pharisees.

If Bauer is right, when we think of the "poor in spirit," we should think of the parable Jesus told in Luke 18:9–14. He contrasts two men who go up to the Temple to pray. One is a Pharisee, who thanks God he is not unjust like other men, including a nearby tax collector. The tax collector stands far off and says only, "God, be merciful to me, a sinner."

Being poor in spirit can mean being humble and having an acute awareness of the need for God's mercy. Matthew's first beatitude, therefore, connects well with the fifth, in verse 7: "Blessed are the merciful, for they shall obtain mercy." If we are poor in spirit, we will be aware of our need for mercy; it should follow that we will be merciful to others and shrink from judging them harshly.

I think it is a good spiritual exercise to remind ourselves regularly of the worst sins we have committed. Not to wallow in guilt. But rather, to wallow in joyful gratitude that God has forgiven us, and to avoid the sin of spiritual pride. Doing this will also help us to be poor in spirit and to look at others with the same mercy God has shown to us.

To be poor in spirit can also mean detachment from wealth—voluntary poverty, according to NJBC. In the Bible, material poverty is an injustice to be corrected, and wealth is not an evil itself, although if we are not careful, riches can lead us to neglect the love of God and neighbor. In this sense, to be poor in spirit would be to realize we need above all to love God and neighbor, no matter how much money we have. If handled properly, money can actually help us love God and neighbor more effectively. We can share our money with the poor.

To be poor in spirit means realizing that having or getting money is not going to satisfy our deepest needs. We realize our money is not going to "save" us or make us special or better than other people. This can be a real trap for many people, rich or not. What is going to save us is God's grace and loving service to God and neighbor.

As we will see, taken as a whole, the beatitudes can enrich and even modify one another. They shed light on one another. They are all good, but sometimes too much of a good thing can become a bad thing. For example, it is good to be meek as a rule, but there are times when we need to let go of our meekness to challenge injustice. Jesus did.

To be poor in spirit connects well with the third beatitude in verse 5, "Blessed are the meek [*praeîs*], for they shall inherit the earth." Abbott-Smith and Bauer list "gentleness" as another synonym; Bauer adds "humble." The gentleness translation is more commonly used when Matthew's Jesus refers to himself as *praeîs* in one of my favorite gospel verses, 11:29: "Take my yoke upon you, and learn from me; for I am gentle [*praûs*] and lowly in heart, and you will find rest for your souls."

What's so great about being meek, humble, or gentle? Does not our world encourage bold ambition, self-assertive confidence? Is not this the way to leading a "happy and productive life"? We are often told not to believe in God but rather, "Believe in yourself!" I suspect the way of the world, worldly wisdom about how to get ahead and make something of oneself, was not so different in Jesus's day. Jesus is congratulating those courageous enough to be gentle, strong enough to buck the conformist pressure "to get ahead."

On the other hand, Jesus was not gentle at all when confronting the Pharisees, injustice, and those responsible for it. Nor was he gentle with Peter when his good friend admonished him to avoid the suffering his mission required (Matthew 16:22–23). There are times to abandon meekness. But if we follow Jesus, we will do this not to "get ahead" but because we "hunger and thirst for righteousness."

This brings us to the second beatitude in verse 4, "Blessed are those who mourn, for they shall be comforted." The Greek word translated as "those who mourn" is *penthoũntes*. When we hear "mourn," we may think first of those who are feeling a subjective sadness—people who are grieving over their own mistakes or because of the loss they feel after a loved one has died. However, Bauer has an interesting gloss on this word that he ties directly to Matthew 5:4. The *penthoũntes* "mourn not for their own sins, but because of the power of the wicked, who oppress the righteous." Do we suffer because every winter in our rich land, many homeless people die in the cold on the street? This is the kind of mourning Matthew's Jesus is talking about.

How will these mourners be "comforted"? The Greek here is *paraklēthḗsontai*. Once again, Bauer adds some nuance to the word. Other meanings include "to encourage, to cheer up." And the comfort "arises through words or a favorable change in the situation." Jesus's kingdom comforts those who sorrow over injustice by informing them that this feeling is appropriate. And in this way, it can spur them and others to improve the situation. This has been my own experience, and I thank God for it. That said, my mourning continues because there is still so much unjust suffering. The Kingdom in its fullness has not arrived yet.

What we have discovered about this second beatitude links up with the fourth, in verse 6, "Blessed are those who hunger and thirst for righteousness, for they shall be satisfied." What is "righteousness" or *dikaiosúnēn*? Abbott-Smith tells us in a broad sense it means "conformity to the Divine will in purpose, thought and action." We are not talking about a secular, reason-based ethic here, but rather a passionate, even personal, devotion to doing God's will on earth. To hunger and thirst for this, Bauer adds, would mean it is "the compelling motive for the conduct of one's whole life."

If we "hunger and thirst for righteousness," it follows we are going to mourn that we have so far to go to fulfill justice on earth. This is no dispassionate, bloodless conclusion about persistent injustice, but rather something that drives us and even eats away at us at times. If you feel this way, Jesus says, "Congratulations!" And I say, "Wow!"

What does it mean to be "pure in heart"? The word, *katharoì*, can also mean "clean." I would suggest it has something to do with confessing our sins to God and receiving God's forgiveness. Jesus was very familiar with the psalms, and when he said this beatitude, I wonder if he had these verses from Psalm 51 in mind:

> HAVE MERCY ON me, O God, according to thy steadfast love; according to thy abundant mercy blot out my transgressions.
>
> Wash me thoroughly from my iniquity and cleanse me from my sin!

> Purge me with hyssop, and I shall be clean; wash me, and I shall be whiter than snow.
>
> Create in me a clean heart, O God, and put a new and right spirit within me.

The bliss of peacemakers seems clear enough not to merit comment. However, let's not forget there is a difference between being a peacemaker and shunning all conflict. I sometimes think Christians believe that all conflict is sinful, so they seem to avoid it at all costs. In order to make peace when there is conflict, we often need to confront people with some painful truths. We may find ourselves under attack for doing so. We should all try to be peaceful, but being a peacemaker may require us to enter into conflicts.

The beatitudes make clear what a revolutionary message Jesus proclaims. The reading from St. Paul highlights the countercultural dimension of the teaching. It is not a message that will appeal to everyone, as Zephaniah makes clear with his notion of a "remnant," a smaller number of humble, lowly people.

These passages are comforting to me. The plausibility of the Christian message sometimes suffers in my mind because at least in the circles I move, not many people take Christianity all that seriously. These verses help explain why. The beatitudes present us with a "transvaluation of moral values," to paraphrase Nietzsche. It is a message that is not for everybody.

FIFTH SUNDAY ORDINARY TIME

Isaiah 58:7–10
1 Corinthians 2:1–5
Matthew 5:13–16

MATTHEW PLACES TODAY'S passage right after the beatitudes we read last week. How does going down those blessed pathways make us like salt and light?

"Nothing is more useful than salt and sunshine," writes Pliny, according to the NJBC.[31] Light allows us to see where we are going as we follow the Way, an early name for Christianity. Light does not force us to go in any specific direction; it is necessary for us to follow our chosen path. Being a light for others is certainly one way we can be useful.

Modern people may have forgotten, but salt is a preservative as well as a spice. Before refrigeration, salt's power to conserve food was essential. A good teacher will take care to preserve the health, spiritual and material, of her students. She will also season them with insights that transcend the bland, everyday status quo.

Salt "imparts resistance to corruption to the meats on which it is sprinkled," Hillary of Poitiers points out.[32] Salt also is very apt to add the sensation of "hidden flavor," he adds. That is a wonderful goal for any teacher! It reminds me of the Socratic "midwife" image, his hope that he could assist the student in giving birth to what was already inside.

Jesus called his disciples the salt of the earth and the light of the world. Chrysostom observes the shift here from proclaiming the Good News to Israel alone to a universal mission that includes everyone on the planet. Matthew's Jesus then tells them, "Let your light shine before men, that they may see your good works and give glory to your Father who is in heaven." Does not this contradict the following message?

> BEWARE OF PRACTICING your piety before men in order to be seen by them; for then you will have no reward from your Father who is in heaven.
>
> Thus, when you give alms, sound no trumpet before you, as the hypocrites do in the synagogues and in the streets, that they may be praised by men. Truly, I say to you, they have their reward. But when you give alms, do not let your left hand know what your right hand is doing, so that your alms may be in secret; and your Father who sees in secret will reward you. (Matthew 6:1–4)

Obviously the two messages seem to give us two contradictory pieces of advice: yet each points to a different, partial truth. Taken together they can illuminate how to navigate between the Scylla of pride and the Charybdis of a false and useless humility. I would go further: the apparent contradiction between these two sayings of Jesus actually points to a deeper spiritual-moral truth.

St. Thomas Aquinas tells us that we can determine the goodness of an action in three ways: our intention or our purpose in doing the action, the immediate object of the act, and the circumstances. Let's say I steal money from the collection plate at church to feed my starving children. My intention is a good one, and the circumstances support it, but the object of the action is bad because I am stealing from the church. Aquinas also asserts that for an action to be good simply, it must be good in all three ways.[33] If any one of these three dimensions goes awry, the action is defective at least to some degree.

For example, if I am a poor woman and I make a large donation into the collection plate in order to impress everyone with my generosity, the object of the act is good, and since I am poor, the circumstances make it still better. But the goodness of the action is spoilt because I am doing a right thing for the wrong reason.

This example, by the way, illustrates why it is important to love both God and neighbor. For this good woman loves her neighbors (or their admiration) too much, and God not enough.

Jesus tells us that good works can lead people to give glory to God. In the passage we read today from St. Paul, 1 Corinthians 2:1–5, Paul wants to minimize his own importance in order to emphasize God's power. I think I have had an experience akin to St. Paul's, and I bet most believers have as well. When I find myself doing a "good work" that is relatively easy, it feels natural, effortless; a kind of self-forgetfulness is at play. When the work is more sacrificial, the natural, effortless feeling is absent; but then I have the sense that Jesus's Holy Spirit is telling me to do it, and so I am just following orders. In these cases, I would really rather not do the act required of me. It is taking me out of my comfort zone.

You can see that in neither case does it make a lot of sense for me to feel proud of my good works. And by the way, my experience is that when the Holy Spirit gets me out of my comfort zone, I usually experience a transcendent reward later. When Jesus speaks in 6:4 of our "reward," it may well refer to a reward in this life, not the next.

What are good works? The fact that today's reading comes right after the beatitudes in Matthew's gospel gives us some idea of how St. Matthew would answer the question. The Church weighs in as well with our first reading from Isaiah, which is mainly about serving the poor. The seven corporal works of mercy, based on Matthew 25:34–36, are further examples. These seven works of mercy are 1) feed the hungry; 2) give drink to the thirsty; 3) shelter the homeless; 4) visit the sick; 5) visit the prisoners; 6) bury the dead; 7) give alms to the poor.

Will those seeing our good works give glory to God? It is maybe one of the most powerful ways we can evangelize. We need to do these things. But we must not be shy about confessing *why* we do them when someone asks. I have sinned in this regard, out of shyness or embarrassment. Whenever we have a natural opportunity to bear witness to our faith, why not do it?

SIXTH SUNDAY ORDINARY TIME

Sirach 15:15–20
1 Corinthians 2:6–10
Matthew 5:17–37

TODAY'S GOSPEL READING presents so many questions! Let's start with the first three verses:

> DO NOT THINK that I came to destroy the Law and the Prophets. I came not to destroy but to fulfill. For, amen, I tell you, until heaven and earth shall pass away, not a single iota or single serif must vanish from the Law, until all things come to pass. Whoever breaks one of the least of the commandments and teaches people to do likewise shall be called least in the Kingdom of the heavens; but whoever performs and teaches it, this one shall be called great in the Kingdom of the heavens.

But Jesus himself repeatedly broke the Law. Here are a few notable examples:

He touched a leper to heal him (Matthew 8:1–4, par. Mark and Luke).

He rejected all Jewish dietary laws by saying "not what goes into the mouth defiles a man, but what comes out of the mouth, this defiles a man" (Matthew 15:11, par. Luke).

He heals on the Sabbath (Matthew 12:9–14, par. Mark and Luke).

Moreover, by affirming the eternal validity of Torah, Jesus contradicts St. Paul (cf. Galatians 2:15–16; Romans 3:21–31). And finally, as NJBC points out, "no major Christian church requires observance of all 613 precepts of the Old Testament law," but only the moral commandments, such as the Decalogue and the duty to love God and neighbor.[34]

The passage I quoted above is found only in Matthew. When such a unique gospel passage is at odds with the clear witness of the rest of the New Testament (including the gospels themselves) and when it contradicts universal Christian practice, I believe we are justified in questioning the authenticity of the words attributed here to Jesus.

We know that St. Matthew and his community were members of the Jewish-Christian party and the early Church suffered conflict between this group and "the Hellenists" (see Acts 6:1–6; 9:29–31). Matthew's community was locked in a still more bitter family feud with the rabbis of Jamnia, who had recently placed them outside of Judaism "through a ban called the *birkat hamminim*."[35] For the Matthean community, Jesus really was the final fulfillment of the Law and the Prophets. Not only was there no ultimate conflict between Judaism and Christianity, but also to be a faithful Jew, you needed to follow Jesus.

There are some battles worth fighting. To me, this is one of them. It is a tragedy that in the end, Matthew's community lost this battle; the separation of the two religions has meant centuries of conflict between Judaism and Christianity and the persecution of Jews at the hands of Christians. The NJBC also suggests that the death of true Jewish-Christianity led to the creation of Islam, and thus centuries of another form of religious strife.[36]

In any event, we can understand that Jesus's fidelity to the Law was a hot-button issue for Matthew and his community. Together with the fact that no other gospel writer has Jesus saying these words, and considering their incompatibility with

St. Paul's and Jesus's own behavior, I think we can conclude these words tell us more about St. Matthew than about Jesus.

It is worth pausing a moment to ponder, and maybe to weep, over these words. Think what it means that Matthew may have put words into Jesus's mouth he never said! Taking such liberties with the Savior of the world is mind-boggling to me. I cannot conceive of doing such a thing. It seems sacrilegious. But Matthew saw fidelity to Jesus differently and experienced the inspiration of the Holy Spirit differently.

I make my peace with Matthew in this way: he and his community did everything they could to bridge the growing gap between early Christianity and Judaism. In the end they failed. But I salute them for trying. In fact, I am grateful. It shows this tragic division that has caused so much human suffering did not "just happen." Many devout and loving believers moved heaven and earth to prevent it. Must we perhaps conclude, with broken hearts and confused minds, that it was God's will? Would that not be strange?

In any case, this is one more example suggesting that when the Bible appears to contradict itself, it is pointing to a deeper truth and more profound mystery than mere literal quibbling can begin to fathom.

It is also worth pointing out that Matthew did not suppress the many examples when Jesus does appear to violate the Law. He must have been tempted to do so. The Matthean "lost cause" of devotion to the Law reminds us that Christian diversity and disagreement was present from the very beginning. It can strengthen us today to accept as natural the continuing doctrinal differences within the larger body of Christ. What unites us is our love of the Father, the Son, and the Holy Ghost.

And now for something (almost) completely different. If we read this passage with the ancient Christians, we can transcend the problems that arise from interpreting Matthew's words perhaps too literally. Listen to Hilary of Poitiers:

> WITH A BEAUTIFUL introduction Christ moves beyond the work of the law. He does not intend to abolish it but to enhance it by fulfilling it. He declares that his apostles will not be able to enter heaven unless their righteousness exceeds that of the Pharisees. *Therefore he bypasses what is laid down in the law, not for the sake of abolishing it, but for the sake of fulfilling it.*[37] (ACCS, 1a, 97, emphasis added)

The Law's moral purpose is to guide us so we will fulfill God's will on earth. The Pharisees sincerely and devoutly attempted to follow the Law, but Jesus clearly saw what they were doing as missing the mark. While it is true that Jesus at times violates some of the concrete behaviors required by the rules of the Law, in this passage we see how by internalizing its requirements, Jesus actually deepens and radicalizes the Law.

Maybe the best example of Jesus's "radicalizing by interiorizing" approach is found in verses 27–28. Jesus here equates lust, or wanting to commit adultery, with actually doing it. We can find a good deal of practical wisdom in this statement because deeds begin with desires. It is usually easier to stop our minds early on from wanting to do something we know is wrong, whether it is adultery or any other evil. Once we allow ourselves to "get used" to the action in our minds, it will be harder to stop it.

Beyond this bit of practical psychological advice, I think Jesus is making a deeper point. The act of adultery is an injustice to the marriage and the married partners. The desire to do it is an injustice to ourselves. Moreover, by not following through on the act but instead allowing ourselves to continue to dwell on the desire, in some ways we can fall into a deeper pit. It is possible to become so obsessed with evil desires—lust, greed, or whatever—that we can lose the "self," our souls, in the process, even if we do not do it.

These verses can easily be misinterpreted in a destructive way, however. As the NJBC points out, Jesus is only talking here about adultery.[38] He is not condemning all thinking about sexual matters, as might be involved in the study of medicine or "simple velleities"—that is, mild wishes. Because I believe Jesus was fully human, I believe Jesus must have at some point felt sexual desire or temptation. As Hebrews 4:15 says, "For we have not a high priest who is unable to sympathize with our weaknesses, but one who in every respect has been tempted as we are, yet without sinning."

It's not the first look that is the problem—it's the second. What I imagine happened was that Jesus saw an attractive woman, felt the attraction, and turned away. That is what he is telling us to do here.

A second, more problematic example of the radical interiorization of the Law is found in verses 21–23. After noting that the Law commands us not to kill, Matthew's Jesus in verse 22 says, "But I say to you that everyone who is angry with his brother shall be liable to judgment; whoever insults his brother shall be liable to the council, and whoever says, 'You fool' [*raka*] shall be liable to the hell of fire."

The main problem with this passage is that Jesus himself appears to violate it. In Matthew 23:13–36 (par. Luke) Jesus actually calls the scribes and the Pharisees "blind fools" (*Mōroì kai tuphloí*, which means "foolish and blind"). The word *raka* that Jesus uses in 4:22 is from Aramaic and literally means "empty" or empty-headed, and although he uses different Greek words when insulting the Pharisees, I don't believe this makes a huge difference. He also insults the Pharisees with other words, repeatedly calling them "hypocrites."

Now, Mark and Luke also have Jesus criticizing the Pharisees and other Jewish religious leaders, but with far milder language. Has Jesus changed his mind about insulting others, or has Matthew changed Jesus? I think it more likely that Matthew has changed Jesus and put these harsh words into his mouth. Chapter 23 is another example of the bitter family feud within Judaism we discussed earlier. By showing Jesus violating his own strictures against insulting others, Matthew has turned him into a hypocrite: the very insult this Jesus throws at the Pharisees!

This shocking inconsistency reveals how deep the split between Matthew's community and the Jamnia rabbis had become. Matthew is evidently so absorbed in the fight with Jamnia that he is blind to the contradiction between the Jesus of chapter 5 and the Jesus of chapter 23.

Yet let's also recognize Matthew's intellectual integrity. If he wanted to preserve the attack of chapter 23 and remove the contradiction, he could have excised Jesus's teaching in chapter 5.

Even though there are no parallels to Matthew's chapter 5, Jesus's teaching here is far more consistent with the Jesus we know from the other gospels than is the enraged and insulting Jesus of chapter 23. If we have to choose between the two, and I think we do, I think it far more likely the teaching of chapter 5 is authentic and the words of chapter 23 reveal more about Matthew's battle with Jamnia than about Jesus.

Even though I think it is authentic, I have a problem with Jesus's teaching in 5:21–22. Is it right to condemn all expressions of anger? Jesus got angry at times, according to the gospels, without calling anyone a fool. Can I not sometimes express love through anger? I was once bicycling in Rock Creek Park when a car passed me on a narrow two-lane road. Another biker was coming in the opposite direction and was forced off the road by the passing car, which almost hit him. I was never in danger, but I yelled angrily at the passing motorist, "You could have killed that guy!" Before continuing my ride I made sure the biker was all right; he was, and I sensed he was grateful for my outburst. Was I wrong to be angry?

Still, I have to confess that most of the times when I get angry, it is not out of love—unless it is self-love. So Jesus is right to call us on this; it is the kind of deep-rooted challenge that makes me love him. Each time I get angry or even annoyed is an opportunity to ask myself: why? I recommend this spiritual exercise to everyone.

SEVENTH SUNDAY ORDINARY TIME

Leviticus 19:1–2, 17–18
1 Corinthians: 3:16–23
Matthew 5:38–48

TODAY'S GOSPEL IS beautiful, and it challenges us both morally and mentally. Must we love all evildoers, not resist injustice, renounce self-defense and even the defense of innocent third parties? One aspect of the problem is easily dispensed with. Jesus here commands us to offer no *violent* resistance to evildoers. What Jesus did on Good Friday clarifies any ambiguity about the words Jesus uses in St. Matthew's gospel.

Jesus resisted the evil and injustice of the Jewish and Roman authorities. He challenged their authority, their methods, and their values. They responded with fear, anger, and violence. Jesus faced up to their threats of violence and did not run away from them as his disciples did. He stood his ground and suffered the unjust torture and execution they inflicted on him. This is the model of nonviolent resistance, later followed by the Christian martyrs, Gandhi, Martin Luther King, Jr., and many others.

If we turn the other cheek to one who strikes us, we are also standing our ground, not fleeing for safety. We are saying, in effect, "Your violence will not affect me. I will not imitate your violence nor allow it to change my position of confronting you face-to-face." It takes far more courage and self-control to maintain this position than it does to fight back with violence, or to run away. The fight-or-flight options are deeply embedded within us, thanks to thousands of years of evolution and natural selection.

One of the most powerful messages of the resurrected Jesus is what he does not say. We would expect a normal human being to tell his disciples to take vengeance on those who tortured and killed him. Or he might be angry with his disciples for abandoning him, even betraying him, when he most needed them.

Instead, Jesus's first and last word to his followers is "peace."

Jesus's own example reveals he wants us to resist injustice and to do so nonviolently. Does Jesus's teaching mean all his followers must always renounce violence, even in self-defense or in the defense of innocent third parties? The answers to these questions may be more complicated.

Jesus in our passage starts off his teaching with "You have heard that it was said." What does this mean? Where have his listeners heard they are to "hate their enemy"? The NJBC tells us this is close to an exegetical formula common in the rabbinic schools.[39] First a Bible quotation, then "You might think this means . . . but I say to you . . ." We should also remember that "it was said" is the theological passive, a polite way of saying that God said something.

Jesus in verse 38 is quoting a legal rule of retaliation (*lex talionis*) found in Exodus 21:22–25; Leviticus 24:19–20; and Deuteronomy 19:21. These are all variations on the famous life for life, eye for eye, tooth for tooth idea also found in the Code of Hammurabi, the Roman Law of Twelve Tables, and Aeschylus.[40] While this law sounds brutal today, the original idea was humane. Its intent was to restrict revenge and to make the punishment fit the crime. Previously, ten people, not one, might be killed as revenge for the one who was murdered.

Jesus boldly transcends this law, and in doing so raises several questions for us. What are we to make of the several Old Testament passages where this law appears? Does the New Testament contradict the Old? I would answer that this reveals the history of salvation as an evolving process. What was humane in one period may need to be altered later. This process continues to our own day.

Verse 43 ("You have heard that it has been said, 'You shall love your neighbor and shall hate your enemy'") raises several more problems. The quotation from Leviticus 19:18 is incomplete and inaccurate, leaving out the crucial "as yourself," while adding the "hate your enemy," which is not found in the passage at all. Fortunately, our first reading this week allows us to directly compare the phrasing. NJBC suggests Jesus may have been correcting a false interpretation of the text rather than commenting on the text itself.

On the one hand, as our first reading indicates, the OT does teach us to be merciful to our enemies, as God is merciful. However, the notion that we could have a religious duty to hate, or even kill, our enemies is certainly also present in the Old Testament and in the Apocrypha, especially the Wisdom tradition (see appendix E).

Jesus tells us in our gospel passage that we are to love our enemies, as God does. God makes the sun rise on the evil as well as the good. But if we read the Bible literally, it is not so clear that God has always loved God's own enemies. For instance, God seems to instruct Moses to be merciless to God's, or Israel's, enemies.

NJBC points to Deuteronomy 7:2. When God brought the Hebrews to the Promised land, they believed God had instructed them to kill their "enemies" who lived in this Promised Land.

> WHEN THE LORD your God brings you into the land which you are entering to take possession of it, and clears away many nations before you, the Hittites, the Girgashites, the Amorites, the Canaanites, the Perizzites, the Hivites, and the Jebusites, seven nations greater and mightier than yourselves, and when the Lord your God

gives them over to you, and you defeat them; then you must utterly destroy them; you shall make no covenant with them, and show no mercy to them. (Deuteronomy 7:1–2)

We may wonder who is speaking here. God or Moses?

Later, in verse 10 of the same chapter in Deuteronomy, Moses tells the Hebrews that God "requites to their face those who hate him, by destroying them; he will not be slack with him who hates him, he will requite him to his face." Destroying an enemy is a concrete expression of hatred. If God does this, must not we?

Our beautiful first reading suggests the Old Testament may contain mixed messages about the commandment to love our enemies and refrain from violent vengeance. One tension I have found is between the attitude toward foreign nations who were the enemies of the Israelite people and the attitude toward a fellow Hebrew individual who is an enemy on a personal level.

Notice how in our first reading Moses commands the Hebrews to "take no revenge and cherish no grudge against any of [their] people." The early books of the Old Testament are filled with accounts of God apparently commanding the utter destruction of Israel's national enemies. The request for divine violence is not limited to Torah. We also find it in Psalms. Psalm 58 is probably the most notorious. It is not clear here whether "the wicked" are Israel's national enemies or simply all evildoers, whatever nation they belong to. Here we read:

> THE WICKED GO astray from the womb,
> they err from their birth, speaking lies
> . . . O God, break the teeth in their mouths;
> tear out the fangs of the young lions, O Lord!
> Let them vanish like water that runs away;
> like grass let them be trodden down and wither.

> Let them be like the snail which dissolves into slime,
> like the untimely birth that never sees the sun.
> ... The righteous will rejoice when he sees the vengeance;
> he will bathe his feet in the blood of the wicked.
> Men will say, "Surely there is a reward for the righteous;
> surely there is a God who judges on earth." (Psalms 58:3, 6–8, 10–11)

The poem suggests that we have a religious duty to ask God to destroy the wicked and to rejoice when God wreaks violence upon them. It is somewhat more defensible to demand violent destruction on "the wicked" than it is on one's personal or national enemies. However, if we are convinced we are on God's side, it can also be easy to define "the wicked" as all those who are our enemies. This has happened throughout the history of religion.

The idea that we have a religious duty to hate evildoers and take delight in their torment was not only present in the Torah and Psalms; it was still very much "in the air" in Jesus's time. The NJBC tells us that it can be found in the Dead Sea Scrolls used by the Qumran community, contemporaries of Jesus: "And that they [the saints] may love all the sons of light each according to his lot in the Council of God; and that they may hate all the sons of darkness, each according to this fault in the vengeance of God."[41]

Jesus's death and resurrection are the ultimate refutation of the Old Testament belief that we need to use violence to destroy all of God's enemies. The commandment to destroy any enemy of God was used to justify the Crucifixion. Yet Jesus was not only innocent—he was also sinless! This reveals the essential problem with the commandment to kill God's enemies. We can never know for certain who God's enemies are.

As if that is not enough, Jesus's resurrection reveals that it is not violence that "wins" in the end anyway, on neither a personal, individual level nor the historical world plane. The

Resurrection launched the Christian movement into world history. And Christian faith in the Resurrection empowers us, as it has empowered martyrs for centuries, to believe that no act of violence will end our lives. These two dimensions are related. As Tertullian once said, "The blood of the martyrs is the seed of the Church."

Our second reading is a good example of the New Testament rebellion against the Jewish Wisdom tradition. St. Paul argues that the "wisdom of this cosmos is folly before God" (1 Corinthians 3:19). Jesus also attacks "wisdom" in the gospels (cf. Matthew 11:25). I explore Jesus's relationship to the Wisdom tradition in more detail in appendix E.

Jesus's command to love our enemies and never resort to violence to combat evil is beautiful, challenging us to transcend our human nature. But is it a practical way to order temporal society? I would argue it is not, because sin is still too powerful in our world. If we followed his teaching, thugs and bullies could run the show, oppressing the weak and innocent. Is it not better to resort to violence if necessary to protect the innocent? To prevent genocide, for example?

I read in *The New York Times* not long ago that the fear of kidnapping by violent gangs now pervades the streets of Haiti, hindering routine activities. People are afraid to let their children go to school, or even to sit outside with neighbors.[42] Do we want to live in a society ruled by such gangs, or in one ruled by law, in which the police have guns and use them when necessary? Of course, we have seen recently how often our police use their guns and kill when it is not necessary. The problem is complicated and certainly beyond my power to resolve. Still, most of us want police who have the power to use deadly force when necessary.

If the presence of sin in our world makes Jesus's nonviolent teaching impractical as a basis for laws regulating our society, is his teaching worthless? No! For two reasons. First, Jesus's teaching is applicable on a personal level. Here is an example of what I mean from my own life experience.

My uncle was murdered years ago, and the murderer was convicted of the crime. I went to the trial and, by the grace of God, ended up pitying the murderer of my uncle. He appeared to be a small, broken man. I testified in the trial against giving him the death penalty. I later wrote to him, telling him I forgave him for his crime.

However, my pardon did not mean I thought he should not be punished and imprisoned for many years. I would say the state-sanctioned punishment of life in prison he received made it easier for me on a personal level to follow Jesus's teachings in this passage. I agreed with Jesus that the murderer's life should not be taken because he took my uncle's. I did, and do, pray for him. I cannot say I love him, but I feel compassion for him; I could see in his eyes great suffering.

On the other hand, putting him in prison for a long time is a kind of violence. Nor would it be possible to incarcerate anyone without the threat of violence the state uses to enforce the rule of law.

Second, Jesus's teaching works as a utopian critique of our current reality that can slowly inspire us to grow in the right direction. This is often how progress in justice works. We go from ten lives for one life to one life for one life, and then to eliminating capital punishment altogether. Replacing this with a life in prison is progress, but I do not think Jesus would approve.

Jesus calls us to move beyond violent punishment to forgiveness, restorative justice, redemption of all sinners, even the end of sin. In business, they call this a "stretch goal." It seems just as unrealistic to most people now as only one eye for one eye may have seemed to our ancestors. Or perhaps as unrealistic as the abolition of slavery once appeared to be.

Is a world without violence imaginable? Surely yes. Is it desirable? Yes! Does a world without violence seem practical to us now? I would say no. But the fact that it is both imaginable and desirable yet not apparently feasible reveals a creative tension that can help move us in the right direction.

Another way to conceive this problem is to say that Jesus's teaching can and does apply to us on a personal level because we all have a soul. But the state does not have a soul; it cannot enter the Kingdom or be judged worthy of purgatory. Jesus's teachings do not apply to the state in the same way they do to persons. This approach to the problem resembles, to some extent, the Old Testament vision that called for vengeance against Israel's national foes, mercy for personal enemies. The difference is Jesus removes divine justification for state violence.

To love our enemies and to respond to violence with forgiveness goes against our human nature. It is only possible with God's help, which we call grace. This is Jesus's consistent challenge to us: to be, to act, to think, and to feel the way God does. This is also where we need to remember Jesus gave us two commandments: to love God and love our neighbor as ourselves. Jesus would say we can't really love our (unjust) neighbor unless we love God and see things God's way, and think like God.

The notion that we are being asked to grow to resemble our Creator, in whose image we already exist, is bolstered by a Greek word in Matthew's gospel. Jesus closes the passage with the command to be "perfect as your heavenly Father is perfect." The Greek word translated as "perfect" is *téleioi*. The word can also be translated as "complete, in various senses of labor or growth: physical, mental, moral character."[43] This suggests that for Jesus, our goal is to be like God, to think like God: to be like Jesus.

What is the meaning and purpose of life? According to a recent poll, 89 percent of young British people (ages sixteen to twenty-nine) believe life has no meaning.[44] Christians have an answer: to become more like God, who created us in God's own image. This is one way to understand Jesus's mission. He was fully human and fully God. He came to us so we could become like him, like God. If we are engaged in this quest, our lives will have meaning. I believe even if we are not explicitly telling ourselves that we are following Jesus, our lives have purpose if we are on the pathway he points out to us.

Let's let Chrysostom have the last word this week.

> HE DID NOT say "do not resist your brother" but "the evil one"! In this way he relaxes and secretly removes most of our anger against the aggressor by transferring the censure to another.
>
> "What then?" one asks. "Should we not resist the evil one at all?" Indeed we should, but not in this way. Rather, as Jesus has commanded, we resist by surrendering ourselves to suffer wrongfully. In this way you shall prevail over him. For one fire is not quenched by another, but fire by water. (The Gospel of Matthew, Homily 18.1, ACCS, 1a, 118)

ASH WEDNESDAY

Joel 2:12–18
2 Corinthians 5:20–6:2
Matthew 6:1–6, 16–18

I HAVE A bone to pick with today's readings. I think the passages are intended to guide us as we begin Lent so that we approach it in the right spirit. Whether they are an appropriate guide for us today is my main question, and I hope you will understand my reservations by the end of this piece.

I love Lent! That may sound strange to some who associate Lent with unpleasant austerities. Traditionally, Lent means prayer, fasting, and alms giving, but I'm not sure everyone is still on board with these traditions. If you aren't planning on a lot of extra prayer, fasting, and alms giving, these readings might seem beside the point.

So today I am going to approach the readings a little differently. Instead of starting with them, I am going to start with how I look at Lent and what I do, and only then get into how these readings help me within this context.

I love Lent because it is the spiritual version of the secular New Year. We are invited to take a good, hard look at our spiritual life, decide what is working and what is not, and make a fresh start. It's exciting! Because spiritual growth never ends. Even in eternity. It is one answer, maybe the best answer, to the meaning of life: to grow in our capacity to give and receive love from God, neighbor, and self (Matthew 22:34–40, par.).

I prepare for Lent by asking the following question: what am I doing and not doing that creates distance between me, God, and my neighbors? I take this all-important question into my prayer life and ask God for direction. It is also good to ask this of your spiritual advisor or confessor if you have one. (If you don't have one, get one!) Or talk about this with anyone close to you who is a Christian fellow traveler. It is all too easy not to be honest with ourselves and with each other.

It takes time to discover true answers to this question, in my experience, and finding them is critical to having a powerful Lent. It's better not to wait until Ash Wednesday to seek these answers. We probably ought to be asking ourselves this question every single day.

One way to know we are on the right track is if what we come up with is at least embarrassing, if not humbling. I will give an example that is, for me, both embarrassing and humbling.

One year I answered the question partially by concluding that I was drinking too much at times. Some nights I don't have anything alcoholic; often I have a glass of wine. But some nights I drink more. As a result, the following day I might lose a good part of the morning, either by sleeping late or not feeling as energetic as I would like. (I am retired.) Alcohol may help us get to sleep, but it means we do not sleep as deeply as we normally do. As a result, I was not as in touch with the Holy Spirit the following day.

Believe it or not, Catholics have a patron saint for hangovers! Her name is St. Bibiana.

At any rate, after drinking more than my usual, I felt a kind of absence. I was still able to do some of what I needed to do, but it was too easy to put off the tough stuff. I felt a lack of motivation and clarity. Alcohol was limiting my ability, on some days, to respond to God, to participate in God's life, to allow God to participate in mine. I also felt more cut off from others.

It would be dishonest of me to try to appear to be a rigid "anti-intoxicant," however. I have found that sometimes staying up late and sipping Calvados, or even having a little marijuana, has led me to insights that I would not have had otherwise. Sometimes these intoxicants help me realize painful truths, to understand I need to do something that makes me uncomfortable. These insights can sometimes lead to a deepened relationship with God and neighbor. I know because I write these thoughts down and look at them the following day. I would say about half of them pass the "sobriety test" I give them.

Still, often it was all too easy for me to pass beyond a certain point of sobriety and into a deliberate escape from the inner emptiness we all carry, a desire for a kind of oblivion. That is where the sin comes in.

I asked myself, *Why am I doing this?* Whatever it is you are doing, or not doing, that seems to be separating you from God and neighbor, I recommend you do the same: why are you doing this? Get to the root of the problem. This is also critical if we are to love ourselves, part of the Great Commandment. We cannot love ourselves if we do not know ourselves. We cannot know ourselves, or stop the self-destructive behavior, if we do not understand why we are doing it. And finally, we cannot love ourselves if we keep doing self-destructive things.

I felt a certain inner emptiness that only God can really fill but which I was seeking to fill through alcohol. I discovered I was using food in much the same way—as a material means to fill an emptiness that matter cannot fill. My Lenten solution was to limit myself to two glasses of wine per day, give up spirits altogether, and to fast on Fridays. I also gave up meat entirely. Like so many of my Lenten practices, I now find I do this every year. Some of the practices I do year-round. This is another reason I love Lent.

What we start doing during Lent is just as important as what we stop doing. After Friday-evening Mass at my parish, we do the stations of the cross, a good prayer discipline to remind us of what Jesus went through for us. After that we all get together for a simple meal of bread and soup and listen to what one local organization is doing to help the needy. And then we give them some money.

Finally, I make a point of putting the money not spent on food into a "rice bowl." Then I give this money to feed the hungry, either directly to people in my own city or to those far away. Fasting and being hungry also helps me to feel at least some physical and spiritual solidarity with the many people in our world who are hungry not by choice, like me, but because of injustice.

For me, fasting is really a trifecta. It allows me to check all the Lenten boxes at once. By fasting, I save time for more prayer and save money for more alms. When I prepare for the fast prayerfully, I don't often feel very hungry. It's a very different feeling from just missing a meal. And the hunger I do inevitably feel is a way to put body and soul back together. Fasting on Fridays also helps me to feel some solidarity with Jesus. He suffered so much on Good Friday that we can easily forget he also had no time to eat anything.

I think we North Americans don't do enough fasting. Catholics used to do it more, but since Vatican II, it has been played down. We don't hear about it from the pulpit so often, nor do I hear about people doing it.

For Lent I also ask myself what I am *not* doing that likewise creates distance between God, me, and my neighbors. My answer often results in several additional activities. I decide I need to pick a book or epistle in the Bible, read some of it every day, and spend some time studying and meditating and praying on it. I also read spiritual writers, like Thomas Merton, or saints.

I look at ways I am not as available to friends, our struggling guests at the Monday-morning program, and family members as I could be. Each year the specifics of this change. My Lenten promise could be spending more time on the telephone, making more time for visits, being more present when I am together with others, and so on. That's enough about my Lent! Now to the scriptural readings.

The first reading from Joel is a powerful reminder of how to approach this season: with a repentant heart, fasting, sorrow for our sins. I also like its emphasis on the communal dimension of repentance. Our Lenten observances should balance private prayer time with connecting more often to our local faith community.

I read St. Paul's message from 2 Corinthians as a reminder that we have a job to do in spreading the Good News. St. Paul writes God is making "a supplication" through us. What is God asking us to do? To be reconciled with God. We need to live life so that when we die, it is clear that what we did would make no sense without our faith in God. We evangelize by what we do and do not do. By baptism, we are ambassadors of Christ. Both readings remind us that Lent is not just about ourselves—it's about the larger faith community and the even larger faithless community.

The passage from Matthew is a useful reminder of the danger of doing the right thing for the wrong reason. It is certainly a danger for us to become so focused on what to do, and not do, that we forget to focus on the proper motivation: deepening our relationship with God, neighbor, and ourselves. In other words, following the Great Commandment (Matthew 22:34–40, par.).

My problem with the Matthew reading is that it presupposes we are taking Lent seriously. Only if we are fasting, giving alms, and praying more do its warnings make sense. However, my hunch is that an even greater danger for many Catholics and Christians is not taking Lent seriously in the first place: not fasting, not praying more than usual, not helping the poor more. Rather than warning us against the dangers of doing these good works for the wrong reasons, I would rather we received more encouragement for doing them in the first place.

Finally, I have a problem with both David Bentley Hart's translation of this passage as well as the RSV's. Both miss the irony of Jesus's warning about practicing piety to win praise from people rather than from God. The RSV uses one word, "reward," to translate two different Greek words: *misthòn* and *apékhō*. This is a problem because the two words have quite different meanings; the translation is right for one word but quite wrong for the other.

The connotation of divine reward for *misthòn* is probably clearest in Matthew 5:12, Jesus's Sermon on the Mount, where it is used to describe the heavenly reward given to those persecuted for Jesus's sake. But *misthòn* is used in our passage in verses 1, 2, 5, and 16 to refer to the "reward" already received in this world by the hypocrites of phony piety. The irony seems clear: these people will not receive the heavenly reward *misthòn* implies, and the reward they do receive on earth pales in comparison to the real deal.

The second Greek word the RSV translates as "reward" is a form of *apékhō*. This word appears several times in Matthew and elsewhere in the New Testament. It means "to give back, restore, return." It also means to render what is due, including debts and wages. This is not at all the same meaning as "reward"! For example, Matthew uses a form of *apékhō* in 20:8 to refer to the wages the owner of the vineyard paid to the laborers. As we may recall, he paid the same amount to those who had toiled all day as to those who worked only an hour.

In Matthew 18: 25–34 a form of *apékhō* is used repeatedly in the story of the unjust steward who owed his lord ten thousand talents but could not repay him. His master forgave the debt completely, but then this servant turned around and demanded those who owed him money to repay him. When his master found out, the unjust steward was jailed until he repaid all his debt.

In Luke 19:8, Zacchaeus says, "If I have defrauded any one of anything, I will restore [*àpothithomi*] it fourfold."

If you still have any doubts that *apékhō* does not mean "reward," Matthew uses a form of this word when Joseph of Arimathea asks Pilate to "give back" (*apothothēnai*) Jesus's corpse. No reward there!

What Matthew's Jesus is suggesting here is that if we pray, fast, and give alms for the right reason—that is, if we do it for God, not human acclaim—God will give us back what God owes us. It is not a reward, and this affects both our action and God's response.

I think the translation of *apékhō* matters because a reward is external to, or even separate from, the action rewarded. You toil not because you love the labor but because of a reward that is external to your action. However, when Matthew tells us God will restore to us what we gave up, it suggests to me that the good of the action is intrinsic to the sacrifice. If you are making the sacrifice for the right reason, this is what you will feel.

My experience confirms this. Ordinarily, when I pray, fast, or give alms, I sense divine energy, life, and blessing flowing into and around me. This seems to happen close to the time of my action, although sometimes there may be a delay. The joy reminds me of Robert Alter's translation of Psalm 23:3: "My life you bring back."

This translation also suggests prayer, fasting, and alms giving is our joy-filled "job." It is not to be seen as something so extraordinary or supererogatory as to call for a reward. God's response therefore is not to reward us for something special but simply to pay us what God owes us.

Have a Spirit-filled Lent!

FIRST SUNDAY OF LENT

Genesis 2:7–9; 3:1–7
Romans 5:12–19
Matthew 4:1–11

THIS WEEK WE have to come to grips with more than the gospel reading; we must contend with the original sin. What is that?

Books have been written on this subject; I can't do full justice to such an important and complicated issue. But I also cannot avoid it. The original sin is hard for us modern people to understand and accept. Yet we cannot really understand Jesus's mission unless we have some understanding of the problem he came to redeem us from. I will limit myself here to grappling only with what our readings tell us about the original sin and Jesus's temptation.

I read the Genesis account as an effort to answer this question: if God is loving and all powerful, why are sin and death in the world? Before we examine its answer to that question, notice the presupposition of the story: the Bible is telling us here that sin and death are the two essential problems with being human. That is already telling us a lot. Do you agree with this assessment of the human condition?

I also read the Genesis story as an answer to the question of what makes us different from the animals God created. The answer given is that we know when we do something wrong, so we can feel guilty. And we know we are going to die. Animals do not want to die, but I don't believe they have our awareness of it. Sometimes dogs appear to look guilty, but I suspect it is more a case of not wanting to get caught and punished.

The story, in passing, answers the smaller questions of why work is so hard and the delivery of babies so painful. Don't miss the presupposition behind all these questions. Sin, death, toil, and painful childbirth should not exist. Genesis affirms God is good and God's creation is good, but these realities are not good at all, and that generates the problem the story of the Fall seeks to answer.

Genesis tells us that sin and death came into the world because of our disobedience to God. That is an unsatisfying answer for a number of reasons. The most important one, in my view, is that as Julian of Norwich points out, God could very well have created a world in which we freely chose never to sin.[45]

The standard answer is that God created us to be free, and because we have free will, we can choose to reject God. Adam and Eve exercised this freedom to be disobedient, and so human freedom is the cause of the Fall, and it is the reason why we still "choose" to sin.

One advantage of this position is it seems to let God off the hook for the existence of moral evil in the world. It's our fault that we have misused the divine freedom God gave us. But I have come to reject this view for theological reasons. To conceive of human freedom as the power to reject God places humans and God on the same level. It means the only way I could avoid sin is if I lost my freedom and were nothing but God's puppet, with God always pulling the strings. This is a typical modern mistake of secular reason's conception of God: God is an entity, a divine puppeteer, rather than "being" itself. And this view exalts sin, distorting it into an exercise in human freedom.

I can only fall into a power struggle with another being like myself, and this is precisely what God is not. In fact, God is the ground of my genuine freedom, and the only true exercise of my freedom is to follow God's will. Far from being an expression of freedom, sin—and especially sinful habits—leads to a loss of freedom, as any addict will tell you.

David Bentley Hart puts this well in his book *That All Shall Be Saved*: "But you cannot reject God except defectively, by having failed to recognize him as the primordial object of all your deepest longings; the very source of their activity. . . . This means also that God could never be, for the rational will, merely some extrinsic causality intruding upon the will's autonomy."[46]

Hart explains later that God gives human beings freedom always by making us freely seek God as the ultimate end in all else that our intentional consciousness seeks.

This understanding of God is quite Catholic and is related to God's universal salvific will (see appendix A). But it does create the problem that Julian of Norwich wrestled with. God could have created us so that we freely choose never to sin. Why did God not do that?

Genesis does not tell us. Julian's answer is that God revealed to her, "All shall be well, and all shall be well, and all manner of thing shall be well." This is hard to swallow when we consider the genocides of Hitler, Pol Pot, Rwanda, not to mention so many other horrible crimes that cry out to heaven. Yet Christ's death and resurrection give us some basis to believe Julian's revelation is true. At any rate, we cannot resolve this thorny problem here, as we have to push on to St. Paul's interpretation of the Genesis Fall in this week's Romans reading.

Here's what David Bentley Hart has to say about Romans 5:12: "A fairly easy verse to follow until one reaches the final four words, whose precise meaning is already obscure, and whose notoriously defective rendering in the Latin Vulgate [*in quo omnes peccaverunt*] *constitutes one of the most consequential mistranslations in Christian history.*"[47]

The standard translation and interpretation of this verse

is that we all somehow participated in Adam's sin and now inherit his guilt when we are born. The Western understanding of original sin, or original guilt, is that we are all born guilty enough to be damned to hell forever because we have somehow sinned in Adam.

The NJBC notes these words are debated by scholars to this day, offers five ways of understanding the verse, and concludes there is no real consensus on how to translate or interpret 5:12.[48] I cannot here delve into the details of Greek grammar that drive this debate; if you are interested in doing so, I recommend consulting NJBC and Hart's translation.

I end up siding with Hart's translation, for grammatical reasons I will not go into, and for theological reasons, which I will. Here is how Hart translates verse 12: "Therefore, just as sin entered into the cosmos through one man, and death through sin, so also death pervaded humanity, whereupon all sinned."[49]

Hart rejects the view that Paul is here telling us we somehow inherit Adam's sin and guilt. Rather, Adam sinned, and because of this, *death*—not sin—spreads to all humankind. As a consequence of death spreading to all human beings, we all became sinners. Paul sees death and sin as a kind of contagious disease which we are all born into, or a civil enslavement from which we need to be "redeemed" to regain our freedom. What Paul does not do here, or elsewhere, is see sin "as an inherited condition of criminal culpability."[50]

This interpretation makes sense exegetically because it sets up the parallel between Adam and Jesus that St. Paul develops in verses 15–20. After Adam, sin and death are built into the human condition. Adam is a mythological person, so it doesn't make any sense to worry about whether we got this way because of what he did. It is undeniable that we all sin and we all die—these are facts.

What Paul asserts is that Christ reverses this contagion. Jesus's reversal of Adam is clearest in verse 18: "Then as one man's trespass led to condemnation for all men, so one man's act of righteousness leads to acquittal and life for all men." Note that just as we are all subject to sin and death after Adam, we all are now freed from sin and death because of Jesus. This reading is incompatible with a hell of eternal torment, but it is of course in line with the universalism I discuss in appendix A.

Seeing sin and death as a kind of contagious disease is also consistent with St. Augustine's marvelous image of Jesus as our physician. If we can "catch" sin and death from Adam, we can also "catch" eternal life and forgiveness of sins from Jesus. Jesus's sinlessness and resurrection are therefore his crucial gifts to us, freeing us from these twin, related evils.

I recognize this reading of original guilt and St. Paul may seem strange to Western Christians, but it is not so for the Orthodox. Why have we Westerners rejected what seems like the plain meaning of verse 18 and so many other passages that promise eternal life to all? Is it because it simply seems too good to be true?

Hart points out that belief in universal salvation was far more widespread in the first five centuries of Christian history than at any time since. He suggests one reason for the decline of this doctrine may have been because there are many people "who can be convinced to be good only through the threat of endless torture at the hands of an indefatigably vindictive God."[51] That is plausible. But while the threat of a hell of eternal punishment might induce some people to be less unjust in this life, it is unfair to God! If we are all spared from the sin-death trap, it is good news. How is it good news if instead we are threatened with a hell of eternal punishment?

Now we are in a position to look at Matthew's account of Jesus's temptation in the desert. We cannot know the basis of this story. Did Jesus confide in his disciples about his temptations, and did this enter the oral or written tradition? Is this the Holy Spirit inspiring the early Church?

I love these temptation stories because I see them as potentially offering us fascinating information about Jesus's inner life. What is more revealing than what tempts us?

The tempter's first two temptations begin with "If you are the Son of God . . ." This suggests two possibilities. Was Jesus sometimes tempted to doubt his mission and status? During his baptism, just before the Spirit drove him out to the desert, God declares, "This is my Son, the beloved, in whom I have delighted" (Matthew 3:17). Jesus may have been waiting for this divine approbation for many years. This may have been what the "hidden years" in his twenties were about.

The very fact that we have this baptism story, that we and Jesus need to hear God say this, tells me that whether Jesus was God's Son was an issue. Surely hearing God's voice would settle the matter once and for all. But in moments of weakness, after days of solitary fasting in the wilderness, we might be tempted to doubt what we heard, or think we heard. Before Jesus can embark on his dangerous mission, he needs to confront any remaining doubts he might have about his status as God's Son. His faith needs to be as powerful as the temporal and spiritual forces he will confront.

In these first two temptations, the slanderer also tempts Jesus to use his divine power to serve his own needs, first for food and second to prove he is God's Son. This makes a lot of sense to me. If I were Jesus, I would be tempted to use my power to serve my own needs, be they material or spiritual. As Jesus's story unfolds, we see again and again that he always uses his power to serve others, never himself. Extraordinary! Jesus appears to have no ego needs. I believe it is because he was clear on who he was: God's beloved Son. What more does he, or anyone, need?

I love that the tempter quotes Scripture. This suggests to me that Jesus, like all of us, wrestles with God's Word. The Bible is not a self-interpreting text. Its meaning is not always clear.

In fact, if misread, it is dangerous! Too often we think reading the Bible is always good for us, never harmful. I disagree. The Bible needs to be read with other believers, living and dead, and in humility with the Holy Spirit. The Catholic Church is sometimes attacked for keeping Scripture from laypeople before the Reformation. I'm glad we got past that, yet this caution about the possible dangers of the Bible points to a profound truth.

Jesus knows how to apply the complicated, various words of Scripture to concrete situations. This is a gift of the Spirit and at the same time the fruit of prolonged study and prayer.

The culminating temptation is the offer to Jesus of glory and world dominion. Despite his divine power, Jesus ended up a failure in the eyes of the world. This temptation brings to mind Jesus's words in Matthew 26:53 when, as he is being arrested, one of those with him pulls out a sword and slices off the ear of the chief priest's slave: "Do you imagine that I cannot ask my Father, and he will at this very moment place more than twelve legions of angels beside me?" Can you imagine having the power to destroy evil and avoid a tortured, humiliating death . . . and not using it?!

God is not violent and will never use force to conform us to God's will. If we are to follow Jesus, we must act the same. This may well be the greatest temptation of all.

SECOND SUNDAY OF LENT

Genesis 12:1–4a
2 Timothy 1:8b–10
Matthew 17:1–9

I WAS DISCUSSING the Transfiguration with some friends not long ago, and one of them, a retired Lutheran pastor, called this event a "booster shot" for Jesus and the disciples. I have long struggled to make sense of the Transfiguration, but this characterization helped frame it for me.

The context suggests Jesus and his friends needed some transcendent support. In Matthew, Jesus has just warned his disciples that he will have to "suffer many things" from the chief priests in Jerusalem and be put to death. When Peter objects to this horrible fate, Jesus attacks him, calling him Satan, viz. devil or accuser. The disciples are doubtless afraid and discouraged by Jesus's fateful prediction. They had hoped Jesus would redeem Israel in his lifetime. Conflict and division between them and Jesus make matters worse. Jesus the man must also have been afraid, or else he would not have called Peter a *skándalon*, or "stumbling block."

Maybe we too, in the middle of Lent, are feeling discouraged by our sacrifices; we too need a vision.

The fundamental mystery of Jesus is his fully divine and human nature. The disciples were fully aware of his humanity. This episode serves as a reminder and proof of his divinity.

These considerations lead to another question: why does

Jesus only bring Peter, James, and John to the mountaintop to experience his transfiguration? Surely all the disciples needed this "booster shot."

One answer to this question is that afterwards Jesus tells these three to keep the event a secret until Jesus rises from the dead. It's obviously easier to keep it a secret if only three, rather than twelve, know about it. But this only raises another question: why keep it a secret?

The early Christian writers can help us out here. Here's what Chrysostom has to say: "For the greater the things said about him, the harder it was for the many at that time to accept them. And the offense of the cross increased all the more thereby. Therefore he told them be silent about the transfiguration."[52]

This leads us to consider another mystery. On the one hand, God the Father transfigures Jesus in this marvelous way and tells the disciples to listen to his beloved Son. And then God turns around and allows this same man to be publicly humiliated, tortured, and crucified! Is it not almost incredible that this is the kind of God we have? After two thousand years, we now take this for granted, but we should not.

These reflections lead me to conclude that Jesus judged Peter, James, and John to have greater faith than the other nine disciples. They could handle this scandal, and in fact, the Transfiguration might even strengthen their faith to hang in there when Jesus hangs on the cross. Jesus will call these three to stay with him during his agony in the Garden of Gethsemane. They don't do very well there, of course, falling asleep when Jesus needs them most. That Jesus placed such trust in these three both then and at the Transfiguration deepens the pathos of the scene.

What's up with the three booths Peter wants to build? The NJBC tells us this has to do with the Jewish feast of booths, Sukkot. This idea goes nowhere. Sukkot was celebrated at a specific time in the autumn; it was a harvest feast. Was it autumn? Who knows? When people are anxious, they often find it necessary to say something, no matter how inane, as a way to allay the anxiety.

Moses and Elijah represent the Law and the Prophets. By proposing the three booths, Peter is implicitly putting Jesus into the same category as Moses and Elijah. But one of the messages of the Transfiguration is that Jesus is both connected to, yet transcendent of, the Law and the Prophets. The disappearance of Moses and Elijah at the end of the story confirms the supremacy of Jesus for Origen: "They saw Jesus only and no other. Moses, the law and Elijah the prophet had become one with the gospel of Jesus. They did not abide as they formerly were as three, but they became one."[53]

The first reading shows the Church connects the Transfiguration to God's call to Abraham to leave his country and journey to the land God will show him. This connection can have two meanings. Objectively, the Genesis passage can connect Jesus's transcendence of the Law and Prophets to the fulfillment of God's promise in Genesis 12:3, "And by you all the families of the earth shall bless themselves."

Subjectively, it can mean that we are called to follow Jesus, to be transfigured out of our own comfortable native place, to go to the strange and unknown promised land. Christians too are to be transfigured, transformed, as St. Paul writes in Romans 12:2 and 2 Corinthians 3:18.

THIRD SUNDAY OF LENT

Exodus 17:3–7
Romans 5:1–2, 5–8
John 4:5–42

TWO THEMES JUMP out of this week's gospel passage, demanding our attention. We encounter here the first missionary-apostle, and she has three strikes against her: she's a woman, a Samaritan, and has had way too many husbands. Jesus does not seem to care. Second, what is meant by the water Jesus gives that will end our thirst forever?

In *The Community of the Blessed Disciple*, Raymond Brown points to the original Greek to support the idea that we should see this unnamed Samaritan woman as akin to Jesus's male disciples.[54] John explains that many Samaritan villagers believe in Jesus because of the woman's word by using the phrase *dia tou logou pisteuein*. These are the same words Jesus uses later (in John 17:20) when, just before his arrest, he prays for those who come to believe through the words of his disciples.

Jesus makes clear that this woman has a missionary function in his conversation with his male disciples at 4:35–38. Earlier, at 4:30, we are told that many Samaritans are now coming out of the city to Jesus because of what the woman told them. Jesus then tells his disciples, "I sent you to reap that for which you did not labor; others have labored, and you have entered into their labor."

The Samaritan woman's testimony to the villagers precedes

the "reaping" of the disciples. Just as women are the first witnesses of Jesus's resurrection, a woman is the first missionary-evangelist. Given the status of women in traditional Judaism, this is a shocking development. We are not shocked by this because we live two thousand years after Jesus's religious revolution. We need to exercise our historical imagination when we read the gospels.

The disciples underscore the strangeness of Jesus even talking with a woman in public in 4:27. Is this because Jesus rarely did it, or because no one was ever supposed to do it? In any event, their astonishment is one reason why I sense a frisson of erotic tension in this exchange.

Jesus and this woman are alone. Robert Alter, the superb translator of the Old Testament, points out, "The drawing of water after encountering a maiden at a well in a foreign land signals to the audience that a betrothal type-scene is unfolding."[55] Alter is commenting on the episode when Jacob meets his future wife, Rachel, at a well—and kisses her. Jesus meets this woman at "Jacob's well." Throughout the Old Testament, men and women frequently met and became engaged at wells. This context would have been obvious to any Jewish person. Here, instead of forming a new marriage, the woman's previous relationships are revealed.

The denouement of this tension comes when Jesus tells her to go and come back with her husband and we learn she is on her sixth husband. Could this be why she is drawing water alone? It is midday, and traditionally women came to collect water in the cool of the morning for the rest of the day. Do the other women in the town want nothing to do with such a woman? Jesus may well have surmised the woman was an outcast and the reason why.

We cannot lose sight of what a shocking reversal of norms this is. The first missionary of the gospel is a loose-living Samaritan woman. The embarrassment the story surely provoked for many early Christians, especially Jewish Christians, is a sign of its historicity. It would strain credulity if the other villagers came to believe in Jesus only because of this tainted evangelist. But we learn in 4:42 that although she got the ball rolling, the other Samaritans came to believe Jesus was the Savior of the world also because of his own testimony.

The story sheds light on the gradual progress of belief. She sees Jesus at first just as an impertinent, thirsty Jewish man. Next, she perceives him to be a prophet. Later, she and many villagers come to believe in Jesus as the Christ and the Savior. Elsewhere in the gospels, belief is often presented as an urgent matter requiring an immediate decision. This story about the gradual growth of faith is more in line with my experience.

What are we to make of Jesus's claim that he can give living water that will make us never thirst again? Water is a metaphor for the gifts that result from faith. The twin evils of sin and death can make this life feel fragile, pointless, or tragic, causing us to "thirst" for something that appears to transcend these horrors (e.g., money, power, fame, status, sex, security, etc.). But as you may have noticed, people pursuing these things never seem to have enough of them; they keep thirsting for more. The empty promises of this false transcendence cannot deliver what only faith can.

What does the Exodus story of Meribah bring to the table? It is an early critique of the anxiety that arises naturally when faith weakens. The people did not believe God was truly with them. Yet can you blame them? People die of thirst in the desert all the time!

The Exodus passage also highlights the common distinction between the Old Testament's focus on the material nature of reality versus the New Testament's tendency to spiritualize reality. This tendency is clearest in John's gospel, where Jesus frequently speaks in metaphors while his Jewish interlocuters misunderstand him to be speaking literally. This is apparent in the Jacob's-well story we read today.

Some of my Jewish friends wonder if Christianity is "too spiritual" and therefore too easily ignores material reality, such as injustice in the here and now. This tension between the material and the spiritual seems to have been part of what separated us from our Jewish brothers and sisters early on, and perhaps it persists to this day. This "Jewish" critique seems valid to me, and something for us Christians to be watchful of. Genuine faith must always affirm the unity of matter and spirit. And of course Christian faith, if not Christian practice, is very "materialistic." We believe God took on human flesh and appeared in history. You cannot get more "materialistic" than that!

FOURTH SUNDAY OF LENT

1 Samuel 16:1b, 6–7, 10–13a
Ephesians 5:8–14
John 9:1–41

THIS WEEK'S READINGS provoke more questions in my mind than answers.

Why must this poor beggar be born blind just so "the works of God might be made manifest in him"? It doesn't seem fair, does it? Perhaps the answer lies in the difference between God's time and our human experience of it. We experience time as a one-way, linear progression; for God, all eternity is continually present. This experience of blindness led to the beggar's healing and something more precious than sight: faith and the experience of Jesus.

The disciples reveal the common presupposition of the Jewish Wisdom tradition. If you are righteous, God will reward you, and if you suffer, it is because God is punishing you for your sins. Job already challenged this view in the Old Testament, and Jesus's crucifixion finally puts it to death for Christians.

I do not want to bring back the "blame the victim" notion that suffering is God's punishment for sin. But if sin is not the cause of suffering, then what is? When a natural disaster or a plague like COVID-19 destroys many lives, we no longer have an explanation. But maybe explaining these horrors is an insult to those who are suffering. What we can say is that no one need suffer alone: Jesus is suffering there with us on our cross.

Curiously, this man does not ask to be cured of his blindness as the others Jesus heals do. How does Jesus know he wants to be cured? Gaining his vision led to problems and a completely different life.

Why does Jesus choose to heal on the Sabbath? Could he not have healed the man on any of the other six days of the week, thereby avoiding antagonizing the Pharisees? Perhaps Jesus's compassion compelled him to do it spontaneously. Or perhaps Jesus wanted to challenge the restrictive Sabbath rules of his day.

How is it good news for Jesus to "come into the cosmos for judgment, that those without sight may see, and those with sight might become blind"? I can understand the good news of the first part of the statement, but not the last. Maybe the idea is not that Jesus makes people blind but rather that he reveals the blindness inherent in thinking we "know all, understand all."

The reading from 1 Samuel also seems to be about the difference between how humans and God see things. But this story has always puzzled me. God first says to Samuel in 16:7, "Do not look on his appearance or on the height of his stature, because I have rejected him; for the Lord sees not as man sees; man looks at outward appearances, but the Lord looks on the heart."

Later, after Samuel has David brought before him, the narrator informs us in verse 12 that David "was ruddy, and had beautiful eyes, and was handsome. And the Lord said, 'Arise, anoint him; for this is he.'" Nothing here about David's heart at all. After telling us that God does not care about outward appearances, the description of David's handsome outward appearance could have been penned by a smitten schoolgirl!

That's all I have this week. Please forgive me. You see, today I finally am fully vaccinated, and so I did tons of shopping! Because of the pandemic, I have not been to a store in months.

FIFTH SUNDAY OF LENT

Ezekiel 37:12–14
Romans 8:8–11
John 11:1–45

THE RAISING OF Lazarus occurs only in John's gospel, and this is fitting. The story shows Jesus at the pinnacle of his power over life and death. While he does restore Jairus's daughter to life (Mark 5:22, par.) as well as the widow's son at Nain (Luke 7:11), those two people had died just before Jesus saw them. Perhaps they had not really died but were in a coma. Jesus's skeptics would certainly have asserted something along these lines.

With Lazarus we have a completely different situation. This is a man who is certifiably dead and buried. NJBC tells us that Lazarus had been dead long enough that rabbinic authorities would have said his soul had departed the vicinity of his body and the corpse's decay had definitely begun. The detail Martha gives us in verse 39 drives the point home graphically: "Lord, by now it gives off a bad odor; for this is the fourth day."

Bringing Lazarus back to life plays a critical narrative role unique to John's gospel. This miracle causes so many people to have faith in Jesus that the Pharisees and the chief priests grow terrified that the Romans will take away the Jews' holy places and their nation. They decide to kill Jesus because as the chief priest Caiaphas explains in 11:49, "It is expedient for us that one man should die for the people and that the whole nation not perish."

This is the classic function of scapegoating violence,

brilliantly diagnosed by Rene Girard.[56] Girard argues that all societies achieve unity and ward off the continual threat of civil war by uniting around the persecution of an innocent scapegoat. The function of religion is to hide the innocence of scapegoats so that we can kill them with a clear conscience. Christianity is unique because it reveals the innocence of the scapegoat: Jesus is sinless. Unfortunately, our need to scapegoat is too deep to go away easily, and despite the revelation of the cross, we continue to do it: burning witches, gassing Jews, lynching African Americans. But increasingly, we can no longer commit these atrocities with the clear conscience of ancient societies.

Unlike the Jesus of the synoptics, John's Jesus is always in control of the situation. He deliberately delays coming to save Lazarus, even when told he is seriously ill, so that Lazarus will be dead long enough to remove any doubt that Jesus is lord of life and of death. Both Mary and Martha reproach him for this: "Lord, had you been here my brother would not have died."

Jesus's deliberate delay seems out of character. His practice is to conceal his miraculous healing powers as much as possible. When he uses them, it is always to serve others. Here, he is deliberately displaying his greatest miracle to further his own mission, and he is doing so at the expense of people he loves. I will return to this problem below.

Perhaps this inner conflict explains Jesus's reaction when confronted with the grief of Mary, Martha, and all the other mourners. Hart translates the description of Jesus after he sees Mary weeping: "he groaned in his spirit and yielded himself to his turmoil." This is as human and out of control as John's Jesus can get!

The key Greek word Hart translates as "groaned in his spirit" is *enebrimésato*. It can also be translated as "to snort as a horse" and thus to speak or act with deep feeling or as an expression of anger. Could Jesus really have been angry with people grieving for his dead friend Lazarus?

Elsewhere in the gospels, Jesus has shown impatience with mourners. We see this in Mark 5:38–40 just before Jesus brings back to life the daughter of Jairus, a ruler of the synagogue: "[Jesus] saw a tumult, and people weeping and wailing loudly. And when he had entered, he said to them, 'Why do you make a tumult and weep? The child is not dead but sleeping.' And they laughed at him."

This episode strikes us as odd. We might cry quietly at a funeral, but making a lot of noise seems tasteless. Plus, how can you switch from loud expressions of grief to laughter in just a few seconds? In ancient Palestine, weeping was a big deal when someone died. You might even hire professional mourners to make a louder ruckus, as doing so showed love and respect for the dead person. Perhaps this explains the abrupt change from tears to derisive laughter at Jesus. It may also explain Jesus's impatience with this phony display.

The most revealing example of Jesus's apparent contempt for Jewish mourning practices is Matthew 8:21–22. Here a disciple asks Jesus if he can first go and bury his father. Jesus replies, "Follow me, and leave the dead to bury their own dead." Even in our day, we would take the command not to give our father a proper funeral, and not to allow some time to mourn his loss, as a shocking lack of feeling for a spiritual leader. Jesus normally is deeply moved with compassion when confronted with the suffering of others. What is going on here?

The key is the phrase "leave the dead to bury their own dead." If we lack faith in eternal life, we are spiritually dead, and we are going to have to suffer and mourn when a loved one dies. Jesus demands his disciples have faith in life: in this life and the life to come. If they do, they are spiritually alive, not dead.

All this helps me understand why Jesus could have been upset, angry, conflicted, or groaning inside when faced with the Lazarus mourners. He must have known this would happen when he deliberately delayed his return, but now he is confronted with it, and it is painful to behold. It is painful first of all because Jesus is moved by other people's suffering; this pain is complicated for him because he knows the sorrow, while real, is based on a misunderstanding about life, death, and betrays a lack of faith. And finally, Jesus is himself the proximate cause of this tumult.

"Jesus wept," verse 35, is the shortest verse in the Bible. We cannot know what made him cry. My guess would be the powerful combination of emotions: compassion for those who were suffering, anger with the "in your face" experience of death's merciless dominion over people's hearts and souls, frustration with his role in bringing about this situation. John's Jesus seems to have already conquered death; perhaps he forgot other people have not reached this level of faith. Now he is experiencing what it's like to be under death's dominion.

Why does Jesus raise Lazarus from the dead? After all, Lazarus is going to die again anyway. The miracle shows Jesus is the "life of the world," an important theme in John's gospel. Jesus has power over life and death and has destroyed death. Death has no ultimate reality, although it does continue to exist.

R. H. Fuller, in *Interpreting Miracles*, points to a reason to wonder if this episode happened as John relates it (91ff). Why would the synoptists omit this powerful story, especially since according to John it was the immediate cause of Jesus's arrest?

John's gospel contains a number of miracles found in the synoptics, but in John the miraculous is heightened. John's Jesus heals the official's son in Capernaum at a distance (4:46ff), just as he heals the centurion's servant in Matthew 8:5–13 and Luke 7:1–10. But in Matthew and Luke, Jesus is just outside Capernaum; in John, Jesus is at Cana, nearly twenty miles away from the official's son. In John, the blind man Jesus healed (9:1) was born blind; the lame man of Bethesda (5:5) had been crippled for thirty-eight years. And, as we pointed out, Lazarus was dead for four days, while in Mark, Jairus's daughter had only just died, and in Luke Jesus met the funeral procession for the widow's son he brought back to life.

Today's first two readings help to steer us away from wondering too much about whether or not Jesus raised Lazarus as John reports. As we approach Holy Week, we remember the joy of Easter is God's destruction of death's apparent finality. This is what Ezekiel's God is telling us.

St. Paul reminds us that faith in Jesus's resurrection completely alters the way we live now. The Holy Spirit that raised Christ from the dead also dwells in us right now.

What does St. Paul mean when he writes in verse 8, "For those existing in the flesh cannot be pleasing to God"? Are not we all existing in flesh until we die? Paul contrasts "flesh" with "spirit." By "spirit" he means our human spirit as well as the way we participate in God's Spirit, through the Holy Spirit and Christ's Spirit which "dwells in [us]." (I capitalize "Spirit" to refer to God's Spirit, and leave it lowercase for our human spirit.) This spirit/Spirit gives eternal life and brings us to a fuller, richer, more intense life right now, even before we die.

If we read Romans 8, we see that Paul connects flesh to sin, death, enmity to God, slavery to fear, pointlessness, and decay. I believe we could read "flesh" to mean the natural selfishness we have when we consider our own material well-being first. This is where we start off in nature; it can be seen as the fruit of evolution—the survival instinct.

We saw back on the first Sunday of Lent in Romans 5:12 that St. Paul believed in what I call the reversal of Adam. Adam sinned and as a result was punished with death. For us, this sequence is reversed: Adam bequeathed death to us, and this death leads us to sin. This helps to understand why Paul connects flesh, death, and sin as he does here and contrasts it with spirit, God's Holy Spirit, and life.

PASSION SUNDAY

(Palm Sunday)
What Jesus Did Not Know

Matthew 21:1–11
Isaiah 50:4–7
Philippians 2:6–11
Matthew 27:11–54

PERHAPS BECAUSE I am a convert, the Catholic celebration of Passion Sunday (Palm Sunday) has always confused me. I am used to celebrating Jesus's triumphant entry into Jerusalem, described in our first reading from Matthew. But we have two gospel readings today, and the second, longer one is about Jesus's passion. Why do we read both on the same day?

The juxtaposition of the two different stories raises another question. How does Jesus fall so quickly in the span of a few days, from receiving a hero's welcome to being the object of the crowd's fury on Good Friday? From "Hosanna!" to "Crucify him!"

Let's take the second question first. The prophecy Matthew believes Jesus fulfills speaks of "your king." The people shouted, "Hosanna to the son of David." David was a king. Throughout history, kings have frequently been murdered. People often turn on leaders in a hurry; crowds are fickle. We see a milder version of this phenomenon in the US. Every president comes to office with approval ratings that gradually decline the first years he is in office. The president's party is normally punished in the midterm elections.

A second answer to the question is that the Good Friday crowd was made up of different people from the Palm Sunday crowd, and they all had different notions of who Jesus was. It is likely the people crying, "Hosanna!" had different ideas about who Jesus was, beyond the son of David or Messiah. We catch a glimpse of this in verse 11 when, in response to a question about who Jesus is, Matthew tells us the crowds respond, "This is the prophet Jesus, the one from Nazareth in Galilee." This verse is found only in Matthew. The reference here to Jesus as a mere prophet—rather than as someone more exalted, like the Son of God or the Son of Man—makes it more likely it is historically accurate.

Reading on the same day the two stories of Jesus's triumphant entry and horrible crucifixion forces us to face the total picture of Jesus's final week in Jerusalem. I have come to think there might even be one answer to both questions.

Hosanna means "Help, I pray!" It can also mean "save."[57] When the crowd cries, "Hosanna to the son of David," they are crying for help from someone like King David, the archetypal Jewish military (and religious) leader. However, Jesus usually shrank from comparisons with King David and with messianic expectations because Jesus was committed to a nonviolent revolution of the spirit.

What did the people of Jerusalem want to be saved from? The Romans. The people of Jerusalem wanted a military leader to eject by force the oppressive Roman rulers and return the holy city to Jewish control. They understood violence was the only language the Romans understood. Jesus's rejection of violence must have disappointed many. Given the oppression suffered by Jews, it is not hard to imagine the disappointment turning to rage: "Crucify him!"

The people may also have wanted deliverance from their own religious leaders, who were cut off from the common people, corrupted, and compromised by their alliance with the Romans.

The people had already showed how much they loved John the Baptist's radical critique of the religious status quo, thereby frightening and infuriating the religious establishment.

Unique to Matthew is the use of two animals, the ass and the colt. Matthew does this because he reads the prophecy too literally. Hebrew poetry and prophecy often use a device known as parallelism. This means using two similar words or phrases to make the same point a little stronger. Zechariah 9:9 foretells Jesus as "humble and riding on an ass, on a colt the foal of an ass." The prophet uses two ways of referring to the same animal. How could Jesus ride on two animals at the same time? This rather pedestrian mistake helps us understand and, at least for me, even like Matthew a little more. I think I can hear him saying, "Oops!" across the centuries.

What is more important than Matthew's humble mistake is the humility and nonviolence involved in Jesus's triumphant entry on an ass. It would be like a president in a motorcade riding in a Volkswagen beetle! Kings and generals ride horses. Horses are larger and more intimidating than asses; they connote violence and oppression. Even today, police ride horses to control crowds and maintain order through fear. By riding an ass Jesus is already signaling the people, "Not your usual messiah king."

The Philippians reading is, to my mind, one of the most important passages in the New Testament. The self-emptying, the kenosis, of the preexistent divine Godhead is one of the foundations for my Christology (see appendix B). Jesus's passion passes beyond humility to utter defeat and humiliation. You cannot empty yourself of your divinity more than that!

The Isaiah verses counter the notion that humiliation is the final word on what Jesus went through. Jesus remained faithful and obedient to the end, even forgiving his tormenters: "For the Lord God helps me . . . and I know that I shall not be put to shame." His faith in God preserved his soul—and of course his body as well, as we will discover on Easter Sunday.

These two readings help support the understanding I have of Jesus's crucifixion—one I have come to believe is crucial for the life of faith and discipleship. Jesus did not *know* he would be raised from the dead on Easter Sunday: he had faith that somehow God would save him. He trusted God would ultimately come to his rescue, but he did not know how. There is evidence that he believed, incorrectly, God would intervene on Good Friday in a definitive and eschatological way.

First, on Good Friday Jesus tells the high priest, "But I tell you, hereafter you will see the Son of man seated at the right hand of Power, and coming on the clouds of heaven" (Matthew 26:64). This is critical to the drama of Jesus's passion, as with these words the high priest tore his robes and declared Jesus had uttered blasphemy that deserved death. But Jesus was mistaken about this. The high priest saw no such thing, nor did anyone else. The Parousia Jesus expected in "his generation" (Matthew 24:34) did not happen.

A second reason I believe Jesus did not know what would happen to him on the cross and afterwards is Matthew 27:46 (par. Mark): "My God, my God, why did you forsake me?"

A third scriptural reason I believe that Jesus did not know what God would do to save him is Matthew 24:36 (par. Mark). Jesus believed that his death would usher in the eschatological intervention of God. But in this Matthew passage, Jesus is speaking to his disciples about the last things—heaven, hell, death, judgment, the Parousia, and the end of the age: "But about that day and hour no one knows—neither the angels of the heavens nor the Son—except the Father only."

The kenosis of Philippians 2:6–8 further supports the idea that Jesus emptied himself of divine omniscience in order to become fully human (see appendices A and B). Not knowing what tomorrow will bring is an essential dimension of what it is to be human. If we know what will happen in the future, we simply cannot be fully human. That would be cheating!

This is clearest, in my mind, when we think of Jesus's passion. If Jesus knew for a fact that in three days he would be raised from the dead, that his followers would later rally and go on to establish a worldwide Church that has lasted longer than any nation or empire, it is not such a big deal to go through excruciating pain for a few hours. To paraphrase Nietzsche, if we have a why, we can handle any what or how.

If, on the other hand, Jesus goes to Calvary just as we would, with only his trust in God to support him, it makes what he did divine! This is the paradoxical truth: it is precisely Jesus's lack of knowledge, his self-emptying, his total faith in God, that makes him divine. Philippians 3:8–10 makes this very point: "He reduced himself, becoming obedient all the way to death, and a death by a cross. For which reason God also exalted him on high and graced him with the name that is above every name, so that at the name of Jesus every knee—of beings heavenly and earthly and subterranean—should bend."

What makes Matthew's account of the scene where Pilate questions Jesus unique is the way Matthew underscores the guilt of the Jewish crowd. He highlights their free choice between Barabbas and Jesus by having Pilate ask the crowd directly if they want him to free Barabbas or Jesus. They call for Barabbas to be freed, while Jesus should be crucified. The principal addition unique to Matthew in this scene are verses 24–25. Here Pilate washes his hands and states he is innocent of this man's blood. The crowd, on the other hand, declares, "His blood be upon us and our children."

Given the long history of Christian anti-Semitism, this verse is an obvious problem. Matthew wrote this verse, however, at a time when his community of Jewish Christians had been ejected from the Jewish synagogue because they accepted Jesus as the Son of

God. The two communities were in the middle of a bitter family feud. I think Matthew would be appalled to learn how these verses were misused in the centuries that followed. Notice the crowd does not say, "His blood be upon us and our children *forever*."

Compared to the well-established Jewish community, the early Christian community was weak and vulnerable to oppression. Sometimes Jewish people would abet Roman persecution of Christians. None of this historical context excuses the far worse crimes professed Christians later inflicted upon Jews. It should alter the way we read Scripture, however. The New Testament arose at a time when Christians, many of whom were themselves Jews, were sometimes being persecuted by Jews—Jesus Christ, of course, being the first.

The silence of Jesus in the synoptic gospel accounts of his "trial" before the Sanhedrin and Pilate has always astonished me as much as it did the governor:

> AND. WHEN HE was accused by the chief priests and elders of the people he made no answer. Then Pilate says to him, "Do you not hear all the things they attest against you?" And he did not answer him, not a single word, so that the governor was greatly astonished. (Matthew 27:12–14)

Maybe I find this unfathomable because I have a big mouth. I cannot conceive of remaining silent when confronted with false accusations that could mean torture and death. Good heavens, I can't let the pettiest unfair accusations go by without objecting!

What do I need to learn from the silence of Jesus? He was not totally silent, as we have seen in his statement to the high priest at Matthew 26:64. This prediction, which turned out to be incorrect anyway, only got him into deeper trouble. Perhaps Jesus learned from this that it was better to keep his mouth shut.

The American theologian John Courtney Murray once commented that a genuine argument is a rare achievement. We must have some basic agreement on fundamentals in order to discuss true differences. Jesus correctly perceived no such common ground existed between himself and those who had the power to execute him. To begin a discussion with them would put him in a false position, as it would imply there was some common ground upon which to build a dialogue. We can learn something from this.

Pilate and the Jewish leaders were driven to preserve their power, and that made them fearful of Jesus and the people who followed him. Truth, guilt, or innocence did not factor into their calculations. What's to talk about?

By maintaining silence, Jesus is able silently to challenge their way of being in the world more effectively than with words that would be twisted and misunderstood to suit their venal purposes. For example, when Pilate asks him if he is "King of the Jews," Jesus does reply, "You have said so." But that cryptic remark is the end of the "conversation." What Pilate understands by King of the Jews is quite different from Jesus's understanding.

Jesus's silence reveals his skepticism, if not contempt, for the entire human project of reason and justice in this case. It also reveals a deeper faith in God's ultimate justice. Jesus's silence means the accusations against him stand unrefuted. Jesus is not afraid of arguing with Pharisees and others about who God is, what God wants. He shows us there is a time for words and a time for silence.

I have tried to learn from this as well. I have tried to recognize the limits of human reason to resolve conflicts. My faith lies not here but in God's justice. At times, the best way to witness your faith is by remaining silent, difficult as that may be.

EASTER SUNDAY VIGIL

Isaiah 55:1–11
Romans 6:3–11
Matthew 28:1–10

THE GOSPEL ACCOUNTS of the empty tomb that first Easter morning differ in a number of details. Was it one, two, or three women who went to anoint him? Did they see one or two angels (or men?) in the empty tomb? And so on.

Rather than trying to make sense of these discrepancies, I am going to focus on the significance of the details about which the gospels agree. What is the meaning of the empty tomb and Jesus's resurrection appearances?

One crucial detail present in all four gospels is that women are the first to discover the empty tomb and experience the resurrected Jesus. This is plausible historically because the male disciples might well have been paralyzed by fear of the authorities and/or guilt over their cowardly abandonment of Jesus in his time of trial.

The women who followed Jesus were perhaps empowered by their powerlessness. They could not have been expected to do much to protect Jesus, nor did they need to fear the authorities, who regarded them as harmless. Could it be that the women were more receptive to the resurrected Jesus because, unlike the men, they were engaged in acts of service as they attempted to anoint his corpse?

By appearing first to women, Jesus displayed his typical

disregard for Jewish rabbinic norms—that "a woman's testimony was discountable in rabbinic law"—and because of this, the story becomes more historically credible.[58] If early Christians wanted to convince their Jewish brothers of Jesus's resurrection, they would not begin with appearances before women.

Women are the ones who start things in the gospels. Redemption began with Mary's "yes" to the angel Gabriel. As we saw in the third Sunday of Lent, the Samaritan woman was the first missionary apostle. The Church begins when these first witnesses to the Resurrection evangelize the evangelists.

The empty tomb and the huge stone are rich symbols found in all four gospels. Peter Chrysologus points out that the enormous stone was not rolled away from the tomb to allow Jesus to rise from the dead: he could have passed through the stone. Rather, the stone was removed for the sake of our faith: "Pray, brothers, that the angel would descend now and roll away all the hardness of our hearts and open up our closed senses and declare to our minds that Christ has risen."[59]

The empty tomb has been offered as "proof" of the Resurrection, but as NJBC points out, logically this is incorrect. Jesus could have risen even if his corpse remained in the tomb. Conversely, Jesus might have not risen at all, and the empty tomb could be the result of disciples stealing his corpse. Still, the empty tomb is a powerful illustration of the Resurrection's "destruction of death."

The four gospels agree that the empty tomb was discovered at dawn on the first day of the week—Sunday. We do not know when Jesus actually rose, but timing it with dawn on the first day of the week is perfect. We connect light with life, and every dawn brings new light to shatter the darkness. Peter Chrysologus writes, "Even as mortality is transformed into immortality, corruption into incorruption and flesh into Word of God, the darkness is transformed into the light, so that the night itself rejoices that it did not die but is transmuted."[60]

We have entered a new era, a new way of looking at time, because with the Resurrection we have the promise of eternity. Therefore, it is fitting that this is announced to us at the dawn of the new week. To signify the transcendence of everyday, immanent time, some people call it "the eighth day." God's creation was completed with the Sabbath rest; its redemption is at dawn of the following day.

The reading from Isaiah 55:1–11 is my favorite Old Testament passage and perfectly expresses this divine transcendence: "For my thoughts are not your thoughts, nor are your ways my ways, says the Lord." That God's Son would suffer crucifixion and then be raised from the dead is a total rupture of our theological expectations and our everyday experience. Furthermore, this event has changed the world forever: "My word shall not return to me void, but shall do my will, achieving the end for which I sent it."

Peculiar to Matthew is that after the women are told by the angel to tell the disciples Jesus has risen, they depart with "great fear and joy." At first these two emotions seem incompatible, but when we stop to consider it, that reaction makes perfect sense. It's akin to the emotions we might feel on our wedding day.

Matthew also has Jesus greet these women on their way back to the disciples. The Greek word he uses is *khaírete*. The RSV translates this as "hail," Hart as "greetings." But *khaírete* has a warmer connotation than these English words. It also means "rejoice, be glad." Jesus must have done something extraordinary to make these women feel at ease if Matthew is correct that after seeing the risen Jesus, instead of running away in fright, they took hold of his feet and prostrated themselves before him. Most people would be terrified to see "a dead man walking."

By touching his feet, the women not only show they are not terrified of the risen Lord, but they also give us a sign that the resurrected Jesus has a body and is not a ghost. I prefer Hart's translation—that the women "prostrated" themselves before

Jesus—rather than the RSV's "worshiped" him, because the former is more objective. We would have to know what they were feeling inside to determine whether they were worshiping Jesus at this point. I suspect they were feeling a range of emotions, as Matthew has already indicated: fear, joy, awe, bewilderment. These women knew Jesus only as a man who walked the earth; the awareness that Jesus is also divine dawned gradually for the early Church.

Matthew agrees with Mark and John that Jesus "is going before [the women] to Galilee; there [they] will see him." What are we to make of that? Everyone was in Jerusalem. Why must they return to Galilee to see Jesus?

"Jesus is going before you": to me, this helps to normalize what we must believe about the Resurrection's meaning for us. Jesus has gone before us; just as he rose from the dead, so will we when our time comes. Jesus also goes before us in the sense of demonstrating how we are to live lives of service to the poor and the marginalized.

Second, Galilee is where Jesus and his disciples began and where they had their early success. The identity of their movement was forged there, in the boondocks, away from the big city of Jerusalem where Jesus was crucified. Jesus's followers—poor, simple, and uneducated people—need to regroup where their roots are in order to face the ordeals awaiting them in Jerusalem and the Roman Empire. Most will end up as martyrs. Perhaps also they needed to retrace the footsteps they took with Jesus, and relive the time of his ministry in order to understand now, in the light of his death and resurrection, the many things he told them about the Kingdom.

How does a small band of cowardly former disciples transform into a courageous group that will face death and change the world? This is one of the most important historical and theological questions posed by the New Testament as well as by the history of the Roman Empire.

On the one hand, it is astonishing that such a thing happened at all. Yet we know that it did. Christianity conquered and outlived the mighty Roman Empire. The most plausible explanation is that these men and women of the early Church experienced something so extraordinary that it totally changed their lives.

We will be returning to this question in the weeks of the coming Easter season.

SECOND SUNDAY OF EASTER

Acts 2:42–47
I Peter 1:3–5
John 20:19–31

EVERY YEAR ON the first Sunday after Easter, we read this passage from John. What is the Church trying to tell us? That belief in Jesus's resurrection is both critical and difficult.

"How blissful those who do not see and who have faith" is then the crucial point. The Greek word Hart translates as "blissful" and the RSV as "blessed" is *makárioi*. It is the same word Matthew uses in the beatitudes. Hart notes it also means "blessed," "happy," "fortunate," even "prosperous," but with a connotation of divine or heavenly bliss.[61] Bauer adds that it usually carries the sense of "a privileged recipient of divine favor."

I like the "blissful" translation because it suggests the feeling we have when we fall in love or are transformed by a stunningly beautiful experience. It could be music, the glory and grandeur of nature, food or wine, a loving action by someone. Unlike "blessed," which seems like a word only fuddy-duddies use and carries the stuffy odor of the sacristy, "bliss" suggests a connection with beauty and another Hart book I recommend, *The Beauty of the Infinite*.

Makárioi can mean the feeling that we are "in heaven" in this life due to a gift from God. How does faith in Jesus's resurrection do this for us? Many people would agree that Jesus's teachings are beautiful: the beatitudes, forgiveness for everyone—even those who crucified him—and loving our enemies. What did those high-minded ideals do for Jesus? Where did they get him? If his death on the cross is the end of the story, his teachings would seem to have been defeated, and we would be tempted to ignore them as unrealistic, or even self-destructive. Many people do this anyway.

Jesus's resurrection vindicates the beauty and truth of his goodness. It means it is not pointless or self-destructive to try to live up to what he teaches. Despite all the suffering it can give us, life is, ultimately, beautiful after all. What bliss!

The wonderful Peggy Lee song "Is That All There Is?" points to a second, more personal reason Jesus's resurrection brings us bliss. In her song, Lee sings of some of her peak experiences in life: going to the circus as a girl, falling in love. But each time, when it's all over, all she can do is ask, "Is that all there is?" Divine discontent.

For many people, life is so hard and unrewarding that it can seem pointless. The minuses outweigh the pluses. Yet the joys of this life can be the most depressing of all, as even they never seem to satisfy us completely. Jesus's resurrection tells us that is *not* all there is. St. Augustine famously wrote, "Our hearts are made for you, O Lord, and they are ever restless until they rest in you." For everyone who feels what this life has to offer is ultimately not enough, the Resurrection is good news.

Faith in the Resurrection, then, can restore our love of *this* life. Now that we don't have to carry all that metaphysical weight, we can delight in the genuine joys this life offers us. This is bliss! As Jesus explains, "I came that they might have life, and have it in abundance" (John 10:10). Faith in Jesus and his resurrection makes us more alive right now.

One question that always perplexed me was why Jesus still had his crucifixion wounds and why this was so important for Thomas as proof it was the risen Jesus. I think I have at least a provisional answer to these questions.

We all have wounds. We all have suffered. I believe my suffering, and how I have dealt with it, plays a huge role in forging my identity. If you take away my wounds, you rob me of who I am. We believe our wounds will be healed and won't be painful, open, or bleeding; Jesus's were visible but apparently no longer painful. If we will still carry our wounds somehow, like Jesus, our friends will recognize us.

Perhaps more important, Jesus does not do what we would expect any other leader to do. He does not tell his disciples to exact revenge upon his persecutors. The Resurrection allows us to transcend the need for vengeance. This is another reason we need to believe in the Resurrection right now: this faith will free us from the natural human desire for revenge in this life.

Today's reading is also the first chapter in the growth of faith and experience of the Holy Spirit for the apostles and the early Church. Note how here, shortly after Jesus's crucifixion, the disciples are in effect cowering behind a locked door "for fear of the Judeans." The disciples had reason to be afraid. The description is utterly believable. Jesus, their leader, has just been crucified. Why should they not be next?

The fact that John does not shrink from revealing embarrassing details about the apostles lends credence to his gospel. He was writing long after the events he describes. How tempting it would be to paint a more heroic picture of our fathers in faith! It reminds me of St. Paul, who often wrote about how God used his weakness to reveal God's own power.

In the coming weeks, we will read of the transformation of these fearful men into fearless apostles and martyrs. This is the great drama of the early Church and, arguably, a historical miracle. It is one proof that the Holy Spirit was working its magic on them.

THIRD SUNDAY OF EASTER

On the Road to Emmaus

Acts 2:14, 22–33
1 Peter 1:17–21
Luke 24:13–35

WHY DO WE read every year the story of doubting Thomas on the first Sunday after Easter? And why this year do we read about the doubting followers of Jesus on the road to Emmaus? John, Luke, and the Church realize that for Christians, faith in the Resurrection is as crucial as it is difficult. St. Paul puts it clearly: "If Christ has not been raised, then our preaching is in vain and your faith is in vain. . . . If Christ has not been raised, your faith is futile and you are still in your sins. . . . If for this life only we have hoped in Christ, we are of all men most to be pitied" (1 Corinthians 15:14–19).

The gospel readings for this week and last reveal how our situation is both similar and different from that of those who witnessed the Resurrection. Thomas, like all the remaining eleven apostles, experienced the risen Lord. Yet Thomas's position is not "superior" to ours. John's Jesus promises us greater bliss than Thomas if we are given the gift of faith without having to see.

Everything, it seems, depends on our receiving this gift of faith in the Resurrection. How do we get there? Is it a pure gift? Do we have a role to play in obtaining it?

Luke's story "On the Road to Emmaus" sheds light on these questions.

The two wayfarers are on a journey and are in community with one another. This is important, as Jesus said, "For where two or three are gathered in my name, there am I in the midst of them" (Matthew 18:20). To be in a good position to receive the gift of faith, we are to understand our life of faith as a journey we take with others.

As they walk, they are not talking about the weather or what celebrities are up to on Instagram. They are talking about Jesus's passion and resurrection. Being "in community" is not enough. We must, at least at times, be discussing the Jesus story.

Yet discussing "real things" about Jesus is also not enough. When Jesus asks them about their conversation, their first reaction is to stop walking and to be sad. As an analogy to this, I sometimes get so absorbed in the details of Scripture study or dealing with my parish community that I lose track of what I am doing and why. If the work is divorced from faith in Jesus, I can get stuck, stop moving, and become sad. It is good when we allow Jesus to ask us, "What are you talking about? What are you doing and why?"

The two wayfarers then explain everything that happened. They know all about the Passion and that Jesus was "a prophet mighty in work and word before God and all the people." They have a fine command of the details but understand nothing! They are contrasted with "the women of our company," who are presented as faithful witnesses to the Resurrection.

Why do all four gospels consistently present women as the first to experience and believe in the Resurrection, and men as far behind them? One possible clue is offered in today's reading when our two men explain the reason for their disappointment in Jesus. After recounting his crucifixion, they add, "But we had been hoping that he was the one about to liberate Israel."

Perhaps men are more focused than women on the external, material, political and military situation. I encounter the same stumbling block to faith at times. What did Jesus really accomplish, either then or in the two thousand years since then? He did not liberate Israel from the Romans. In fact, soon that situation got far worse! Proclaiming the Kingdom of God was his mission. Where is it? What is it? This story offers an answer.

True faith in the living risen Jesus, as opposed to a man "who was a prophet," begins with the proper interpretation of Scripture. Jesus "opens up" the Scriptures to them, and they later realize, "Our heart was burning within us" as he did so along the way. Simply reading the Bible is not enough, as the devil can quote Scripture. One clue we are interpreting the Bible aright is that it elicits a powerful response in our hearts, as happens here.

A second clue is what happens next. The two men offer hospitality to this stranger. We can discern if we are interpreting the Bible correctly if it leads to good actions, as here. The climax comes when they share a meal together. It is only then that "their eyes were opened and they recognized him."

The experience of recognizing the risen Jesus could be related to the eucharistic sacrament. It can also simply be a basic human reality: breaking bread with another means sharing and experiencing our common humanity, as we all need to eat to live. When we recognize the fully humanity of the Other, especially a stranger, we are likely in the presence of the living Jesus.

I can vouch for this. I struggled for years with recognizing the humanity of the unhoused panhandlers I met every time I went to work or to church. Sometimes I walked quickly by, fearful or repulsed. Sometimes I gave them money out of guilt. Rarely did I engage with them as human beings. Occasionally, when I had the time, I would invite one to a fast food restaurant and we would share a meal. That made a huge difference! But then I found something even better.

After I retired, I made a commitment to join my parish's homeless ministry program. As I mentioned in the introduction, on Monday mornings, we give our guests a hot meal, a bag lunch, clothing, and toiletries. After breakfast, many guests and volunteers stay to discuss the gospel reading for the previous Sunday.

Volunteering every week at this program, eating and drinking coffee with the unhoused, gave me a safe space and the time to get to know many of our guests more intimately. This was a game-changer. I no longer saw unhoused people as the Other. A few of them became my friends. I learned that each unhoused person is unique; they are as different from one another as those of us who have a place to live are. By seeing and feeling their humanity, I saved my own.

Now I feel neither fear nor guilt when I encounter panhandlers. I feel frustrated that this rich country of ours has not figured out how to build enough affordable housing.

One time during a discussion, we were trying to figure out the meaning of Jesus's Kingdom of God. One of our guests said, "I feel like the Kingdom of God is right here, on Monday mornings."

Luke begins today's story by giving us a picture of what it is like to love and follow Jesus but not believe in the Resurrection. I think this picture applies to everyone at some point, believers and nonbelievers alike. What the two wayfarers learned is what I needed to learn about Jesus's kingdom: it begins in one's "burning heart," not in the political-military-economic world outside of us. But if that is where the Kingdom begins, it certainly cannot end there. The proof that our hearts are really on fire is when they lead us to work to transform the outer world in line with agape, which will be explained in next week's reading. If we do not, that fire will go out. These disciples did by offering hospitality to the unknown traveler. It is important that they did not recognize the traveler to be Jesus at first, as it would have been too easy for the two disciples to offer hospitality to Jesus.

Why did Jesus vanish from their sight as soon as they recognized him? I don't know. But I do know that this is also my experience with Jesus and God the Father. (Maybe less so with the Holy Spirit.) It can sometimes feel like a game of hide-and-go-seek! We certainly can never possess God, or control Jesus. Maybe Jesus's constant presence would be too overwhelming for us. At any rate, it is comforting to know that this is the way Jesus has been right from the start of his risen life.

My biggest question comes from verses 26–27: "Was it not necessary for the Anointed to endure these things and to enter into his glory? And beginning with Moses and with all the prophets, he expounded to them the things concerning himself in all the scriptures."

Of course, "The Suffering Servant" of Isaiah, especially 53:1ff, can certainly be seen as a prophetic anticipation of Jesus's passion. But I do not know of other passages from the Old Testament that foretell a messiah who suffers in order to enter into glory. And even in Isaiah, there is nothing about resurrection.

In our first reading from Acts, Peter quotes a Greek translation of Psalms 16:8–11 to show that King David foretells the resurrection of the Messiah. But his argument does not hold up to scrutiny. We know David did not write the psalms, and the original Hebrew of this psalm has been mistranslated into Greek to support Peter's argument.[62]

Peter's speech in today's first reading may not pass muster as proof that the Old Testament predicts Jesus's passion and resurrection. But it does show a remarkable transformation in St. Peter. Gone is the man cowering behind a locked door "for fear of the Jews." This transformation of Peter is better evidence for Jesus's resurrection and the outpouring of the Holy Spirit than twisted Old Testament citations.

When the prophets talk about the future messiah, their words usually bear little resemblance to what we know about Jesus. In discussing messianic expectations in the later prophets, NJBC says: "We should emphasize that these 'Messiahs' are not transcendent savior figures in the Christian sense. They are functionaries who hold offices in the restored Jewish community."[63]

Jesus was rejected by most Jews precisely because he was not the kind of messiah they were expecting. They, like our two wayfarers, had been led to believe in a messiah who would liberate Israel from Roman rule and restore its political-religious independence along the lines of King David. In his ministry, Jesus often resisted these messianic expectations. Moreover, resurrection of the body is alien to the Old Testament. Concern for the fate of the individual after death does not become important until the end of the Old Testament period, in the apocalyptic and apocryphal literature, and then it is usually discussed in the context of national and cosmic expectations.

Rene Girard, however, has shown how a deeper reading of the Old Testament does indeed lead to seeing Jesus's death as the culmination of a long process of revelation. He argues religion has always told stories to justify the persecution of innocent victims. The Old Testament slowly reveals the innocence of the victim, and with the tortured death of the sinless Jesus, we reach the final stage in this revelation.[64]

At the Last Supper, Jesus says he won't share food with them until God's kingdom comes. That Jesus does so now shows God's kingdom has started to arrive with his resurrection.

FOURTH SUNDAY OF EASTER

Acts 2:14a, 36–41
1 Peter 2:20b–25
John 10:1–10

TODAY'S GOSPEL ENDS with one of my favorite passage in the entire Bible: "I came that they might have life and might have it in abundance." As we are still in the Easter season, it answers one obvious question posed by the Good Shepherd Sunday readings: what does the Good Shepherd have to do with Easter?

The word Hart translates as "abundance" is *perisson*. It can mean "more than sufficient," and "out of the common, pre-eminent, superior" or "superabundant (in quantity) or superior (in quality)." Bauer adds "extraordinary, remarkable, superfluous, [even] unnecessary."

God is the Creator of life, of course, and God saw that it was good, even "very good" (Gen 1:31), so it is logical that God would want us to have as much of it as possible. Indeed, there is an abundance of life all around us. How do Jesus and the Easter resurrection give us all this extra, superfluous life?

The deaths of those we love, the fear of our own deaths, cast a depressing shadow of sorrow and futility on the lives we live right now. We alone, perhaps, among all God's creatures know our bodies will perish. That's a problem. The fear, anxiety, and depression it logically causes diminishes our ability to live life to the fullest.

Yet if we believe Jesus rose from the dead, and believe his

promise, we no longer need to worry so much about death. Now, I know it is not always so easy to hold on to this hope. Plus, faith and hope are not the same thing as knowing death has been killed. However, this is where that third theological virtue, love, comes into play. And this brings us more directly to today's reading.

Jesus contrasts his personal relationship to his flock with that of a stranger. The sheep will not follow a stranger's voice but will follow the recognizable voice of their shepherd. But the Good Shepherd metaphor goes beyond this personal relationship.

It is hard to understand fully today's reading without reading up through verse 13, where Jesus contrasts the Good Shepherd with the hireling. A hireling could also have a personal relationship with the sheep, but a person who works for wages is doing x to obtain y. There is nothing wrong with this; we all need to make a living. But often those who need to be paid for doing something are not doing it because they love it. In this week's passage, Jesus contrasts his personal connection with, and caring for, his sheep with the thieves, robbers, or hired hands who are motivated by money. We know of religious leaders in Jesus's time and our own who have exploited the faithful.

The test of religious leadership is that it is not undertaken for an extrinsic reason. We don't do x to obtain y. Even if we do get paid, we do it above all out of love. This issue of extrinsic motivation returns us to the theme of *perisson* life. If we need to make a living, we are often forced to do x to obtain y. The medieval scholastics called this a *bonum utile*. This is part of life, and there is nothing inherently evil about it. However, the more our time is devoted to a *bonum utile*, the less *perisson* life we will have.

The scholastics contrasted a *bonum utile* with a *bonum honestum*, or something we do for its own sake. Any other rewards we receive apart from the activity itself are secondary. This is what the Good Shepherd does in caring for the sheep, and it leads to *perisson* life—just as we don't have a friend primarily because of something that friend can do for us. Jesus of course goes one step further than this: he is willing to die for his sheep. It is agape love that we are talking about here. This kind of love is based on equal regard for everyone, unlike eros.

Remember falling in (erotic) love with someone? During that blissful time, we definitely feel *perisson* alive! Everything is more intensely beautiful, all our senses make the world sparkle with joy, and we feel wonders we never dreamed of. Our souls expand up through the sky, and we want to tell everyone we meet, "I'm in love! I'm in love with the most wonderful person who ever existed!"

Well, agape is not like that! The joys of eros are way more intense than those of agape. In the early days of my conversion to Christianity and Catholicism, I did have intense moments of "falling in love with God" that were in some ways analogous to falling in love with a person. And now I sometimes have flashes or waves of similar feelings. But still, it's not the same, and it is understandable that most people prefer to fall in love and marry rather than become a monk or nun.

While agape, this love for God and neighbor, is less intense than eros, it is likely to last longer. If we are lucky, eros will fade into something calmer and, usually, more complicated; we are unlikely to stay in that wonderful "I'm in love!" state for long. I also believe there can be a tension, even a competition, between the two forms of love. We have no evidence that Jesus ever experienced eros at all. But the silence of the biblical writers on this issue is revealing. We have a limited amount of spiritual energy. If much of it is focused on eros, there is going to be less left for agape. St. Paul was well aware of this, as he explained in 1 Corinthians 7:32–38.

If, like me, you are not involved in an eros relationship, you will have not only more energy for agape but more need for it as well. We were created to love and to be loved, and if we are missing out on eros, we are in danger of drying up inside without some other kind of love, or even dying spiritually. Rainer Werner Fassbinder, the great German film director, was warned that if he did not cut back on his drinking and drug abuse, he would soon be dead. No doubt the advice was good, but I have never forgotten his reply: "Most people are already dead."

When we think about spiritual life and death, it is obvious most of us are somewhere in the middle—or muddle! Maybe we are tempted to keep bumbling and muddling along, doing the best we can to keep body and soul together. Yet I think it's valuable to be mindful that something akin to inner death is possible, so we want to avoid choices that deaden our spirits and pay attention to what makes us more spiritually alive. As Jesus often says, in a slightly different context, "Keep watch!" (Mark 13:33–37, par. Matthew; 24:42–44, par. Luke; Matthew 26:41, par. Mark).

Put more positively, falling in agape-love with God and neighbor is what Jesus was getting at with the words I quoted from verse 10: *perisson* life. This feeling is echoed in Psalm 23: "my cup overflows."

A good example of *perisson* life is St. Peter in our first reading today. Contrast this Peter with the fearful Peter during and immediately after Jesus's crucifixion. He is an excellent case study in how faith in Jesus leads to more abundant life.

One of the many reasons why I converted to Catholicism years ago was that it seemed to me most of my friends were Catholics, and I was drawn to them because they somehow seemed more alive than did other people I knew. This is a rejoinder to one of Nietzsche's critiques of Christianity: he wrote Christians don't seem redeemed. We are all called to evangelize, and I think one of the best ways to do it is to allow ourselves to experience the joy of *perisson* life.

The Good Shepherd metaphor is clearly a rich one, but does it have limitations? It does, because the flock of sheep are passive animals, not human beings with free will. I don't want to be thought of as a sheep! This is why we have to read the Bible not literally but analogically or metaphorically. That said, there may be times when we think of ourselves as lost sheep, when we simply want to be taken care of. This may be a somewhat embarrassing confession for a modern individualist to make. But, at least in my case, it has sometimes been true.

If we can "own" our "lost-sheep" selves, we can also be better shepherds to others when they need it.

FIFTH SUNDAY OF EASTER

Acts 6:1–7
1 Peter 2:4–9
John 14:1–12

AS A CHILD, I loved the King James version of today's gospel: "In my Father's house are many mansions." For one thing, I loved the idea of living in a mansion. The notion that there were many such mansions inside the Father's house captured my imagination precisely because it doesn't make literal sense. And it suggests an abundance, a generosity that, as we saw last week, is absolutely appropriate to what Jesus reveals about the Father.

The Greek word is *monaì*. It does not appear to mean "mansions," alas! It can mean either the act of staying or a place to stay; Abbott-Smith may capture this twofold sense by noting it can mean "abiding" or "an abode." Bauer adds to this "a dwelling place." The NAB follows this and accurately translates *monaì* as "dwelling places."

I hate the RSV's translation: "In my Father's house there are many rooms." Hart is a little better: "In my Father's house there are many places of rest." But what I don't like about "places of rest" is that it doesn't suggest a place we would want to stay in: we come for a rest and then move on. *Monaì* is tied to staying or abiding. After all this, "mansion" seems better than ever, as a mansion is exactly the kind of place where I would like to stay!

Jesus is referring here to our eternal home, so it is theologically important to convey the idea of a place we will enjoy forever.

Equally important, there will be many such mansions. As I mentioned earlier, this reminds us of the Father's generosity. But it also affirms the diversity of God's human creation. We are all so different that we each need to have our own mansion! I don't envision spending all my time alone inside this mansion, although sometimes it might be nice. I think of the marvelous parties I will be able to throw in my mansion for everyone I have ever known. Faith and imagination must be partners. Why else, I wonder, did God give us an imagination?

John's Jesus tells us, "I am going to make a place ready for you" in Hart's translation. What can this mean? I take this also to be another "imagination opportunity," so here goes. I imagine two different activities of Jesus. First, he is going to help us prepare for the place, by guiding us and being with us in this life. I do think that for Christians, this life is to be seen as a preparation for eternal life.

By staying with us throughout our lives, Jesus will create and modify each individual's personal mansion so that it will suit us perfectly. This is something we all do for ourselves to some extent with where we happen to live now. We can go too far with this, as we can with virtually anything, but to some extent, creating a fit dwelling place for oneself is a holy, sacred activity. "Dwelling is not primarily inhabiting but taking care of and creating that space within which something comes into its own and flourishes," Martin Heidegger writes. This is one reason why I believe housing is a human right. No one should be homeless.

That said, Martin Heidegger also writes, "We are all homeless now." We can read something similar already in Hebrews 13:14, "For here we have no lasting city, but we seek the city which is to come." I believe if we are honest, we all have a built-in estrangement from the towns and even the houses where we live, and so we have a longing for *monaì* where we will be truly at home. Today's gospel speaks to this in-built longing.

Good old, down-to-earth Thomas asks how we can find our way to this place. Jesus's answer is personal, not a list of directions. In what way is Jesus himself "the way, the truth and the life"? Just a few verses after today's reading ends, at verse 15, John's Jesus tells us, "If you love me, you will keep my commandments." In 15:12 he spells it out further: "This is my commandment, that you love [*agapãté*] one another as I have loved you." And finally, a culmination for me of John's gospel lies in 15:15 where Jesus calls us his "friends [*phílous*]." Friendship with God! And how do you "become a friend" with someone who died two thousand years ago?

Now, friendship, as Aristotle tells us, connotes a kind of equality. Equality with God is, it would seem, inconceivable. And for most religions, it certainly is. Christianity is unique in offering this possibility, this insight into the kind of relationship God wants to have with us. This is only possible for Christianity because Jesus is both human and divine. The Christians of the East have a long, rich tradition of seeing the Christian life as an opportunity for the human person to become divine.

The most problematic part of today's reading for me is when Jesus adds, "No one comes to the Father, but by me." Don't all religions claim they are the greatest, and every other one is second best? And is it possible to respect other religious traditions if we believe only ours is "the way, the truth and the life," and the only way to God the Father?

I do not have the answer to these questions, but I do have some responses. Number one, if this claim is truly of God, God will sort it out in God's way and in God's time; we do not need to worry too much about it.

Number two, I refer back to the notion that Christianity offers us friendship with God through Jesus. God does not want us to cringe in guilt-ridden fear before the Almighty, as has often been the case with religions—including Christianity! These words of

John's Jesus pose a deeper problem for our relationship with our Jewish brothers and sisters. How can we have a respectful dialogue with them if we hold on to these words? They have had a relationship with Jesus's Father for thousands of years, and then we come along with Jesus and say, "From now on, you have to go through us." Wow!

I confess I do not have an answer to this one. If you do, please let me know!

SIXTH SUNDAY OF EASTER

Acts 8:5–8, 14–17
1 Peter 3:15–18
John 14:15–21

THE GOSPEL OF John shines a light on Christ from a very different angle than the other three gospels. We can be grateful for this. We need two eyes to see in three dimensions. John allows us to see Christ, and the Church, with the depth of three dimensions.

Agape love and the Advocate (*paráklēton*) are the two realities that shine this light in today's readings. "If you love me," Jesus says in this gospel reading, "you will keep my commandments." And what are Jesus's commandments? That "you love one another as I have loved you" (John 15:12).

Can it make any sense at all to "command" someone to love? Yes! We explored agape some last week, and I discuss it further in appendix F. But some points bear repeating. Agape begins with God's love for us. Jesus says, "You did not choose me, but I chose you" (John 15:16). And in 1 John 4:10, "Herein is love, not that we loved God, but rather that he loved us and sent his Son as atonement for our sins."

Unlike other forms of love, such as eros, God does not love us because of our merits or out of desire for something from us. And unlike eros, or even a mother's love for her children, God's love is not limited to a few people. It is equal, unconditional, universal, and unmerited. First John 4:11 closes the circle: "Beloved ones, if

God loved us so, we also ought to love one another." Our human agape for one another is then the second moment in the story of God's creative love for us: it is our response.

Our response-ability to love others then rests on our first having experienced God's love for us. If we have not felt this, the commandment to love others equally, unconditionally, universally, and despite their faults, expecting nothing in return, will make no sense. There is a logic to this two-step reality, and agape is made easier because we humans are natural imitators. I should also add that the love we have experienced from creatures will also shape our understanding and experience of God's love for us. God's love transcends all human love, yet human love is an image of God's love, as we are created in God's image. It is obviously more difficult for someone without many loving relationships to experience God's love.

Because God's love for us is foundational to all our relationships, morality always comes second for Christians, and spirituality—our lived experience of receiving God's love—must come first. Yet we are also in the domain of morality here because agape resides in the human will, not, like eros, in the heart. Can we choose who we fall in love with? Does a mother choose her children? But agape is a choice we can, and must, make once we have experienced God's love. I explore this further in appendix F.

Agape is central to the synoptic gospels as well, of course. But none of them makes Jesus's agape command so central as John does. Nor do these three gospels make it as clear that agape is nothing more nor less than our imitation-response to the love Jesus has already given us.

This brings us to the Advocate, *paráklēton*. The word is used for the Holy Spirit only in John, so once again we are in the unique light this gospel sheds on Jesus. I have sometimes been put off by John's poetic language and the exalted, otherworldly image of Jesus he conveys. But I have come to learn that in one key respect,

John is actually closer to us and our situation than the synoptics.

The synoptics were written when Jesus was still a living memory. People who knew him were still alive. The oral traditions, the stories about him, were fresh and evolving. By the time John was written, the historical Jesus had faded away, just as he has for us. I think this is one reason there is so much focus in John on "abiding in Jesus." John's community reveals two ways to do this, and both are relevant for us today, who face the same problem of how to remain in Jesus.

We have already touched on the first, which is to obey Jesus's love commandment. The Paraclete is the second. This word means someone called to one's aid in a legal case—for example, a friend of the accused person, called to speak to his character or enlist sympathy in his favor. Something like a lawyer, but without the professional credentials or the financial remuneration.

John also calls this the Holy Spirit, and of course we know about the Holy Spirit from the synoptics. There are similarities and differences between the synoptic Holy Spirit and John's Paraclete; I want to focus here on the differences.

John's community faced persecution, from "the Jews" and the Romans. The Paraclete's role as defender and comforter of the accused connects faith in Jesus with Jesus's ongoing love for us through whatever problems face us now. In the US we don't have to worry about this kind of persecution, but Christians elsewhere are always being martyred.

Beyond that, we all are going to face unjust accusations from time to time, and this can be one of the hardest experiences in life to deal with. Rage is a natural, human response to this injustice. Faith in Jesus and contact with the Paraclete is the way to transcend this all-too-human response. I would say it is even necessary if we are to follow Jesus's path of nonviolence. We can be comforted to know that many others before us—including Jesus himself—have faced similar, or even worse, unjust accusations. We cannot control this, but with God's help, we can shape our response to it.

John's Jesus also tells his disciples that when "the Spirit of truth comes, he will guide [them] into all truth" (16:13). As the memory of the historical Jesus fades, John's community has found two criteria for authentic discipleship: love of God and neighbor, and living in the Spirit. The Paraclete of John may differ from the Holy Spirit in the synoptics because John's Paraclete has a somewhat different function. It is through the Paraclete that his community experienced the revelation of the Father that Jesus provided. They understood that the Paraclete doesn't bring a new revelation but applies and elucidates what Jesus already did.

The Paraclete is thus a kind of successor to Jesus, as indicated by verse 16. Unlike Jesus, the Paraclete does not have a human body, so unlike Jesus, she will remain with us throughout history. Raymond E. Brown, in *The Community of the Blessed Disciple*, believes that the Paraclete so resembles the Johannine Jesus that we may say that the Paraclete is the abiding presence of Jesus after Jesus has gone to heaven, and that the Paraclete plays the same revelatory role in relation to Jesus that Jesus played in relation to the Father.[65]

In his book, Brown argues that John's community of Christians likely included a large number of Samaritans.[66] It is therefore appropriate that we have a record in our first reading of both the mission to the Samaritans as well as how important the Holy Spirit was to them. In the synoptics and in the many epistles of the New Testament, we hear about the apostles and the emerging church structure as the way to remain faithful to Jesus. Raymond Brown, working with John's gospel but also especially the letters of John, presents a convincing argument that these two criteria, agape and the Holy Spirit, were ultimately not enough to prevent a fracturing of the community. The problem with relying on the Holy Spirit for church order and discipline is that anyone can claim to be "in the Spirit." This led to division in John's community, as can be seen from John's epistles.

A church structure based on apostolic authority, creeds, and more objective sources of accountability lead to greater stability and continuity. Eventually, the faithful remnant of John's community merged into apostolic Christianity. The Holy Spirit lost its status as the principal guarantee of communion with Jesus.

While John's vision of Christian community may not be adequate to ensure unity and fidelity to Jesus, it is also obvious that the more centralized, hierarchical church structure that developed over time has its limitations as well. Even in Acts we can see that people motivated by greed or status may seek to gain power in the Church. Christian history has been blighted by this phenomenon.

One reason I am convinced the Holy Spirit was deeply involved in the creation of our New Testament canon is that both John and the synoptics are right! To be faithful to Jesus, we need to envision the Church both apostolically and as a community based in love and communion with the Holy Spirit. The structure and discipline of the apostolic church helps ensure unity and an objective continuity with the Jesus tradition. John's emphasis on love and the Spirit is more "loosey goosey," but it is equally essential that our inner spiritual lives are authentic efforts to live the life Jesus has shown us.

ASCENSION SUNDAY

Acts 1:1–11
Ephesians 1:17–23
Matthew 28:16–20

I CONFESS THE ascension of Jesus made little sense to me until the last few years. It seemed so mythological, so difficult to believe. And what was the point?

The incarnation and resurrection of Jesus also "strain credulity," as my sister likes to say. But at least I could understand how important those doctrines are for shaping the way we live and treat others. I could see how those who knew Jesus and saw how he forgave and miraculously healed others could come to perceive he was God's Son. They talked and ate with the risen Lord. We have some lived experience to back up both the Incarnation and the Resurrection.

Even if it is true, what difference can this apparent theological abstraction make in how we live our lives? In what follows, I will try to answer this question.

Who has seen Jesus sitting at the right hand of the Father in heaven (Mark 16:19)? And where is the evidence for these words of Jesus: "All power in heaven and on earth has been given to me" (Matthew 28:18)? I have come to believe those words from Matthew express the meaning, and the challenge, of the Ascension. The use of the theological passive means God the Father has given Jesus this power, and thus we are now living in the Kingdom of God.[67] More concretely this means that

Christians are committed to the story that the peace flowing from forgiveness of enemies and nonviolence *is more powerful* than the counter-narrative that violence rules the world.

It is easy to find examples of how we do not, even in supposedly Christian America, really believe the Christian story. To protect our security, we don't love our enemies; we spend more money on the military than many other nations combined. To protect our safety, we arm the police with deadly force, which they use to kill civilians, often at the drop of a hat, especially dark-skinned ones. Our incarceration rate is the highest in the world. Many of us buy lots and lots of guns, supposedly to protect ourselves and our loved ones. And so on.

All this is true, and this is why the Ascension, far from being an incredible mythological, theological abstraction, is a challenge to our operating assumptions and habits. The apparent dominance of violence in our world is also further evidence that the fullness of the Kingdom of God is not yet here. It awaits the second coming of Jesus. And this is why the ascension of Jesus is connected to our belief that he will come again in glory.

Yet I also want to question the dominance of the "violence narrative" I just outlined. To some degree, our vision of the world is shaped by our general fascination with violence rather than the "boringness of peace." You may be familiar with the journalistic cliché "If it bleeds, it leads." If we pay attention to what is considered "news," we discover it is usually violent or at least conflictual.

In rare cases, extraordinary forgiveness might make the headlines. One example is the Charleston church massacre of 2015, when white supremacist Dylann Roof shot and killed nine African Americans during a Bible study at the Emanuel African Methodist Episcopal Church. ABC News, among other major news organizations, did a story on how the mother of one of the victims said she forgave Dylann Roof as he was sentenced to death.[68]

This was a powerful story, and I am glad the mainstream news media paid attention. On the other hand, one could argue this story is the exception that proves the rule. This extraordinary act of forgiveness by Christians victimized by racial violence does reveal that Jesus, sitting at the right hand of the Father, has power on earth. We must be mindful, however, that the news is not going to provide us this narrative very often. Even in this case, the forgiveness was tied to a horrific act of violence.

We may read about peace talks. What we rarely see in the news is how conflict is avoided because two people, two communities, or two nations work out their differences before violence. Why is this not news? In a strange way, the tendency to ignore these stories may actually testify to how often Jesus's message of peace rules our world. It is not news. That said, we humans are wired to pay attention to violence. It may have something to do with our survival and evolution. If you are in a field watching butterflies flutter over wildflowers and there is a sudden train wreck nearby, I can guarantee your gaze will shift to the train wreck!

It is up to us, therefore, to keep our gaze firmly set on the way in which the Jesus of peace, forgiveness of enemies, and nonviolence rules the world. And it is up to us to try to change those violent practices I mentioned above that are also embedded in our fallen world. All power has been given to the one who renounced all power and died helpless. Every time we forgive someone else, make peace, avoid violence, we are affirming that Jesus is seated at God's right hand with all the power of the universe.

Right after Jesus says all power has been given to him, he tells the apostles—and us—to go therefore, to instruct all the nations and to baptize them. The "therefore" is there most directly because Jesus has said "all power" has been given to him. Indirectly, it may be seen as a reason for the apostles to have faith and courage when confronted with the persecution and martyrdom they faced spreading the gospel. We can have the courage to do this if we trust that ultimately Jesus, not the rulers of this world, has the power.

This adds meaning and power to my favorite verse in the Bible when I was a child, the final words of Matthew's gospel: "I am with you every day until the consummation of the age." Jesus is with us every day to help us follow his path, and the more we do, the more he is with us.

Even seeing the risen Jesus did not remove all doubt, as we read in verse 17: "And seeing him they prostrated themselves; but some doubted." Once again, embarrassing details like this highlight the likely historicity of these events; as the ACCS puts it, "And if some doubted, herein again admire the Evangelists' truthfulness. Even up to the last day, they were determined not to conceal even their own shortcomings."[69] That some doubted is doubly comforting. It tells me doubt is really part of faith, just as light must cast a shadow. It also tells me that the apostles are in essentially the same position as I am with respect to having faith in Jesus. We are all in the same boat, even though they knew the historical Jesus and saw the risen one.

Their doubt also shows the power of the later work of the Holy Spirit. Most of these doubters would become martyrs for the faith!

PENTECOST

Acts 2:1–11
1 Corinthians 12:3b–7, 12–15
John 20:19–23

A PRIEST FRIEND of mine once said the Holy Spirit is "the forgotten person" of the Trinity. I think this may be true. I do not hear many people speak about the Holy Spirit. Pentecost is a day to ask what the Holy Spirit is doing in our lives; what does she mean to each of us?

I use the pronoun "she" because in the East there is a tradition of linking the Holy Spirit with Wisdom, or Sophia, which is feminine. Moreover, since the Father and the Son are both referred to as "he," we make the anthropomorphic mistake of identifying God with a human gender if we consider the Holy Spirit also as masculine. God transcends human genders.

The reading from Acts serves as an answer to an important historical question. How do we go from a small band of traumatized and confused disciples of Jesus after his crucifixion to a group of followers who bravely face down death to spread his message and found a religion that changes the world?

I was a history major in college, and this question was a crucial part of my intellectual conversion to Christianity. Something extraordinary, miraculous, had to have happened. The New Testament record shows us again and again that Jesus's resurrection appearances did not change the disciples very much. The action of the Holy Spirit is the deepest, most comprehensive answer to the question of what transformed the disciples, and the world.

We looked at the Holy Spirit as it is understood in John's gospel on the sixth Sunday of Easter. Now it is time to look at the Holy Spirit from our point of view. What difference does the Holy Spirit make in how we live our lives? Although, as I have said before, I am "a recovering moral theologian," to answer this question I need to put back on my moral theologian's hat.

The seven gifts of the Holy Spirit developed by St. Thomas in the *Summa* and based on the prophecy of Isaiah 11:2 are wisdom, understanding, counsel, courage (or fortitude), knowledge, piety, and fear of God. These gifts are infused into every Christian at baptism, yet they need to be nurtured by the practice of the seven virtues as well as participation in the sacraments and an active faith life. The seven virtues are divided into four moral virtues: temperance, courage, justice, prudence; and three theological virtues: faith, hope, and love.

Aquinas holds that the moral virtues are directed to the good as defined by human reason, and so we can develop them by our good actions. If we keep doing good things, it becomes a habit after a while. A virtue is nothing more than a good habit. We can grow the moral virtues by using our reason.

But our ultimate purpose is not in this natural world. We are created for a supernatural destiny, to be with God, and reason alone cannot get us there. To fulfill our supernatural destiny, we need God's help, and this is where the theological virtues come in. Unlike the moral virtues, we cannot cultivate these by our actions. Quoting St. Augustine, Aquinas writes that when it comes to developing the theological virtues, "God works in us without us."

The gifts of the Holy Spirit are like the theological virtues, according to St. Thomas.[70] They are given to us by God rather than cultivated ourselves using our own reason and will. St. Thomas is a huge fan of human reason, God bless him, so I think his explanation of why we need the gifts of the Holy Spirit is powerful. He asks whether the gifts are necessary to man for salvation (*Summa* I, II, Q68, a2). After examining both sides of the question he writes: "I answer that, as stated above [a.1] the gifts are perfections of man, whereby he is disposed so as to be amenable to the promptings of God. Wherefore in those matters where the prompting of reason is not sufficient, and there is need for the prompting of the Holy Ghost, there is, in consequence, need for a gift."

The toughest part of the spiritual life for me has always been knowing what God's will is for me and then doing it. Faith in the Holy Spirit and her gifts helps me to grow in my life's participation in God's life. Reason, much as I love it, is not going to get me there.

Here is one practical illustration of how the gifts operate. One of the gifts is courage, or fortitude. Courage is the strength it takes to move toward danger. Fortitude is the strength it takes to endure suffering. The two are related yet distinct. Many of the apostles and early Christians were martyrs for Christ. This means they had to overcome their reason and its devotion to self-preservation. They had to endure torture and not run away from the dangers of persecution. To unbelievers, they are behaving irrationally, of course. In a way, they are.

Yet the martyrs are witnesses to our belief that we have a supernatural destiny, one that transcends this world. We can only get there if we have gifts that transcend natural reason. The martyrs received this gift of courage from the Holy Spirit.

If the Holy Spirit is the forgotten person of the Trinity, maybe that is because we have forgotten about her seven gifts. One way to answer the question I started out with (what is the Holy Spirit doing in our lives?) is to see if we are experiencing any of her gifts. We can deepen our relationship with her, and our knowledge of her, by regularly asking ourselves if we have experienced any of these gifts in a way that seems to surpass the normal operation of our reason.

Now, if you are reading this, I would say you have! Because one of the gifts is knowledge, and another is piety. It is not, strictly speaking, "reasonable" for you to be spending so much time trying to gain more knowledge of Scripture by reading these pages! It also shows a good deal of piety.

I really should explore all seven gifts in greater detail, but I also think that is up to every believer to do for him or herself. I have spent a little time on three of them to help get us started. I will end with one more.

I have come to connect the gift of understanding with a concept that has become a celebrated area of psychological research: emotional intelligence. This is the ability to understand unspoken indicators of how another person is feeling, what her emotional needs or hurts are. It also entails understanding and managing or directing our own emotions to build stronger connections with others. It is a divine union or integration of the heart and the mind.

I believe it is a gift because when I have such an insight, it seems to come from somewhere else. The gift of understanding doubtless includes more than emotional intelligence, but I hope the connection can help point the way to a deeper experience of this gift—and all the gifts.

TRINITY SUNDAY

Exodus 34:4b–6, 8–9
2 Corinthians 13:11–13
John 3:16–18

TODAY IS TRINITY Sunday, yet it is difficult to perceive how today's readings connect with the Holy Trinity. Before tackling that question, however, I want to begin with the problem I have with the text itself.

John starts out well in verse 16 with one of the most famous sentences in all Scripture: "God so loved the cosmos as to give the Son, the only one, so that everyone having faith in him might not perish, but have the life of the Age." So far, so good. But then, in some translations, John seems to contradict himself. I will quote in full Hart's translation of verses 17 and 18: "For God sent the Son into the cosmos not that he might pass judgment on the cosmos, but that the cosmos might be saved through him. Whoever has faith in him is not judged; whoever has not had faith has already been judged because he has not had faith in the only Son of God."

This makes it seem like God has good intentions: he wants to save everyone and condemn no one. But if we cannot or choose not to believe in the name of God's only Son, too bad for us, as God will judge us. In some translations it is even worse, as they have "condemn" instead of "judge." Yet God surely knew ahead of time that most people who have ever lived have not heard of Jesus, let alone believed in him.

If we believe in a hell of eternal punishment, this passage is especially troubling. If we believe in Jesus, great; we're in. But if not, we will burn in hell forever. John's God can say, "Eternal hellfire torture for unbelievers was not my intention with Jesus: it's not my fault, but yours, if you do not have faith."

Shall we say of God, "The road to hell is paved with good intentions"?

David Bentley Hart, and his Greek translation, to the rescue! The word often translated as "condemned" is *krínēi*. It has a rich range of meanings. Here is what Abbott-Smith tells us *krínēi* can mean: to save from peril, injury, or suffering; healing, restoring to (physical) health, salvation from spiritual disease and death. It can refer to the past, present, or future. Bauer lists no fewer than six meanings: 1) separate, distinguish, then select, prefer; 2) judge, think, consider; 3) reach a decision, decide, propose; 4) legal, to judge, decide, condemn, hand over for judicial punishment, including divine judgment, to judge each by what he has done, condemn, punish; 5) see to it justice is done; 6) pass judgment, especially in an unfavorable sense.

The word is clearly more complicated than "condemn." Yet it does have a somewhat scary connotation. I think the English word "judge" comes very close to the meaning of *krínēi*. To judge another person does not necessarily mean to condemn her. But still, we often say, "Don't judge me!" Who likes judgment? In Matthew and Luke, Jesus even commands us not to judge so that we may not be judged (Matthew 7:1).

But there is huge difference between judging and condemning. And there is nothing at all here about a negative judgment leading to eternal hellfire. That is something we may choose to bring to the text. I choose not to.

Hart's translation certainly helps, but it still raises questions for me. Let's start with what "faith in him" means. The New Testament is consistent in holding that genuine faith cannot remain in our heads but is connected to loving service to God and neighbor. See, for example, the letter of James as well as 1 John and the gospels. Not to have faith, therefore, means not to live a life of loving service to God and neighbor but rather to live primarily to serve ourselves. It also means not to have any kind of a relationship with God.

When we die, we will be judged by God. Although this belief does fill me with some trepidation, I embrace it. For one thing, it means I do not need to judge other people—that's God job. It is better for my soul, and a huge relief as well. It is liberating.

I also believe it is good for me to live my life under the shadow of God's judgment. A moderate amount of anxiety improves performance, as social psychologists tell us. Based on my reading of the gospels, we need not cower in terror of God, as God is loving and forgiving. But God does expect us to serve others because that is what we are made for, and we are going to be more joyful in this life, as well as the next, if we follow this plan. I do not know how much we are supposed to give up for others, but I do believe we need to give until it hurts—or until we are at least a little uncomfortable. Get out of your comfort zone!

The most incredible claim of Christianity is the doctrine that God took human form. Just as creation tells us much about the God who created it, our bodies can tell us much about the spiritual life, because body and spirit are "united in difference." I know that to maintain physical fitness, I need to stretch until it hurts a little bit; I need to do aerobics until I am out of breath; I need to use my muscles until I feel them burn.

Why should maintaining spiritual health be any different from maintaining physical health? We need to exercise our spirits to keep them healthy.

The way I make sense of today's reading, then, is that it is intended to help me lead a healthier spiritual life now. Doing so will be better for me now, and after I die. Those who ignore the advice to serve God and neighbor faithfully until it hurts at least a little bit will, I believe, have a less fulfilling life here below, and a tougher time after death. Will they be condemned to a hell of eternal punishment? I do not see scriptural support for this here.

Instead of having Jesus speak of eternal life, Hart translates it as "life in the Age." This is helpful in two ways. First, it clarifies that we are talking about our life right now, in the present. It also suggests that the time we are talking about will likely extend for a long, unspecified period of time—but not forever. Eternity is when we reach the end of the age, the end of time as we know it. At that point, I believe, all will be saved (see appendix A).

I believe those who do not love and serve God and neighbor will have farther to go to reach spiritual health, and I trust God will know how to lead them there. That is about as far as I can go, and that is as far as I need to go. Chucking certainty in a hell of eternal torture for unbelievers helps me to have a more respectful dialogue with them. I believe it helps, rather than hurts, evangelization.

Now to the most challenging dimension of today's reading: Why bother to believe in the difficult mystery of the Trinity? What difference does this complicated doctrine make in how we live our lives? Why not go the simpler, easier route of Unitarians, Muslims, and Jews, and affirm God is one and leave it at that?

The greatest challenge any community faces is living together peacefully and with justice. The challenge is far greater when the community is made up of people with different cultures, religions, races, and political views. This is the problem secular postmodern philosophers call "difference." You can find a good Christian discussion of this in David Bentley Hart's *The Beauty of the Infinite* (pp 35ff).

The postmodern consensus seems to be that the only way to deal with difference is violence. The world is by its nature violent, and human beings are no different. Every effort to maintain peace or order is founded upon violence. Even the supposed peaceful dialogue of democracy is based on the violence of hidden oppression, inequality, and mendacity. It is more honest, the postmodernists assert, to accept the violence of difference than to deny it with oppressive lies. "Foundational narratives" about the gradual progress of peace and justice are debunked as no more than oppressive deceit.

Christians cannot accept this because we believe God created the world and that the world God created is good. Violence is not a necessary built-in feature of nature, or our nature, but a privation of the good.

The Holy Trinity reveals a loving unity in diversity that counters the postmodern myth of the violence of difference. If, on the other hand, we believe God is simply an undivided One, are we not going to be more tempted to resort to violence toward those who differ from us? Christian history is littered with violence toward those who are different. And many Christians, maybe most, do not take the Trinity very seriously or think about it very much. I believe there is a connection.

I converted to Catholicism partly because of the beauty of Renaissance polyphony. My soul said to me, "Anything so beautiful must be true!" Part of the beauty of polyphony is the harmony of difference. Polyphony shows us that far from requiring violence, difference can be beautiful!

Jesus's entire life of nonviolent, forgiving service to others is a historical expression and a practical model for how to make this loving unity in diversity real.

CORPUS CHRISTI

Deuteronomy 8:2–3, 14b–16a
1 Corinthians 10:16–17
John 6:51–58

ON CORPUS CHRISTI we Catholics celebrate the Real Presence of the body and blood of Jesus Christ in the bread and wine of the Eucharist.

This is tough even for most Catholics to believe. A 2019 study conducted by Pew found that just 31 percent of US Catholics they surveyed believe that the bread and wine in the Eucharist become the body and blood of Christ.[71] Instead of believing in the Real Presence, 69 percent of the Catholics surveyed reported they believe the bread and wine are symbols of the body and blood of Jesus. A majority of Catholics in every age group reported this belief.

Our reading from John does not offer much wriggle room here, as Jesus states in verse 53, "If you do not eat the flesh of the Son of Man and drink his blood, you do not have life in you." If you have trouble swallowing this doctrine, you are not alone. A little further on in John, just after the end of our reading, we read at verse 60 that many of Jesus's disciples are complaining about this teaching: "This word is hard; who can listen to it?"

At verse 66 it gets worse! "At this many of his disciples departed, going back, and no longer walked with him." Possibly shaken by this sudden drop in his popularity, John's Jesus even wonders if the Twelve will also desert him over the "eat my flesh and drink my blood" teaching. The stalwart Peter speaks for all of them, evidently, when he replies, "Lord to whom shall we go away? You have the words of life in the Age."

All the same, I do believe in the Real Presence of Jesus's body and blood in the sacrament. Here's why.

I start with the fact that this belief has been part of our Christian tradition from the very beginning. That's a good point of departure, but it's not enough. For me the key to accepting this mystery is to ask what the Eucharist means.

During the Last Supper, as Jesus broke bread with his friends and prepared himself to die, his final command to the disciples, including us, is "Do this in my memory" (Luke 22:19; 1 Corinthians 11:24). Now, when someone tells us to do something just before he dies, we feel a powerful obligation to obey the command. And in fact, probably no command of Jesus has been followed so universally for the past two thousand years as this one. Mass has been said millions of times all over the world for a very long time.

Why did Jesus command us to do this? And why has the Holy Spirit seen to it that we obey it so faithfully? The most obvious answer is that the Mass is a reenactment of Jesus's sacrificial death on the cross. The Mass is first a reminder that Jesus practiced what he preached: he sacrificed his life out of love for us. His message was always that to find real life, we must give it up in loving service to others. He did this throughout his ministry, and ultimately on Good Friday.

Jesus's death on the cross happened once in history, a long time ago. The question for us is, does Jesus's death still mean anything to us two thousand years later? Does Jesus's message still change lives? Or is it just one more obscure event that happened long ago and far away?

For believers, the answer is no! We have to make Jesus's sacrifice real and present now if we are to change our lives, abandon our selfish habits in order to follow him, and find life through loving, sacrificial service to others.

Mass starts with our gifts of bread and wine, "the fruit of the vine and the work of human hands." What happens at the Mass is that Christ takes over our gifts. The meaning changes from their being signs of us and our imperfect self-giving to being signs of Christ and his perfect self-giving. A change in meaning seems to require a change in what the gifts actually are.[72]

Unlike us, Christ gives himself totally: body, blood, soul, divinity. This total self-giving in the world of sacramental signs means the change of bread and wine into Christ's very self. Nothing less than this will do!

Why will nothing less do? I am reminded of a question once asked by a liturgical theologian: "What good is it if the bread and wine are transformed but we are not?" We could also ask this question the other way around. If we are just eating the bread and wine we have offered, how will that change our lives? The gospel is about changed lives.

At every Mass we hear Jesus's request-command, "Do this in memory of me." Why did Jesus want us to do this in his memory? So that we will have life and have it more abundantly (John 10:10), in this life and the next, as Jesus clearly says in our passage today. Why will eating and drinking Jesus give us life? Jesus tells us that to gain life, we must give it up (Matthew 10:39, par. John 12:25). Jesus, "the man for others," did this throughout his ministry with loving service to those who needed help.

Dying to self to live for others is not easy and does not come naturally for most of us. We need God's grace to move in this direction. By eating and drinking Jesus's flesh and blood, we physically participate in Jesus's total self-giving. This is very strong medicine! What could be a stronger challenge to our natural self-centeredness? I know I need medicine this strong to nudge me in the right direction, the direction of life. Even with this medicine, progress can be slow, at least in my case.

Still, receiving the blessed sacrament regularly, at least twice a week for many years, has helped me to move toward more abundant life. I may not be ready yet to die a horrible death, as Jesus was. But at least I am more open to making the small sacrifices that give life "in the age." After a while, some do not feel like sacrifices any longer.

Most translations of our passage translate *aiōna* in verses 51 and 58 as "forever," or "eternal." Jesus promises eternal life to anyone who eats this bread. But this Greek noun has a number of meanings, and it primarily means an indefinitely long period of time. It generally does not mean eternity. Think of the English word "eon," which obviously comes from the Greek word. We can say, "I haven't seen a movie in eons," to mean probably a few years. But we can also say, "Glaciers formed, advanced, and retreated over eons." In this case, we are talking about thousands or maybe millions of years. In neither case does "eon" mean "eternity."

Hart generally translates *aiōn* as "age." When the word is not capitalized, its primary sense is the present age; when capitalized, it suggests time in an otherworldly or eschatological sense. Hart translates verse 51 this way: "I am the living bread that has descended out of heaven; if anyone eats of this bread he will live throughout the age; and the bread I shall give for the life of the cosmos is my flesh." In a footnote he writes that "throughout the age" could also be translated as "until the Age [to come]."

If Jesus here promises us life (only!) until the end of time and the beginning of the new age of his second coming, the words of verse 54 now make sense, whereas before they did not: "Whoever feeds upon my flesh and drinks of my blood has life in the Age, and I will raise him up on the last day." Why would he need to raise us up on the last day if we already had eternal life?

This discussion of eternal life is the flip side of the issue of hell, or eternal punishment, because the same Greek word is generally used in passages supposedly threatening eternal punishment and in promises of eternal life. Jesus does, I believe, offer us eternal life in a number of passages from Scripture, as we can see in verse 54 today. But because *aiōn* is routinely, and wrongly, translated as "eternal," the issue is more complicated than we might think.

One important theological result of the true meaning of *aiōn* is to heighten the sense that Jesus is talking about the here and now of present time, extended indefinitely. The life he offers for eating and drinking his flesh and blood has to do with our current lifespan and after our bodies die, until the end of time itself.

The Eucharist is ultimately God's gift of God's self to us, empowering us to give ourselves to others. It also allows us to be aware of how we participate in God's life, and God in our lives. Otherwise, God can seem too distant and immaterial, as we are creatures with bodies, while God is the Creator and is Spirit.

We can only experience the Eucharist through the Church, of course. Christianity is never a solo performance but always a choir. The Eucharist also then deepens our connection to God as well as to the Church community.

The reading from Deuteronomy is a reminder of the Old Covenant God established with Israel. God delivered the Hebrews from slavery by leading them through the desert and feeding them manna, the bread from heaven. When John's Jesus says, "I am the living bread that has descended out of heaven," it is a reminder of manna.

Moses says in Deuteronomy 8:3 that God humbled the Hebrews and fed them manna "that he might make you know that man does not live by bread alone, but that man lives by everything that proceeds out of the mouth of God." Jesus quotes this verse when tempted by Satan in the desert to turn stones into bread. But I do not understand how God giving the hungry Hebrews manna teaches them that we do not live by bread alone. The manna was a gift from God, but its primary purpose was to avoid hunger and starvation. It is not clear to me how manna is connected to "everything that proceeds out of the mouth of God."

The Eucharist is, however, the answer to my question. The bread of communion is both real bread and at the same time Jesus, God's Word for us. Our hunger to eat the body of Christ reveals the truth that we do not live by bread alone.

TWELFTH SUNDAY ORDINARY TIME

Jeremiah 20:10–13
Romans 5:12–15
Matthew 10:26–33

TODAY'S GOSPEL PASSAGE is clearly meant as a message to Jesus's first disciples, contrasting Jesus's way of delivering his message to them with their mission to the world. It also is about empowering them to take what risks they must in order to spread the gospel. Our job is therefore not only to understand what Jesus is saying here but also to figure out how it might apply to our very different situation two thousand years later.

Fear is the overt focus of this passage: the word "fear" or "afraid" is used explicitly four times in these eight verses, and it colors the entire passage. Yet our attention is drawn to fear, it seems, to reveal something about its opposite, faith.

I want to start with the scariest part of this passage, verse 28: "And do not fear those who kill the body but cannot kill the soul; but rather fear the one who can destroy both soul and body in the Vale of Hinnom."

This is the David Bentley Hart translation. Most translations have "hell" for "Vale of Hinnom." The Aramaic form of the Hebrew Ge-Hinnom, Valley of Hinnom, is "the Gehenna," and some translations do reference this as a footnote. This is a valley to the south and west of Jerusalem. Why it had become a place associated with punishment and/or purification by the time of Christ is hard to say.

A crucial point to bear in mind is that, according to Hart, "there is no single Greek term in the New Testament that quite corresponds—or corresponds at all, really—to the Anglo-Saxon word 'hell.'" Nor can we find anywhere in Scripture any mention of a discrete concept that corresponds to the image we have of hell: a realm of eternal and excruciating tortures ruled by Satan.[73] For a fuller discussion of "the hell problem," see appendix A.

God is here depicted as one who "can destroy both body and soul" in the Vale of Hinnom. If Jesus is talking about hell here, notice this version of hell is one not of eternal punishment but of total annihilation. Still bad, but certainly not quite so bad! Many secular people believe that is what will happen to them when they die anyway.

The Greek word translated as "destroy" is *apolésai*. It means "to destroy utterly." When used of persons, it means loss of eternal life; it also means to be lost, alienated from God. Notice that Jesus says here that God "can" destroy both body and soul, not that God will. What Jesus says is surely true: God can do anything! This divine capacity is a good reason to be God-fearing.

Another way to interpret the verse is that this is a purifying, or purgatorial, form of punishment that evildoers may have to undergo to prepare them for eternal life with God. We sometimes hear people speak about "soul-crushing" events or experiences. Or how someone has "sold his soul" to achieve some temporal benefit. Jesus may have been speaking in this manner. And of course, we all know our bodies will eventually turn to dust.

I believe the best way to understand verse 10:28 is by referring to the opening verse of this passage, 26: "Therefore do not fear them." The "them" here means the Pharisees who in 9:34 accused Jesus of casting out demons by the prince of demons. Jesus will of course allow his own body to be killed because of the hostility of Jewish religious leaders.

Faith casts out fear. But then how can we reconcile faith in

God with the fear of God? The analogy of human relationships sheds light on this question. If I love someone, I must have some fear that I could do something to hurt him or her. I may have some fear of losing the relationship entirely, either because of something I have done or failed to do or perhaps because of some terrible accident or disease.

I do not believe we can ever lose God's love in an ultimate or final sense. But we can certainly do things that damage the relationship, to the point where it feels like we may have lost something forever. We can "lose" our faith. God can seem to withdraw, especially when we are in mortal sin. We should be afraid of these things because ironically this fear will grant us the courage we need to avoid them. I believe this is what Jesus is trying to tell us.

Jesus's intention here is to inspire his listeners to be God-fearers and therefore fearless in this life. Why is fearing God the antidote to fearing people? If we fear damaging our relationship with God above all else, we will stand up to people opposed to God's will and to the truth. The courage it takes to stand up to bullies and defend the truth is rarely seen in the city where I live, Washington, DC. However, we did see it in the brave defense of the US Capitol by the police on January 6, 2021.

Chrysostom reminds us of a second way a loving faith in God strengthens our courage in this world. He begins with Jesus's statement that since God is aware even of every sparrow that falls, nothing that occurs is hidden from God. He continues:

> THEREFORE, IF GOD both knows all things that happen to us and is able to save us and is willing to do so, then whatever we may be suffering, we need not think that God has forsaken us in our suffering. For it is not God's will to keep us wholly separated from that which elicits dread but rather to persuade us not to make

an idol out of whatever we dread. It is this, more than anything else, that constitutes deliverance from dread. Therefore, don't be afraid.... For even if that which you dread prevails, it prevails only over your body; this is the limited part of yourself, which nature will surely take in due time and bring to an end.[74]

French philosopher Gabriel Marcel makes a similar point in distinguishing between optimism and hope.[75] If I am optimistic, I will recover from cancer; that means if I do not, my optimism was mistaken. Everything rides on whether I recover or not. If instead of optimism I have hope, it means that I believe my ultimate destiny will not be determined by my cancer, whatever happens.

The reading from Jeremiah rhymes with the gospel passage. We see how faith in God grounds the prophet's courage when faced with unjust persecution and the betrayal of his friends. One critical difference: Jeremiah wants to witness the vengeance he is certain God will take on the prophet's persecutors. He even asks God to let him see it! Jesus on the cross instead asks God to forgive his tormentors.

I think this is the message from today's gospel that is most relevant to us today: if we are afraid of doing what we need to do to follow Jesus, we need to take steps to strengthen our faith muscles. Go to Mass, pray for God's help, talk to fellow believers, read the Bible. These activities have worked for me; you may discover other ways that work for you.

I want to add that if we feel afraid, or at least uncomfortable, about doing something that God is calling us to do, this is a good sign. Our souls need the exercise! We cannot maintain bodily health unless we push ourselves beyond our comfort zone, viz. by getting out of breath, feeling the burn in our muscles, and so on. God created our bodies and our souls. Why would our souls be any different from our bodies? If we don't at least occasionally push our souls beyond their comfort zone, our faith muscles will become weak, unhealthy.

A more historical message, perhaps less relevant to us but still revealing of Jesus's ministry, is also embedded in today's passage. Or revealing of Matthew's take on Jesus's ministry, at least. Luke has a parallel passage where Jesus tells his disciples that whatever they have said in the dark shall be heard in the light (12:3). But in Matthew's version, in verse 27, Jesus says, "What I tell you in the dark, utter in the light."

The gospels tell us that, for a while at least, Jesus was very popular, with thousands of people following him all over Palestine. But the gospels also tell us that Jesus spoke in parables to the crowds and explained everything only to his disciples (Matthew 13:10ff, par.). We can also think about how, especially in Mark, Jesus wants to keep his healings and his messianic identity a secret. But we can see this in Matthew as well—for example, 12:15–16.

This is a pattern I see repeated in the synoptic gospels. (I am here assuming as correct the scholarly consensus that Mark is the earliest gospel and that Matthew and Luke both used Mark as a source document in writing their gospels.) The pattern is as follows: Mark includes something that seems to have made Matthew and Luke uncomfortable; Matthew softens the language; Luke often goes one step further and may even leave out the passage.[76]

I would argue that the hidden and secretive nature of Jesus's message became more and more problematic for Christians after Jesus's death. We certainly see this process at work: in Mark, the "messianic secret" is quite prominent; it is less so in Matthew, and appears wholly absent in Luke.

Given how difficult and shocking Jesus's message is, rather than allowing ourselves to be shocked by Jesus's originally secretive methods, we should be grateful that whatever he did seems to have worked! Against all odds, the "secret" revolutionary message has been spread throughout the world. The problem is not so much that we have not heard it. The problem is in doing it.

Jesus often deals in parables concerning the mysterious way in which the Kingdom of God starts in a small or even secret manner and then gradually grows large and powerful. I am thinking especially of the parable of the mustard seed (Matthew 13:31–32, par.) and the leaven a woman "hid" in three measures of meal (Matthew 13:33, par. Luke 13:20–21). These parables can also be seen as remarkably accurate prophetic forecasts: the gospel is preached and Mass is celebrated across the planet today.

Despite all of the above, we still might wonder if Matthew and Mark are accurately telling us how Jesus operated when they have him saying he "whispered" his message in the dark. Chrysostom sheds some light on this question.

> THE POINT IS not that Jesus was literally whispering into their ears or speaking in physical darkness. Rather, he was here pressing a strong figure of speech. He was conversing with them quietly and alone in a small corner of Palestine. In contrast with this tone of voice, they would soon be preaching with a boldness of speech that would in due time be conferred upon them. . . . For they were soon to be commissioned to speak not to one or two or three cities but to the whole world. They would soon be traversing land and sea, amid inhabited countries and across deserts, addressing both princes and tribes, philosophers and orators, telling it like it is with an open face and with all boldness of speech.[77]

Nearly all of Jesus's disciples were martyred for proclaiming the Good News. They needed to have a very strong faith to transcend the fearful tortures and punishments they faced for following Jesus. I think this is the context for Jesus's words in verse 33, where Jesus threatens those who deny him that he will deny them to his Father in the heavens.

On the one hand, this kind of tit-for-tat revenge seems out of character for Jesus. But the stakes are high here. Without the courage of the early followers of Jesus, his message could have been lost in the graveyard of history's many lost causes. Verse 33 may have been something that Matthew's community needed to hear to strengthen their faith and courage against persecution. The warning is stern, but Jesus is not threatening eternal punishment or hellfire to those who deny him.

The Church faced persecution for centuries. Jesus's words in Matthew are intended to strengthen the faith of Christ's followers then, but they are just important for us to hear today. More Christians were martyred in the twentieth century than in any previous century. Estimates on the numbers killed vary from fifteen to forty-five million; at the higher range of estimates, twentieth-century Christian martyrs would outnumber all previous centuries combined.[78]

For us North Americans today, it may seem far-fetched to imagine we could be martyred for proclaiming the gospel. However, even in modern America, to proclaim faith in the gospel still requires a certain amount of bravery at times. It does for me. Living in the nation's capital, I find that when I go to any social gathering outside of a church, I find few believers. When I do talk about my faith, I have learned to inure myself to the "martyrdom" of the blank look and the awkward silence. I realize this is paltry compared to the tortures endured by genuine martyrs. But I confess at times I have lacked the courage it takes to withstand even this mild social embarrassment. Who knows, maybe that blank look covers a seed which will sprout later.

This is another way in which this week's gospel reading

is relevant to us today. Remember, the world is hungry for meaning. When appropriate, we must not hide our vision out of pusillanimous politeness.

THIRTEENTH SUNDAY ORDINARY TIME

2 Kings 4:8–11, 14–16a
Romans 6:3–4, 8–11
Matthew 10:37–42

I PROPOSE A little editing of today's gospel passage. The reading from Matthew has a parallel in Luke, and they each have made a good decision; let's combine them and take the better reading from each. This is what they did, after all.

Matthew has Jesus saying, "He who loves father or mother more than me is not worthy of me; and he who loves son or daughter more than me is not worthy of me." Luke's version is "If anyone comes to me and does not hate his own father and mother and wife and children and brothers and sisters, yes and even his own life, he cannot be my disciple."

It sounds as though Luke is resorting to "Semitic hyperbole" when he tells us we have to "hate" everyone in our own family to be worthy of Jesus. Exaggeration in order to shock and make a point was a way of speaking in Jesus's milieu. His listeners would have known better than to take him literally here. Still, some of us, sometimes, are all too ready to hate our parents—we don't need the gospels to encourage us! Kidding aside, there is a deeper point at work here; more about that later.

Matthew surely is on firmer ground with his "He who loves father or mother . . . son or daughter more than me . . ." That makes a lot of sense; it is challenging enough for most of us most of the time. Especially the "loves son or daughter" part. As Aristotle observed, it is natural for parents to love their children more than children love their parents.

But Matthew's version is harsher at a different point in the passage when he writes that a family-loving disciple is "not worthy" of Jesus. Luke's matter-of-fact "cannot be my disciple" is better. Putting together the best of Luke with the best of Matthew we have "He who loves father or mother more than me cannot be my disciple; and he who loves son or daughter, brother or sisters, yes and even his own life more than me, cannot be my disciple."

Both Luke and Matthew have language about the need to lose our lives for Christ's sake in order to find them, while if we find (or, in Luke, "seek to gain") our lives, we will lose them. Mark does too, at 8:35. This prompts NJBC to believe these verses are old and significant.[79]

What does this mean? Matthew and Luke link this with loving Jesus more than one's mother, father, etc. I'm lucky because this is one of the easiest gospel passages for me to understand. Of course, following through and really doing it is tougher—I don't mean to suggest it's easy at all! French philosopher Gabriel Marcel once wrote that a crucial insight in his intellectual and spiritual journey was the sense that "this is not it!" To use the pilgrimage metaphor, it means the certainty that we have taken a wrong turn. We are still lost and don't know the right way, but we do know we have to turn around and retrace our steps back to where we took the wrong turn.

Until I was twenty-three years old, my unacknowledged religion was to please my parents, or at least not disappoint them. Therefore, I went to law school. Not because I truly wanted to be a lawyer, but because that's what they wanted me to do and I didn't have any better ideas. My father was a lawyer and was well established in the best law firm in our little town, a firm that my great-grandfather started and where my grandfather also worked his entire life. I would have had a job for life, along with a well-respected position in the community.

Halfway through my first year of law school, I realized, "This is not it." Many people like law school, and our nation needs more honest lawyers, but it was not for me. I was there for the wrong reasons. The demanding intellectual work, the relentless, rationalistic analysis of minutiae, the law's obsession with technique and disinterest in deeper questions was killing my soul.

I was terrified of dropping out, however. First because I knew my parents would be furious. Second, I was afraid of failure, of "losing." Third because I had no idea what to do instead of law school.

Thank you, Jesus, that during this excruciating period of soul-searching, I recalled these lines from the gospels. It was liberating to have recourse to an authority that transcended— that "trumped"—my parents! Fortunately, they also were churchgoers; my mother was devout, and my father went along for his reasons. Naturally, they still didn't buy my exegesis, or its application, but it helped me to find the courage to "lose" my life and drop out of law school.

I worry that I "know" what this passage means so well in my life that I have no clue about what it might mean for others. But I will try all the same.

Jesus's central message was the arrival of the Kingdom of God. This kingdom transcends ordinary, natural life. It is natural for us to want to please our parents, be well thought of by the community, have a prestigious career, start a family. I think Jesus might even agree these are good things. We can pursue them, and they can be compatible with our faith, but they must come second to our following Jesus.

The first reading from 2 Kings is a reminder of how important having children was for Jewish people. There was no belief in the afterlife in Old Testament times, and one way people dealt with death was through having children. We can see how important children were in the story of Abraham. God entices Abraham to leave his native land by promising him as many descendants as the stars in the sky. Sons were also important for mothers because if they became widows, they could become penniless, since they were generally unable to earn money through work.

Jesus's point is that the goals of ordinary natural life can be so beguiling that we will lose ourselves, lose our souls, lose our "life" in pursuing them too single-mindedly. It is easy to see people doing this in Washington today, in 2021! The goals and community Jesus is talking about are at odds with the goals of ordinary life. The Kingdom of God transcends the immanent kingdom of this world.

This is one of the reasons I converted to Catholicism. The Protestant Reformation was about a lot of things, but one of its principal goals was to establish that there is no ultimate conflict between the ordinary life of work, marriage, and family and the gospel. Therefore, no religious orders, no monks, no nuns, no priestly celibacy, and so on. The Protestants had a point. Back in the sixteenth century, it could seem like only priests and religious were "real" Christians; lay folk were second-rate "amateurs." This whole issue is too complicated for me to pursue here.

But with the Reformation, something precious was lost: the inherent, inevitable, and, yes, creative tension between the gospel of Jesus Christ and "ordinary secular life." I was raised to conflate career and social status with faith in Jesus. And that did not work.

I like Luke's "cannot be my disciple" because it is a simple, sober statement of fact. No need to get judgmental. Plenty of good people appear to be content to love mother, father, sister, brother, son, daughter, and even themselves more than Jesus. We could do far worse with our lives, and many people do that, too. Jesus himself repeatedly says that following him is not for everyone.

What Jesus is saying in essence is that unless we know what Peggy Lee is singing about in "Is That All There Is?" we are never going to get it. We must feel deep down, all the way down, that for every true follower of Jesus, "everyday life" without that constant, transcendent call-and-response to season it is empty.

This raises a question, a question I cannot answer. Should we all feel the emptiness of mere everyday life without any transcendent connection? St. Thomas and St. Augustine would answer yes. We are created for communion with God, and our hearts will be ever restless, deeply unsatisfied, until they rest in God.

Our secular age is not so sure about this, though, and neither is Charles Taylor in *A Secular Age*.[80] He would say both faith and the lack of it are fragile. The practical, self-satisfied, functional atheism of modernity has created a new dilemma for us, one that St. Thomas and St. Augustine did not imagine. Some folks will read our gospel passage and respond, "Fine! I cannot be your disciple then. I love my family and I love my life. And just what is wrong with that?!" Plenty of good people seem to lead meaningful lives without experiencing this "metaphysical deficit" that only a relationship with God can fill. All I know for certain is that I am not one of them.

FOURTEENTH SUNDAY ORDINARY TIME

Zechariah 9:9–10
Romans 8:9, 11–13
Matthew 11:25–30

JESUS BEGINS THIS week's reading with a shocking statement. He actually gives thanks to God that God has hidden "these things from the wise and understanding and revealed them to babes; yea, Father, for such was your gracious will."

What are "these things" that God has hidden? Earlier in Matthew 11, Jesus upbraids the cities where he has done most of his mighty works because despite these miracles, no one there repented, the condition for entering the Kingdom of God—the heart of Jesus's mission. But "these things" also have to do with the radical nature of Jesus's message, a message that upended much of Jewish tradition.

Who are "the wise"? There was a long and venerable Wisdom tradition in Israel. The books of Job, Proverbs, Ecclesiastes, Sirach, and Wisdom of Solomon belong to this tradition. The Jewish leaders—the scribes, Pharisees, and Sadducees—would have been familiar with this tradition; for them it was a crucial component of following the Lord. Jerusalem was the center of this learned tradition, and it required money to study. Jesus was a poor man from Galilee; most of his disciples were too.

I have come to believe we cannot truly understand Jesus without understanding the Wisdom tradition (see appendix E).

As a devout Jew, Jesus would have been familiar with this. The Wisdom tradition has many wonderful insights. The form of writing is poetic, not prosaic. It is concerned with how to live well and with practical wisdom, and it arises out of Israel's deep faith in Yahweh. The point of departure for this tradition: "The fear of the Lord is the beginning of Wisdom" (Proverbs 1:7). Wisdom is divine since the created world declares the wisdom of its Creator (Proverbs 3:19–20).

Yet Jesus never quotes a single passage from a Wisdom book in any gospel.

If we want to understand someone, we need to understand what he rejects. (This reminds me of what I wrote last Sunday about dropping out of law school.) I don't think we can understand Jesus without understanding the Hebrew Wisdom tradition because it seems to me Jesus rejected it—and it rejected him! This could be what's going on in today's gospel reading.

In order to understand Jesus, I especially recommend reading Sirach because it was written less than two hundred years before Jesus was born; it paints us a portrait of what wise and devout Jewish men (and they were all men) thought and believed. Sirach deepens the tradition in beautiful ways—see Sirach 39:16–35 and also the discussion of this passage in Gerhard von Rad's wonderful book *Wisdom in Israel*.[81]

I think that we Christians, precisely because we are followers of Jesus, have been biased against the "Jewish leaders," the "scribes and the Pharisees," that Jesus so often attacks. Reading Sirach and learning more about the entire Wisdom tradition is an important corrective.

But why, then, does Jesus seem to reject it, at times vehemently? Relying on Sirach, I can point to at least five reasons. First, Sirach's attitude toward sinners is contrary to Jesus's: "Give to the godly man, but do not help the sinner. . . . For the Most High also hates sinners and will inflict punishment on the ungodly" (12:4, 6). Sirach urges the wise man to avoid all contact with sinners, lest he be corrupted by the contact: "What fellowship has a wolf with a lamb? No more has a sinner with a godly man" (13:17); "No one will pity a man who associates with a sinner" (12:14).

Can you not hear in these verses the echoes of the attacks on Jesus for hanging out with sinners? Check out the verse just before our reading today, Matthew 11:19: "The Son of man came eating and drinking and they say, 'Behold a glutton and a drunkard, a friend of tax collectors and sinners!' Yet wisdom is justified by her deeds." Notice how Jesus here explicitly responds to the attack of Wisdom for befriending sinners: "Wisdom is justified by her deeds." Jesus's mission was centered on inviting sinners into the Kingdom.

Second, worldly success and happiness in this life is an essential goal of Sirach and the entire Wisdom tradition. These verses are typical: "Do not give yourself over to sorrow, and do not afflict yourself deliberately. Gladness of heart is the life of man, and the rejoicing of a man is length of days. Delight your soul and comfort your heart and remove sorrow far from you, for sorrow has destroyed many and there is no profit in it" (30:21–23).

Jesus tells us exactly the opposite in the beatitudes (Matthew 5), and he advises us to lose our lives in order to find them. And he lived this message: at least in his final years, he was a homeless vagabond relying on the kindness of his friends, and he died nailed to a cross.

Third, Sirach does not tell us to love our enemies. Instead, he calls upon God violently to attack and completely destroy Israel's foes: "Rouse thy anger and pour out thy wrath, destroy the adversary and wipe out the enemy. . . . Let him who survives be consumed in the fiery wrath, and may those who harm thy people meet destruction" (36:7, 9).

Fourth, Jesus shattered many taboos by spending time with

women and treating them like equals. Sirach was a misogynist. The book has many examples of this, but the following is the most brutal: "Better is the wickedness of a man than a woman who does good; and it is a woman who brings shame and disgrace" (42:14). It is important to remember, when reading the gospels, that Sirach was typical of the time. It is Jesus who was not.

Finally, Sirach was an elitist. He believed that the "wisdom of the scribe depends on the opportunity of leisure; and he who has little business may become wise" (38:24); in other words, we have to be rich and have leisure to be wise. Those who need to work with their hands—he "who handles the plow and who glories in the shaft of a goad, who drives oxen and is occupied with their work and whose talk is about bulls"—can never be wise and successful (38:25).

This takes us back to Jesus's words in today's reading, where he thanks God for hiding "these things" from the wise and revealing them to *nepios*. This word is often translated as "babes." It means a young child and, by extension, the simple, the innocent, the childlike—the opposite of the wise. Several of Jesus's closest disciples were fishermen, of course. And St. Paul confirms that most of the early Christians were not well educated nor powerful nor of noble birth (1 Corinthians 1:26).

The first reading reminds us of Passion Sunday and emphasizes the humility of Jesus himself. Jesus was not from an established family in Jerusalem. He was from a tiny town in "the sticks" of Galilee. It is not clear how well educated he was, but it does not seem he spent much time in the fancy schools of Jerusalem where all the best and the brightest learned about Torah. So, in terms of his background and education, to paraphrase what Winston Churchill once said of Clement Atlee, Jesus "was a humble man with much to be humble about." This may well have added to his alienation from the Wisdom tradition.

Now we can see why Jesus rejects the tradition. We can also

understand why it rejects him. The fraught relationship Jesus has with Jewish Wisdom reminds me of the one he has with the Law; this will come up elsewhere.

Above all, Jesus's rejection of Wisdom makes me love him more deeply and with greater understanding. A child of the 1960s, I know how I, and many in my generation, were formed by what we rejected, by what we rebelled against. On the other hand, I do not think we can understand the Wisdom tradition by only listening to Jesus. Rebels never are fair to what they reject. The importance of his mission transcended fairness to Wisdom.

We are now in a better position to understand why Matthew has Jesus follow this up with verses 28–29, which are found only in Matthew. We have seen that those who do hard labor cannot be wise, according to Sirach. Jesus invites these hardworking folks in, to learn from him. And he promises them rest because the yoke he proffers is easy.

The rabbis spoke of the yoke of Torah, according to NJBC. Jesus could mean that his yoke, his interpretation of the Law, is easier because it is simpler quantitatively. We only have to love God and neighbor as ourselves! But this is very hard in a different way because these demands are inexhaustible. Matthew 5 makes this clear, and in 5:20 Jesus insists that unless our righteousness exceeds that of the scribes and the Pharisees, we cannot enter the Kingdom.

In what way is Jesus's yoke easy and his burden light? My answer is that Jesus calls for us to internalize the Law, by loving him, God, and neighbor. Now, those who have been in love with someone know that it is actually a joy to do things for the beloved. Not a burden at all! The same is true if we love our children. At least up to a point. Jesus's message is about love. If we allow ourselves to be possessed by love, then many things become easy.

Note also that Jesus speaks here of "life-long learning" when he invites us to learn from him. This is one reason to fall in love with Jesus. It really does take a lifetime to learn from him. And the love of learning is one way we can remain truly alive, just like an ever-curious *nepios*, a child.

Finally, Jesus speaks of giving us rest. The notion of rest is related to the Sabbath, to the Kingdom. It means the opposite of laboring, of effort. Love is the opposite of labor. It is God's great gift to us. It is what those who work hard for a living need most of all.

FIFTEENTH SUNDAY ORDINARY TIME

Isaiah 55:10–11
Romans 8:18–23
Matthew 13:1–23

TODAY'S GOSPEL CONCERNS a mystery that has long perplexed me. Why is it that so many people just don't seem to "get it" when it comes to Jesus's message? And then there is the attendant concern that if most people do not comprehend the gospel, how can I be so sure I am one of the lucky few? The indifference of so many may threaten the plausibility of the faith. This question has dogged believers from the beginning, but it is raised with new urgency by our own secular age (cf. Charles Taylor's *A Secular Age*). In the circles I travel in, agnosticism is the default position. Forget about Jesus and the many tough things he asks us to swallow—most people cannot even bring themselves to take the existence of God seriously.

I think that all of today's readings shed light on the mystery of Jesus's reception. Let's start with the paradoxical fact that at the beginning of today's gospel, Jesus's main problem is that too many people want to hear what he has to say! He has to take the extreme measure of speaking to them from a boat on the lake. Perhaps this was so the crowd would not get so close to him that his words wouldn't carry far enough. There were no microphones in those days.

The rise and fall of Jesus's popularity with the people is one of the constant rhythms of the gospels. It culminates during Holy Week. On Palm Sunday the crowds cheer his entrance into Jerusalem. Five days later, they jeer at him and demand his crucifixion.

I imagine Jesus himself may have wondered, "What are all these people doing here? They all can't possibly understand what I'm talking about." If so, the parable Jesus then told could be his way of working this out, a kind of reality check, for himself and others. "Let's not get carried away with all this momentary popularity," he might be saying to himself and his disciples. Lots of people may want to hear the Word, but few are going to understand it; fewer still will put it into practice and stick with it when sacrifices are demanded. And even among those who are true believers and actors, some will be far more fruitful than others: "thirtyfold, sixtyfold, and a hundredfold."

Yet another layer of complexity to this whole question is raised by the fact that Christianity is still the most popular religion on the planet, weighing in at well over two billion people. That's almost one-third of the world's current population. On the other hand, how many of those would Jesus count as true believers, willing to sacrifice or even die for the gospel? Far fewer.

If you have been following my train of thought, by now you may feel like a ping-pong ball, going back and forth between opposing perspectives. One way to bring some of these tensions together is to understand that there are, in fact, many ways of following Jesus, many degrees of devotion and discipleship. We can even see this in the gospels.

We do not need to feel like we all have to be just like the twelve, or rather the eleven, devoted disciples, who gave up everything to follow him and most of whom died for the faith. There is also Joseph of Arimathea, whom John calls a "secret" disciple of Jesus out of fear of what "the Jews" would do to him (John 19:38). I'm afraid that's closer to the kind of disciple I might have been with persecution likely. We have options. And our level of devotion to the gospel can change over time; it can grow, and it can also decay.

The toughest part of the gospel reading is when Jesus explains why he speaks in parables. The parallel Mark passage (4:10–12) is even harsher than Matthew. Mark has Jesus saying he speaks in parables "so that they may indeed see but not perceive, and may indeed hear but not understand, lest they should turn again, and be forgiven." Luke (8:9–10) more or less follows Mark. These two writers are suggesting that the whole intention of Jesus's use of parables is to obfuscate! Jesus wants to make his message incomprehensible and make it impossible for people to repent and be forgiven so they may enter the Kingdom.

Is it Jesus's intention that the people not understand his message, as Mark and Luke would have it? Matthew's rendering in verses 13ff suggests it is rather the unintended result in many cases. I prefer his version. It appears to be more consistent with Jesus's message elsewhere. Jesus does frequently express frustration that so many people do not accept his offer of repentance, forgiveness, and a new community based on love. We can see signs of this in today's passage starting at verse 14, and also at Matthew 11:20ff.

Given his frustration with the wooden-headedness of so many, why would Jesus deliberately make the offer harder to receive?

Chrysostom points out that Jesus taught clearly in the Sermon on the Mount and elsewhere, while here he weaves parables into his discourse. Chrysostom believes the parables are for the learned, the scribes and Pharisees, who were absent at the Sermon on the Mount.[82] The resistance of the learned to Jesus's message is a constant in the gospels (as in Matthew 11:25, par. Luke, which we read last week). Their inability to understand Jesus's clear teaching may have prompted him to try parables. St. Jerome suggests that by using both what is clear and what is obscure, Jesus allows people to be drawn from what they understand to things they do not yet understand, an example of how following Jesus entails lifelong learning.

Verse 12 appears unfair: "For to him who has it shall be given and shall be more than is needed; but from him who does not have even what he has shall be taken away." If Jesus were talking about the material world, this would be unjust, but he is talking about the spiritual life where things are quite different. Chrysostom explains:

> WHEN ANYONE HAS zeal and eagerness, there will be given to him on God's part all things sufficient for his needs. But if he lacks any responsiveness and is not ready to contribute his own share, neither are God's gifts bestowed. In that case even "what he seems to have," so Jesus says, "shall be taken away from him." Here it is not so much God taking something away from him as it is his own unreadiness to receive these gifts.
>
> We ourselves do this all the time. When we see someone listening carelessly and when with much effort we cannot persuade him to listen at all, then it remains for us to be silent. For if we continue, even his carelessness is aggravated. But for someone who is striving to learn, we lead on and pour in much.[83]

As a former teacher, I understand Chrysostom's point perfectly. This seems to be another way of saying, "Seek and you shall find, knock and it will be opened to you." Notice how everything here seems to depend on our receptiveness to God's Word. It is mostly a case of our needing to clear away the obstacles inside of us that prevent God's message from penetrating into our hearts.

Jesus wants us to feel compassion for others. I think we should have some compassion for the people who were listening to him, trying to figure him out. When we read the beatitudes of Matthew 5, we must realize Jesus is asking people to turn upside down all their assumptions about how to live and pursue happiness: love your enemies, turn the other cheek, rejoice when you are reviled and persecuted, lose your life in order to find it. We have heard these ideas before, and they are still difficult to understand and put into practice. In Jesus's time, this teaching was bizarre, shocking.

Jesus's also invites everyone to join a new kind of community, one that is based not on violence and fear but on love. It is difficult enough for us, two thousand years later, to understand and receive this message. For the people of first-century Palestine, this was a revolutionary message completely alien to their lived experience—nothing so shallow as a political revolution, but rather something far deeper and longer lasting. This revolutionary message is also why Jesus again and again stresses the importance of faith. A revolution requires faith because it is about the future, not the present. The disciples did not fully grasp it until Pentecost. How can we not have compassion for the incomprehension of so many to what Jesus was saying? The miracle is that anyone understood and believed.

In our passage, the disciples ask Jesus why he speaks in parables. I think his use of parables is quite logical. If he speaks in clear prose, listeners can be passive and will place what they hear into their existing framework. But Jesus's message requires a clean break with the status quo. Speaking in parables also requires listeners to do some work, and this is appropriate because we cannot begin to follow Jesus if we remain passive in our minds and our hearts. The parable form challenges our existing mental-spiritual framework, our received assumptions. Many parables can have multiple interpretations and point to the mystery inherent in embracing an unknown and revolutionary future.

This particular parable was probably helpful to Jesus's

disciples and to his later followers in St. Matthew's community because it helped them to deal with those who rejected Jesus, or who fell away when persecution got hot. The latter would have been a particular trial for later followers of Jesus.

The seed that fell on rocky ground seems to have the problems of St. Matthew's community written all over it. Those who heard Jesus by the lake would not have faced immediate persecution risks. But by the end of the first century, when St. Matthew was writing, it had become a real and ever-present danger. It is harder to remain faithful when many in a community drop out due to fear of persecution. This parable, in part, is intended to strengthen the faith of those who came later—including us.

Today's gospel reading helps us to accept the diversity of responses to Jesus's message, in his day and in our own. Isaiah confirms this by assuring us that God is, and has always been, in charge both of the message and its results.

In this context, St. Paul in Romans leads me to think that a crucial prerequisite for anyone to be receptive to Jesus's message is the awareness of the "pointlessness" of creation. It is beautiful. The immanent created order cannot be explained from within its own framework but only by means of a reality that transcends it.

SIXTEENTH SUNDAY ORDINARY TIME

The Weed People

Wisdom of Solomon 12:13, 16–19
Romans 8:26–7
Matthew 13:24–43

JESUS'S MISSION WAS to announce the arrival of the Kingdom of God. All of today's parables are telling us what the Kingdom of God "is like," so they are extremely important.

Notice that in Matthew (and all the parallels) Jesus is not telling us explicitly and prosaically what the Kingdom is. Rather he uses metaphors to tell us what the Kingdom is like. As I wrote last week, parables and poetry invite listeners to participate actively in the message. It takes some effort even to understand the Kingdom Jesus is talking about.

Second, because of the individual work it takes to understand the parable, we place our own personal stamp on it. To some extent, this can make the parable our own.

Finally, parables challenge listeners to "conceive the inconceivable." They invite people to imagine the Kingdom in creative ways rather than reducing the message to an existing mental paradigm or social framework, as a clearly stated, prosaic message might. A parable is a story, and like all good stories, it can never be exhausted by one interpretation. Every time you hear it, you may have a fresh understanding of its message. The story exists as a whole; its different characters and elements play a role. They do not simply "stand for" something else outside of the parable, as in fables and allegories.

No parable's message can be reduced to a simple propositional statement. For example, today's parable of the good seed and the weeds does not mean "only" that at the end of time God will separate out good people from evildoers and that in the meantime we must be patient with apparent evildoers among us because we aren't very good at distinguishing good folks from bad. This rather literal point is certainly part of the parable's message, but it does not exhaust it. Unlike prose, parables preserve something of the mystery and open-endedness of the Kingdom.

Jesus was part of an existing tradition of Jewish rabbis who used parables to instruct and illustrate. Jesus used parables for these purposes but also as a form of proclamation, especially about the Kingdom of God.

All of this may help explain verse 34: "Indeed he said nothing to them without a parable."

Scripture scholars tell us that while Jesus spoke in parables, the early Church often recast them as allegories. We have a perfect example of this allegorizing phenomenon in today's gospel: Matthew 13:36–43. The fact that the parable and its "interpretation" is found only in Matthew offers further reason to believe Matthew was inspired to use it in order to serve the needs of his community.

As I mentioned earlier in my introduction to Matthew, this is what he does: he is serving the needs of his church. No doubt some members of Matthew's community were upset with other members and wanted them out of the Church. We do not have any good information on what was going on, but we know from the letters of St. Paul that the early Church was not always one big happy family.

The advantage of allegories is they make the message clear and univocal. In times of crisis, that can be essential, but that is their disadvantage as well. Everything in an allegory stands for one particular person or thing. Once we discern what it stands for, we do not even need to bother with the story anymore; we can simply translate the message into straightforward, prosaic language.

I do a lot of gardening, and I know very well that if I'm not careful, my weeding can uproot desirable plants, especially if the roots are entangled. Are not people also entangled, the good with the bad, husband with wife, mother with son? If we "root" out one, we may end up hurting another who has done nothing. Not only that, but most individuals are a mixture of good and sinful inclinations. God can sort this out far better than can mere human beings.

We could see the parable as telling us something about the Church. The Church has a long, complicated history filled with saints, martyrs—and scoundrels! In our own time, everyone is scandalized by the sex abuse horrors. Why would anyone want to join or remain a Catholic?

I can think of many answers to that question, but today's parable gives us one. Human judgment is flawed. It is actually more difficult to make good judgments about people than it is about weeds! The Church does excommunicate people, but that doesn't always go very well either. It seems as though we are going to have live with sinners as well as saints.

Still, last week's parable told us of how thorns can choke and destroy good seed. The difference there is that the thorns are not other people but "worldly anxiety and the lure of riches." Jesus does not suggest that the "weed people" of today's gospel have the power to destroy the faith-action of the children of the Kingdom. I worry that he might be too optimistic.

People with weak faith can be demoralized by the evil behavior of others. Maybe this parable can help people to understand that if we are going to remain faithful to the Kingdom, we have to be patient and tolerant—not of evil itself, but of the fact that Jesus's kingdom is not a neat, clean, sanitized place where nothing horrible ever happens. That is going to test our faith at times. It can be too much for some people, and they will leave. For those of us who stick with it, we have to make prudential judgments about safety and behaviors, but we also have to leave ultimate judgments about people to God. Doing this requires faith that God remains in ultimate control of the situation.

Another complication: as the first reading from Wisdom reminds us, the weed people may repent.

I have been writing as if the Kingdom and the Church were the same thing, and of course they are not. The Church is the place where the Kingdom is especially present, but the Kingdom exists in the world as well. This is also a test of faith for many—including, once upon a time, me! How is the Kingdom already present in our world? That's a question to stay with. I hope to get to it at some point.

What about the other two parables in today's gospel? The first parable was about a man, the second a seed, and the third concerns a woman. Jesus's habit of including women in his parables was uncommon at the time. There is a reason why so many of his first followers were women.

Both parables invite us to savor the wonder of commonplace, natural processes we are too likely to take for granted. I love to garden, and it does still knock me out. Any transformation of a tiny seed into a plant is amazing! This mustard seed parable reveals something of Jesus's faith. Not only that he was alive to the miracles of the everyday, but it is also a kind of prophecy. It shows how he believes his message will grow to welcome everyone who needs "a nest." The Church does offer that to everyone on the planet. He was right about that. How did he know?

One element that links all three parables together is the hiddenness and the effortlessness of the natural transformations. When we bake bread, the leaven slowly raises all the dough when we aren't watching. All we have to do is knead it in there. Even though dough and leaven are different and remain different, the leaven alters the dough, makes it rise to new heights. This is a beautiful metaphor for what the apostles, martyrs, and many Christians have done throughout the years. The metaphor suggests that the world is transformed by the faithful of the Kingdom even though the Kingdom remains part of the world.

Again, because I am a recovering moral theologian, I too often catch myself thinking about how I did this or that and then some grace befell me. It can happen that way. But it is easy to miss how the life of faith can also transform us, and others, slowly over time without our even being fully aware of it. It may take another person, or God, to notice because the change has happened so gradually. When I look at the huge plants in my garden, I have to remind myself sometimes, "That was a tiny seed I planted!"

This is what St. Paul is getting at in our Romans reading today: Don't worry too much about getting the words right when you pray. We have "inexpressible groanings" and longings. We don't always know what we want, what we need. Sometimes we just know we are hurting, missing something crucial. I have found that if I am able to take that strange lump of hurt-need and lay it at God's feet, over time God helps me with it. It can take time, though, just as plants and bread do.

Faith enables us to be patient and wait for the growth we need. And if we are paying attention, the end result will in turn strengthen our faith. Nature is full of these slow, gradual, effortless wonders. Look for them! Jesus did. Being his disciple does not only mean loving people as he did. It also means seeing things as he saw them.

Think about the miracle of healing. Think what a bloody mess we all would be but for the miracle of healing. We could have been created in such a way that no wound or illness ever healed. In fact, some wounds do not, as if to make us aware of the miracle.

The last two verses today might seem to confirm the view that unbelievers will burn in the furnace (of hell) forever. But there is nothing in this passage about eternity; we are reading that into the text. "There will be weeping and grinding of teeth there": as I construe this, it means that when we die, we will face judgment and perhaps some punishment—if we need it in order to be made worthy to enter God's presence.

SEVENTEENTH SUNDAY ORDINARY TIME

1 Kings 3:5, 7–12
Romans 8:28–30
Matthew 13:44–52

IN TODAY'S GOSPEL reading we have three parables and a final conversation between Jesus and his disciples, all unique to Matthew. The first two parables, the buried treasure and the pearl of great price, clearly belong together. It seems Jesus liked to double up on his parables, as we saw last week with the parables of the mustard seed and the leaven.

Most of Jesus's parables tell us something about the Kingdom of God. What I like about our first two parables this week is that they reveal how we are going to feel and behave if we truly "get" Jesus's message. I do not want to say how we "should" feel. I believe these two stories are rather a reality check: if we don't feel something akin to this about the Kingdom, then we haven't entered into its fullness yet.

The hidden treasure story has the key phrase in verse 44: "And from his joy he goes and sells the things he owns and purchases that field." And the crucial word here is *charãs*, translated usually to mean "joy." If, like me, you were raised to associate religion with a heavy dose of moral duty and even guilt, you have to love this parable! The message is consonant with what Jesus says elsewhere: our motivation for following him matters, and if it's anything other than the joy that springs from love, it's not the real thing. Moral duty, as in Puritanism or

Immanuel Kant, is out of the question, thank God!

Still, we could say we have a "duty" to preserve our joy. This raises a spiritual challenge. At times we may not feel a lot of joy about praying, going to Mass, serving the poor, or whatever we are doing to follow the Lord. Feelings come and go. On the other hand, joy may seem to differ from mere happiness because joy can be tied to something deeper than ephemeral emotions: our deepest commitment and identity, our faith, and transcendent experiences. I think it is possible to feel a deeper form of joy even when, at a shallower level, we are not "enjoying" what we are doing for the Kingdom. "Joy" and "enjoy" have the same root.

Charãs occurs fifty-nine times in the New Testament. Matthew uses it in a couple other contexts that are illuminating. In the parable of the sower (13:20), which we just looked at a couple weeks ago, he uses it to describe the way someone with "rocky soil" receives the word of the Kingdom at first. But because he "has no root in himself," he falls away when the going gets tough.

Therefore, our initial joy at receiving the gospel is not enough. We can pass through periods where we lose touch with this joy. It is not really our possession but rather a kind of gift we can lose or a reality that possesses us. We can lose it for all sorts of reasons. Losing it is, I believe, akin to the early warning signs our body gives us when we are coming down with a cold. If we listen to what our body is telling us, we will slow down, get lots of rest, keep warm, and take care of ourselves. That way we may not get so sick.

In the same way, if we start to lose track of the joy of the gospel, our spirit is telling us to make some changes in our spiritual life. We might be doing too much—or too little. We might need to go on retreat. Find a spiritual adviser. Ask for God's help in prayer: in my experience God will give us direction.

It may seem counter to all the moralistic junk rammed down our throats about religion. But Jesus here is insisting that we will feel joy when we find and enter the Kingdom. It's a requirement!

If we do not continue to experience joy, our faith may be in peril.

Charãs is also used by Matthew (28:8) and Luke (24:41) to express what the disciples felt when they saw the resurrected Jesus. I would say, therefore, that there is an eschatological element of joy; it is an anticipation of what we will experience when we die and come face-to-face with God. We can and do experience it already, but it is also a looking forward to what lies ahead. It reminds me of being a kid and looking forward to Christmas. The anticipation was almost as good as Christmas itself.

Luke (15:7) uses *charãs* in one other way that supports this eschatological vision: "There will be more joy in heaven over one sinner who repents than over ninety-nine righteous persons who need no repentance." So *charãs* is something that God and the angels experience. When we feel *charãs*, we are already participating in the reality of heaven.

The parable of the net is similar to last week's parable of the weeds. From the very beginning, devoted followers of Jesus wanted to create a community consisting only of the devout, and that excluded those who appeared to be less committed. The lure of creating a community of the pure has continued throughout Christian history and affects all religions. A critical part of America, New England, was founded by such a movement, the Puritans. It is one reason we Americans still believe we are special, exceptional. (We aren't, though!)

The longing for the perfect community was in the air in Jesus's time as well. John the Baptist predicted the Messiah would winnow the chaff from the wheat, and burn the chaff with "unquenchable fire" (Matthew 3:12). This prophecy turned out to be false. Instead, Jesus invited sinners to repent and join the new community.

Why did Jesus do this? It scandalized people then, just as it does today when some complain about how many awful people go to church. Jesus answered this objection with two parables that have essentially the same meaning: last week's one about the weeds and this week's parable of the dragnet. The key phrase in the dragnet parable is in verse 47: "It gathered fish of every kind."

One of the toughest parts of being a Christian is loving our neighbor. Who is our neighbor? Unlike our friends, whom we get to choose, our neighbor is the person we do not choose. Our neighbor is presented to us by God, as the Good Samaritan found his neighbor close to death in a ditch.

It is perfectly appropriate, therefore, that the Church be filled with "fish of every kind." Especially with those who are tough to love. And, of course, we have the same obligation to love those outside the Church. It is not for us to separate the good fish from the bad.

This is good news! It is such a burden to judge other people, is it not? We do have to make tentative judgments about people. Is Bill violent? Should I ever be alone with him? I call these penultimate judgments. They are not certain; they are open to revision. We make them to protect our health and safety. They have some importance, but they have no ultimate value.

The final verses of today's gospel long perplexed me. The NJBC has helped me to understand it better.[84] On one level, it is the conclusion to the seven parables we have been exploring for the past two weeks.

I am struck by Matthew calling those trained for the Kingdom "scribes." I am used to thinking of scribes as Jesus's enemies, those who were narrow-minded, unloving rule worshipers. Our gospel passages this week are found only in Matthew. I love the metaphor Matthew's Jesus uses to describe what is going on in his gospel: a householder who brings out of his treasure what is new and what is old. I can relate to that, as I am myself a householder, and I have a modest wine collection. I love to share both old bottles and new with my guests. More important, however, is discerning how the two-thousand-year-old words of Matthew's gospel reveal brand-new treasures right now! Is not

Matthew inviting us to look for new treasure in what is old? The other gospel writers do not do this.

Matthew was part of a Jewish-Christian community, so he might have meant this to refer to the Jewish tradition (Law, Prophets, and Wisdom) and Jesus's gospel. Matthew's Jesus could also be inviting us to tell our own "new" stories. Every generation, every person, will experience the Kingdom in a unique way. Does it not fall to us, then, to express our experience with stories just as Jesus did? Is he not inviting us to do so here?

What does today's gospel have to do with Solomon's request to God for wisdom? The final verses of Matthew provide one possible answer. Israel's Wisdom tradition was ancient by Jesus's time, so it would count as old treasure even then, and the notion of "scribes" could connect the old with the new. On the other hand, as we have seen, Jesus seems to have had, at best, an ambivalent relationship with the Wisdom tradition. Matthew 11:25ff, which we explored three weeks ago, has Jesus praising God for hiding his message from the wise.

For these reasons, I am not entirely satisfied with this answer. The relationship between Jesus and the Hebrew tradition, specifically the Law and Wisdom elements of that tradition—not the Prophets—is complicated. As we have and will see.

Another connection is that in both cases the person in question values something immaterial over something material. Solomon is praised by God for asking for wisdom rather than riches, a long life, or revenge on his enemies. The protagonists of Jesus's first two parables value the Kingdom more than their material possessions. If this is so, then the Church is asking us to see Wisdom and the Kingdom as analogous. In some ways they are, but I think the Kingdom differs greatly from the Jewish Wisdom tradition (see appendix E or week fourteen of Ordinary Time).

EIGHTEENTH SUNDAY ORDINARY TIME

Isaiah 55:1–3
Romans 8:35, 37–39
Matthew 14:13–21

TODAY'S GOSPEL BEGINS with Jesus learning of the death of John the Baptist and then withdrawing in a boat to a "deserted place by himself." Why did Jesus do this?

Herod Antipas, the tetrarch, had imprisoned John because he criticized Antipas for marrying Herodias, his brother Philip's wife, while Philip was still alive. Such a union was adulterous and incestuous, prohibited in Leviticus 20:10, 21. Matthew tells us in 14:5 that Antipas wanted to execute John but feared to do so because the people saw John as a prophet.

When Antipas killed John anyway, thanks to the subterfuge of Herodias and the beguiling dance of her daughter Salome, Jesus may well have asked himself, "Am I next?" Jesus also was widely regarded as a prophet, and some even came to view him as John raised from the dead (Matthew 16:13–14). I think it likely Jesus withdrew to a lonely place to pray, asking God for guidance about his next move, perhaps also to grieve. Certainly, the killing of John raised the risks and the stakes for Jesus's mission.

Jesus's alone time on his retreat ended when the crowds found out and followed him on foot from the surrounding towns. Matthew suggests the people pursuing Jesus had gone to a lot of trouble to chase him down. I wonder if more people felt drawn to Jesus because John was now dead. In any case, Jesus's focus shifts from inward to outward. When he saw "a large crowd," Jesus "was moved inwardly with compassion for them."

I love this little snapshot of Jesus's ministry because I suspect it captures a revealing moment, a certain tension he must have experienced. The gospels often tell us he goes off, usually before sunrise, to a lonely place to pray alone. He had an intimate relationship with God the Father, and this means, in part, he spent lots of time praying alone. Yet he was also a man who lived to serve others. One cannot do both at the same time.

The Greek word translated to mean "compassion" is *esplankhnísthē*. This word is related to a person's bowels or entrails. For Greeks this was the seat of emotion, akin to our "heart." Another way to translate what Jesus felt could be that "his heart was moved by love and sympathy" for the people going to such trouble to follow him. We could also say he felt this in his gut.

Reading between the lines, I believe we just might be seeing here the internal vibrations of Jesus's two natures: the human and the divine. It is entirely natural for human beings to worry about life, death, and physical safety. The death of John the Baptist has cast this shadow of anxiety over Jesus; his withdrawal to a lonely place to pray to God is what he will do when death is far closer, at Gethsemane (Matthew 26:36ff). At Gethsemane, Jesus actually does not want to be entirely alone, but that is what ends up happening as James, John, and Peter cannot stay awake.

Jesus's discovery that so many people are so hungry for him that they are pursuing him even into such a deserted place confronts him with his divine mission: proclaiming the arrival of God's kingdom, making it real for people. Matthew's Jesus responds by healing them, not by teaching as in Mark. (Luke has Jesus teaching and healing.) I like how Matthew puts it, noting dryly, as if it were by now nothing extraordinary, "He healed their sick."

The Greek word translated as "lonely" or "deserted" *is*

erēmon. It means desolated, a wasteland where no one goes or wants to go. It can also mean a place in the desert. Why did so many people go to such trouble to follow Jesus into the wasteland? One reason could well be that they too had heard of John's execution, as I suggested above. For the people who longed for God's deliverance from the misery of everyday life, Jesus was now the last man standing.

The centerpiece of this gospel story is the feeding of the five thousand. As NJBC points out, this episode points forward to the Eucharist and the messianic banquet of the Kingdom, as well as backward to the way God fed the Hebrews in the desert with manna and quail (Exodus 16; Numbers 11). The reading from Isaiah is another example of what Jewish people, and Jesus especially, understood: food connects the material with the spiritual.

We can understand the miracle of feeding five thousand men and many thousands more women and children in a number of ways, and they are not all mutually exclusive. This could be a nature miracle, akin to many healing miracles or Jesus walking on water, which immediately follows in Mark and Matthew.

In Mark and Luke's account, Jesus orders everyone to sit in companies of fifty to one hundred; Matthew omits this. I believe this detail could be important if we imagine the miracle to be a moral one. It is possible that by sharing, the people had enough food for everyone. After all, we know the disciples themselves had five loaves and two fish. It is reasonable to expect that many of the people in the crowd brought food also as they pursued Jesus into the desert. Wouldn't we do the same if we were going to a lonely place?

If I have a small amount of food, I am far more likely to share it with a smaller group than I am with thousands of people. My bit of food will have little impact in a crowd, but in a small group it can make a real difference. Jesus breaking people up into small groups was a brilliant piece of crowd psychology, making possible what we could call a moral miracle.

Notice also how Jesus's form of leadership is to empower his disciples to become self-reliant leaders themselves: "They need not go away; you give them something to eat." It starts with the disciples sharing what little they have, inspiring others to do the same.

Matthew adds one detail missing from Mark and Luke: the five thousand who ate does not include all the women and children present. We do not know how many women and children were there, but it is important that they came also; this was not an all-male affair.

Even more important is that we now may be talking about as many as twenty to thirty thousand people in all, according to the NJBC. When you add this to the subsequent feeding of four thousand men (Matthew 15:38), you arrive at a total figure that approaches one-tenth of Palestine's total population, estimated at half a million.

The feeding of the five thousand is the only miracle of Jesus recorded by all four gospels! Check out John 6:1–15 to read his rather different account. Not only should that make us feel more confident that it happened, but it also underscores how important everyone thought it was. Why did all the gospel writers feel compelled to write about this miracle story? One possibility is that, assuming the NJBC's math is accurate, Jesus feeding a significant portion of the Palestinian population would have been "headline news" back then.

Eating is also enormously important for Christians. Sharing food and eating with others, whether for the Eucharist or a regular meal, carries tremendous symbolic and spiritual power and allows us to participate in the Kingdom of God, now and in anticipation of what is to come. It is one reason to pray and give thanks before and after every meal we eat.

It is one reason my volunteer work at my church's Monday-morning breakfast program for people in need is so meaningful to me, our other volunteers, and to those we serve. It feeds our souls as well as our bodies. Feeding hungry people is at the heart of what it means to be a Christian.

NINETEENTH SUNDAY ORDINARY TIME

1 Kings 19:9, 11–13
Romans 9:1–5
Matthew 14:22–33

CERTUM EST. QUIA impossible est. Today's gospel account of Jesus walking on water brings these famous words of Tertullian to my mind once again: "This is certain, because it is impossible." Tertullian was referring to the Resurrection, but it works just as well here. I think there is a deeper truth lurking inside this elegant paradox. A modern person might say, "Who could make this stuff up?" Walking on water is so ridiculous no rational person would invent such a preposterous tale.

Besides, if you believe in the Incarnation, that Jesus was truly God and truly man, and if you believe he rose from the dead, then a little water-walking is easy to swallow.

In the four gospels, Jesus ordinarily shows remarkable restraint about using his divine powers. In this case, I don't think he was showing off; walking on water solved a practical problem for him.

After feeding the five thousand men and many more women and children, Jesus wanted to be alone. After all, that was why he came to the "deserted place" in the first place. He allowed the crowds who pursued him to interrupt his alone time with God. But after feeding them, he "dismissed them" and sent his disciples across the lake on the boat, into Gentile country.

Finally, he was able to go up the mountain alone to pray. Jesus prayed with others, and he also prayed alone in contact with nature, often on mountaintops. Christians are probably more likely to follow his example about praying with others than they are to pray alone outside. Both are equally important, in my experience. You might, like Jesus, find it easier to feel close to God the Creator outside in the world God created than in church.

After his time praying alone on the mountain, how was he to reunite with his disciples across the lake? It was a dark and stormy night! No boats were available, and even if they were, it would not be safe. Jesus's decision to walk on the water solved a logistical problem; he was not merely showing off his divine powers.

The gospel story is really about faith. I am grateful Matthew has added to Mark's account the verses about Peter walking on the water (28–31). Matthew alone has two other sections devoted to Peter, both favorable: 16:17–19 and 17:24–27. It seems Matthew had special affection for Peter.

The tension between the divine and the human, which we saw last week, is present here, thanks to the relationship of Jesus with Peter. Jesus shows us two dimensions of his divine nature. First, his command over nature in his ability to walk on water. The story resembles Matthew 8:18–27 (par.), when Jesus stills a lake storm threatening to capsize the boat he is on with the disciples. Jesus's faith also makes him divine. I know I have faith, but I would not dream of walking out onto a lake at night in the middle of a storm!

Peter shows us what it is to be human. He sees Jesus doing this, and he wants to imitate him. Good instinct. What incredible faith Peter had to have in order get out of the boat and walk over to Jesus on stormy waters in utter darkness! He does well for a while, but then he starts to get scared and begins to sink. The scene reminds me of those old Road Runner and Wiley Coyote cartoons. Often Coyote would run off the edge of a canyon cliff and be fine until he looked down and realized he had no ground under him. Only then did he start to fall.

For this reason, I am a little surprised, even annoyed, that Jesus calls him a "man of little faith" and asks him why he doubted. To me this shows Jesus's divine nature losing touch with his human nature. And let's not forget the other disciples were so scared that they stayed in the boat. Should not Peter be commended, not rebuked? Why did Jesus criticize Peter?

Peter shows that if we have faith, we will take risks, apparently foolish ones. I love how Matthew does not turn Peter into an incredible superhero of faith but reveals that he starts to doubt and as a result starts to sink. Maybe the greater the risk our faith leads us to take, the more doubt will assail us. Have you ever felt that same "sinking feeling" of doubt when you are in the middle of a frightening storm challenging your faith?

Matthew shows us the living, unending dialogue of faith and fearful doubt. Peter hears the call to get out of the boat and asks for Jesus's help. By pairing this story with the story of Elijah, the Church is urging us to see a parallel between Peter hearing the voice of Jesus in the middle of the storm and Elijah's hearing the "still small voice" amid all the natural turbulence going on at Mount Horeb.

Peter responds by taking the enormous chance of imitating Jesus by walking on the water. Then he doubts, and his doubts threaten to destroy him, so he cries out, "Lord, save me!" And Jesus does. This story is an anticipation of Peter's behavior during Jesus's passion. Peter is the only disciple who has the courage to follow Jesus along the way to his crucifixion. Yet on the way he loses his faith-courage, denies Jesus, sinks, and falls away. After that, he repents, no doubt begging Jesus again, "Lord, save me!"

This episode points to the limitations of reading the Bible only at the shallow, literal level. If you understand this story to be "only" about an incident that did really happen two thousand years ago, what does that mean for you today? If you read this story on the symbolic level, it offers all sorts of challenges and insights. If we have faith, we need at times to take absurd risks, like walking on water in the middle of a storm. Otherwise, what kind of faith do we have? Faith can perform surprising miracles, like walking on the water. With God, anything is possible.

As I read Peter's response to Jesus, it reveals the silliness of setting up any opposition between "faith" and "works," as occurred during the Protestant Reformation. I believe Jesus insists on the importance of our having faith *because* of the courageous actions that flow from it. And when we talk about faith here, it isn't primarily whether we believe in God or not. Biblical writers did not conceive of genuine atheism as a plausible option. The question, rather, is whether our faith is going to be strong enough to empower us to act fearlessly in following Jesus.

The crucial condition for faith-miracles is to be in relationship with the Holy Spirit of Jesus. Peter first was open to the Spirit of Jesus: he sensed that Jesus wanted him to come to him. He asked Jesus to confirm this: "Lord, if it is you, bid me come to you on the water." Jesus did: "Come." This dialogue can be a model for us. Through prayer, we have to develop a relationship with Christ that allows us to hear what the Holy Spirit is asking us to do. If it seems perilous, we will want to confirm it. But if the only messages we get are "safe" ones, something is not right.

Elijah certainly was not playing it safe before he came to Mount Horeb (called Mount Sinai in Judean tradition) and heard the "still small voice" of God. Jezebel, Queen of Israel, was out to kill him because Elijah had been "jealous" for the Lord (1 Kings 19:10). In fact, Elijah was in such despair as he ran away from her that he asked God to "take away [his] life" (19:4).

Ancient people tended to associate God with powerful natural phenomena. We see traces of this in the Old Testament. This story of Elijah is something of a breakthrough because it affirms God is not in the wind, the fire, nor the earthquake. God speaks to Elijah, as he speaks to most of us, in a "tiny whispering sound." For this reason, Elijah on Mount Horeb is one of my favorite Old Testament stories. I remember my mother talking about the "still small voice."

God speaks to most of us in this way. How can we hear this tiny whispering sound if our lives are filled with noise, clutter, and distraction? For this reason, I realized long ago I needed to cultivate an inner silence in order to hear this voice. This means at least fifteen minutes of silent, centering prayer every day; lately it is more like half an hour (see appendix C). I have been doing this for twenty years, and sure enough, I sense God's voice and presence far more often than before. At first, I thought God would speak to me only during these meditative periods. After a few years, God let me know that was too limiting. I am now often blessed with God's voice and presence throughout the day.

We make so many decisions every day! Some may seem trivial, but I'm not so sure of this anymore. I try to let the Holy Spirit, Jesus's Spirit, guide me in decisions large and small. Before I spent the time to develop this inner silence, I had no idea how to begin to do this.

Chrysostom points out the moral instruction Jesus delivers to the disciples in this episode. Jesus does not present himself to them at once but only in the final fourth watch of the night: "He was instructing them not too hastily to seek for deliverance from their pressing dangers but to bear all challenges courageously."

Then, when Jesus does come to the rescue, he frightens them all the more. Now they are not only afraid of the storm, but they also think they are seeing a ghost! Chrysostom goes on to explain:

> THIS IS THE way he constantly deals with our fears. He does not hesitate to bring on worse things, even more alarming than those before. They were troubled here not only by the storm but also by the distance from the land.

> Note that he did not too easily remove the darkness. He was training them, as I said, by the continuance of these fears and instructing them to be ready to endure.[85]

I don't recommend trying to walk on water during a storm as Peter did. But Jesus calls on us to undertake many actions that will make us uncomfortable. Like praying for our enemies, or loving our enemies. Or forgiving seventy times seven. Being a good Samaritan to someone in need who despises us and "our kind." It's all there in the gospels, easy to find and hard to do. Especially without faith.

TWENTIETH SUNDAY ORDINARY TIME

Isaiah 56:1, 6–7
Romans 11:13–15, 29–32
Matthew 15:21–28

JESUS DOES NOT come off well in today's gospel, and that is what I most like about it.

Number one because this story that Matthew picked up from Mark and which Luke chose to exclude builds trust in our gospel writers. We often read of incidents where the disciples look bad; today we see one where Jesus does. The fact that our evangelists do not sugarcoat their account of Jesus makes me believe what they write.

Jesus calls the Canaanite woman a dog. That is bad—let's not deny it.

But. The Greek word is *kunaríois*. It is a diminutive of dog, so it could be translated as "doggy." Still bad, but less so. *Kunaríois* means a house dog or lapdog—in other words, a pet dog—as opposed to a dog of the street or farm. This lessens the insult somewhat, as for the most part Jews did not like dogs and street dogs were half wild.

Matthew alone also has Jesus say, "Do not give dogs what is holy; and do not throw your pearls before swine, lest they trample them under foot and turn to attack you" (Matthew 7:6). This verse seems to scan with our reading today and suggests dogs and swine were placed by Jews on the same disgusting level. The word for dog in 7:6, though, is *kusin* and can be used metaphorically as a word of reproach.

Matthew calls her a Canaanite woman; Mark writes she is "a Greek, a Syrophoenician by birth." Matthew's term is an anachronism, using an Old Testament name that calls to mind the ancient hostility between the Hebrews and the Canaanites who occupied the Promised Land. Mark's term is more accurate and neutral. But Matthew, unlike Mark, has the woman say, "Have mercy on me, O Lord, Son of David; my daughter is severely possessed by a demon." Mark simply reports that she begged Jesus to cast the demon out of her daughter.

By calling to mind the ancient hostility between the Jews and their neighbors while having the woman confess Jesus as Lord, it seems as though Matthew sees this episode as a way Jesus can heal old hostilities. Matthew's community was composed mainly of Greek-speaking Jews, and many early Christians were Samaritans and Greek Gentiles, so the Jesus movement was bridging sectarian divides.

The historical Jesus did see his primary mission as seeking out and saving the lost children of Israel. Jesus's choice of precisely twelve disciples symbolizes his mission to regather the twelve tribes of Israel. When he sends them out, he tells them, only in Matthew, "Go nowhere among the Gentiles, and enter no town of the Samaritans, but go rather to the lost sheep of the house of Israel" (Matthew 10:5–6).

It is important to realize, however, that the Old Testament is full of passages revealing that Israel's mission as the Chosen People was not simply to hang on to its special status as a prized possession. On the contrary, Israel's essential mission was always to attract all the nations to worship the one Lord. Today's first reading from Isaiah is a perfect example of this.

Moreover, while the historical Jesus saw his mission as gathering the "lost sheep of Israel," the risen Lord in Matthew calls on his followers to "make disciples of all nations" (Matthew 28:19). And this is precisely what did happen.

Jesus grew and changed over time, as all human beings do; this story may be an example of Jesus's growth. During his earthly ministry, he did not completely ignore Gentiles. He performed exorcisms or miracles for them, not only in this episode but in several others (Mark 5:1–20, 7:24–30, par. Matthew 8:5–13; Luke 17:11–19).

Today we get to spend time with a second Greek word, from Philippians 2:7: *ekénōsen*, "to empty." Paul writes that Jesus "emptied himself, taking the form of a servant." What precisely this means is a subject of theological debate, but I suggest it means that when incarnated as the historical Jesus, the second person of the Trinity, he emptied himself of some divine attributes. How much and to what extent is an open question I explore in appendix B.

But at least we see here that the historical Jesus appears to lack foreknowledge, can change his mind over time, and betrays some of the negative views his countrymen had toward foreigners. This passage is a wonderful corrective for those who would deny his humanity in favor of his divinity. Jesus here also appears to be somewhat out of character in his treatment of this doubly marginalized—she is a woman and a Gentile—suffering mother. In other cases, Jesus shows compassion for such people, especially women. Here, at first, he remains silent to her appeals for help, claiming, "I was sent only to the lost sheep of the house of Israel." What changes for Jesus, perhaps starting right here, is the "only" part of that statement. And that brings us to the second theme of today's gospel: faith-prayer.

I link those two words because that's what this story invites us to do. The Canaanite woman reminds me of the widow in the parable of the unjust judge in Luke 18:1–8. A widow keeps pestering an unjust judge to deliver justice for her. The judge couldn't care less about her or justice but finally concludes he will give her what she wants just to get her off his back. Jesus asks: if this unjust judge delivers justice, will not God do the same to those who cry to God day and night?

The Canaanite woman does not give up. Jesus ignores her, the disciples try to get rid of her, and Jesus then gives her the dog insult. But this woman turns the tables on Jesus by saying that even dogs get to eat the crumbs that fall off the table.

Is Jesus "converted" by her faith, her persistence, and her resourcefulness? I think it is possible. What does this tell us about prayer?

We all have had the experience of not getting what we prayed for. It is hard for us modern people to believe that God intervenes in the real world and that our prayers can change outcomes. Some spiritual writers tell us that prayer is not about changing what is outside of us but rather about changing what is inside.

These writers are correct in many cases, but the Canaanite woman tells us that is not the whole story either. She appears to have changed Jesus's heart by her "dogged" (sorry!) persistence and by her faith. The parable of the unjust judge also praises persistence. That ought to tell us something about prayer.

This story also reveals that for Jesus, faith is what matters most. Once he sees how powerful her faith was, he changes in an instant from calling her a dog to praising her faith and saying, "As you desire, so let it happen to you." Notice he does not say, "I will cure your daughter." He makes it seem as though her desire-powered faith cures her daughter. The woman's faith transcends her non-Jewish ethnic status. In this way she is an archetype of the Church.

Having strong faith does not guarantee God will answer our prayers as we desire. Notice, however, the woman was not praying for herself but for her daughter. God did not answer Jesus's own prayer in Gethsemane to spare him from being crucified. We have to accept that sometimes God is not going to give us what we want, especially if the prayer is for ourselves.

TWENTY-FIRST SUNDAY ORDINARY TIME

Isaiah 22:19–23
Romans 11:33–36
Matthew 16:13–20

TODAY JESUS ASKS his disciples the fundamental question "But who do you say that I am?" It is a question he asks all of us, of everyone who has ever heard of him.

He starts out by asking them, "Who do men say that I am?" (The more inclusive Luke substitutes "the people" for "men.") This is the point of departure for all of us: what do most other people have to say about Jesus? Some people may choose to leave it there. But we all begin with what "the others" have to say about Jesus. This is one reason I love today's gospel: the narrative and sequential logic of Jesus's two questions must be repeated in every generation, by every person who hears his name.

Of course, the way most people answer the first question will change over time and throughout space. In the days of medieval Christendom, the answer would have been akin to Matthew's Peter: "the son of the living God." In other times and places, the consensus might be "a great moral teacher." I think this is probably the answer for most "post-Christians" where I live. It is an answer I would expect to hear from those who belong to other religions.

One difficulty with this position is that as we have seen and will see, Jesus emphasizes that *faith* is what matters the most and that all his moral teachings are inextricably tied to this living faith. The moral teaching is the necessary consequence of faith; faith is the empowering engine we need to execute the tough moral demands. We cannot, according to Jesus, have the one without the other.

No matter the consensus view surrounding us, each of us must answer the second question for ourselves: "Who do I say that Jesus is?" We can, of course, default to the view of others, or try to skip answering the question entirely, but in that case, no answer or "I don't know" becomes our answer.

On the other hand, maybe we live surrounded by believers. But even if we conform to the prevailing view that Jesus is the Son of the living God, we are not going to go very far or very deep in following Jesus unless we make this judgment "our own." We cannot easily depersonalize or weasel out of this question. That is one message of today's gospel.

Still, I don't mean to suggest that this answer we cannot avoid is made in utter isolation. Jesus is asking this question of his twelve disciples, although he does imply that Peter reached his own conclusion because of a special revelation from God the Father. The reading is also about the origin of the Church, and as an intentional community of faithful people, the Church mediates between everyone and the isolated individual. The Church helps each one of us determine who Jesus is. So does reading the gospels.

Simon Peter's confession is found in all three synoptic gospels, but only Matthew adds the Jesus–Peter dialogue in verses 17–19. Let's spend a little time with these verses. Again and again, Jesus praises people because of their faith and the actions that flow from this faith. In this case, Jesus praises Peter not exactly for his faith but for the relationship he has with God the Father and, implicitly, with Jesus as well. This is good for us to reflect on: the quality of our faith can be gauged by the depth and richness of our relationship with Father, Son, and Holy Spirit. How to build this relationship is important, but for now let's stay with this specific reading.

Notice also that Jesus does not praise Peter the way we might, by saying, "Peter what a smart guy you are! You are special!" No, what makes Peter "blissful" is not Peter qua individual, but Peter-as-related-to-God-the-Father. We live in a world that worships the lonely, original, creative individual. We should, rather, follow Jesus and praise people for their relationships, especially with God. But do we?

How does Jesus know that it is "not flesh and blood" but "my Father who is in heaven" who revealed to Peter that Jesus is the Christ and, as Matthew adds to Mark, "the Son of the living God"? The word "Christ" is the Greek word for the Hebrew "messiah," and it means "the anointed one." Jewish messianic expectations tilted toward a military-national savior along the lines of King David. The Christ would not be a divine figure but a great leader who would rescue the Jews from the oppression of the Romans by military force. The Christ would then establish a powerful and just new Kingdom of Israel that would not be beholden to its neighbors.

Jesus was not this kind of messiah!

Therefore, if Peter recognized that Jesus was the Christ, and the Son of the living God, he was flying in the face of received wisdom and "who men say that I am." Jesus concludes that God the Father must have been the source of Peter's unique insight. Matthew's inclusion of "Son of the living God" in Peter's confession can lead to confusion, as we will see.

Notice too how Jesus demands the disciples tell no one Jesus is the Anointed. Jesus did not want people to have misleading messianic expectations of him. But Matthew's Peter calling him Son of the living God is quite different.

The Church leaders who established the order of the gospels placed Matthew first because Matthew placed the Church first in his gospel. We see that here, in the verses found only in Matthew:

Jesus declares he will build his church on Peter, which means "rock" in Greek—*Kepa* in Aramaic.

Matthew paints a lively and generally positive portrait of Peter, partly because Matthew is concerned about serving the Church. But Peter's insight into Jesus's unique messiahship had its limits. Not only was Jesus not going to deliver his people from Roman oppression with military force, but Jesus was himself going to be beaten, tortured, and die a humiliating death at the hands of the Romans! A more complete reversal of common messianic expectations is inconceivable. This was too much even for Peter to swallow, as we see in the verses that follow immediately on today's reading (Matthew 16:21–23).

When Peter protests at Jesus's prediction that he will suffer many things from the chief priests and be killed, Jesus rebukes him. "You are not on the side of God," Jesus tells him, "but of men." This is an about-face to what he said earlier in praising Peter because God, not flesh and blood, had revealed to him that Jesus was "the Anointed, the Son of the living God." What is going on here?

Peter may have understood that Jesus's message of love, forgiveness of sinners, and his miraculous healing of the sick and feeding the hungry transcended messianic expectations. But he still did not grasp that Jesus's mission involved transcending violence itself. Nor did Peter understand that Jesus's kingdom was not of this world—at least, not entirely of this world. In other words, Peter had not yet untangled the meaning of the traditional understanding of the "Anointed" from the reality of Jesus as the "Son of the living God."

What does it mean to be "on the side of men"? I think it means to be on the side of immanence rather than transcendence when confronted with violence and injustice. It means that rather than transcending the violence, one participates in it and thereby perpetuates it. This is the way "the world" normally works. It certainly worked that way in Jesus's time, and even after Jesus, violence is not giving up without a fight! Jesus correctly realizes the only way to stop violence is to stop being violent.

This insight is one reason to believe Jesus is the Son of God.

The first reading echoes the gospel in certain respects, with a parallel between Eliakim and Peter. Peter is given the keys to the Kingdom; what he binds on earth will be bound in heaven, and what he loosens on earth will be loosed in heaven. The prophet tells us that God wants to replace Shebna with Eliakim, who will be "father to the inhabitants of Jerusalem." God says, "I will place the key of the House of David on Eliakim's shoulder. When he opens no one shall shut, when he shuts, no one shall open."

In Jesus's day the high priest was God's intermediary. For Christians, the involvement of the high priests in Jesus's execution means Peter replaces them. Catholic Christians can connect to their Jewish roots by seeing the successors to St. Peter—the popes—as successors to the high priests in Jerusalem.

Why does Jesus "strictly charge" the disciples to tell no one that he is the Christ? This command is found in all three synoptics, although Mathew adds the "strictly" part. I can think of two good reasons Jesus wanted no one to know he was the Christ. First, because Jesus was himself ambivalent about the military and nationalistic implications of this title. He saw his mission quite differently. He did not want to be another King David.

Second, the Christ title would only compound the popular misunderstanding of Jesus. If Jesus and his followers went around proclaiming him as the Messiah, the people of Israel would want to see his armies and his military victories. And they definitely would not want to see him crucified!

The more profound, eternal victory Jesus won on the cross was, and is, hard enough to grasp after the fact, looking backward. It is simply impossible to understand it looking forward. Jesus did not need divine omniscience to figure that out.

TWENTY-SECOND SUNDAY ORDINARY TIME

Jeremiah 20:7–9
Romans 12:1–2
Matthew 16:21–27

TODAY'S GOSPEL RAISES an issue that has come up before: did Jesus, as the Son of God, know what would happen in the future as God the Father does? The question of whether Jesus had divine foreknowledge is complicated, and I explore it in greater detail in appendix B, but we have to tackle it here today to some extent.

Jesus makes predictions elsewhere in the gospels, and we will see a similar passage on the twenty-sixth Sunday of Ordinary Time. A few thoughts on these prophecies: First, Jesus clearly possessed a brilliant and perceptive mind, so it makes perfect sense that he would have an acute sense of what was going to happen. Second, we have to be careful in reading these predictions too literally because they were written long after the events they describe. The writers may sometimes have read some of their hindsight knowledge into the sayings of Jesus. Finally, we ourselves have to be careful about how we read the gospels because we also know how it turned out, and so we often read more into a passage than is actually there.

For example, notice Jesus does not predict he will be crucified by the Romans, which is in fact what happened; yet we may read this into the passage without being aware we are doing so. He tells his disciples he will suffer "many things" from the elders, ruling priests, and scribes, "be put to death," and then be "raised on the third day."

Except for the prediction of being raised on the third day, all the other predictions could have been foreseen by a sagacious person without any divine powers. Jesus's predecessor, John the Baptist, had already been executed. The three groups Jesus identified comprised the Sanhedrin, and Jesus knew he had antagonized the religious establishment. Notice the Pharisees are not mentioned here. Yet Matthew later tells us the Pharisees tried to arrest Jesus in Jerusalem (Matthew 21:45–46) and to "ensnare him in words" (Matthew 22:15).

I believe there are solid theological and scriptural reasons for doubting the historical Jesus knew he would be raised on the third day. Jesus is both fully human and fully divine. I do not believe you can be fully human if you know what will happen in the future.

The kenosis, or self-emptying, St. Paul discusses in Philippians 2:7–8 gives additional theological and scriptural support for the idea that God gave up omniscience and other divine powers to become man. Finally, if Jesus knew for certain he would be raised in a couple days, why would he sweat blood (Luke 22:44) in the Garden of Gethsemane, pray to God to let him avoid crucifixion, and cry out on the cross that God had forsaken him?

I believe Jesus's divinity rests, in part, on the extraordinary faith he had in the Father. Faith is not knowledge. Jesus trusted the Father totally, unto death. If Jesus knew he would be raised on the third day, trust and faith in the Father would not have been necessary. His sacrifice on the cross is greatly diminished if he knew he just had to put up with that for a few hours in order to be resurrected a few days later. I could even imagine doing that myself!

If Jesus knew in advance that his life and death would have a happy Easter ending, his life and message are less relevant to me. Because I don't have that kind of knowledge. Emphasizing

Jesus's divinity at the expense of his humanity "let's us off the hook" of the challenge his sinless life poses to us. The specific challenge here is to trust that God will not abandon us no matter what happens to us in this life.

In St. Matthew's gospel, Jesus has just finished praising Peter in verse 16 for receiving God's revelation that Jesus is the Anointed, the Son of the living God. Jesus goes so far as to tell him that he is a rock that Jesus will build his Church upon. Almost immediately, Jesus turns on Peter. Now Jesus tells the "rock" that he has become a stumbling stone for him. The irony is obvious and bitter. The Greek word is *skanthalon*, related to our word "scandal." The stumbling block that causes one to trip also refers to something that is the cause of error or sin. Jesus attacks Peter even more harshly when he calls him *Satanã*, which means "the Adversary," "the Accuser." Could Jesus have said anything worse to his best friend?

Why does Jesus turn on Peter so suddenly, so harshly? How is Peter a potential cause of sin, Jesus's dangerous adversary? This exchange, found in Mark as well, reveals another dimension of Jesus's full humanity. When Peter denies that Jesus must suffer and die, he is of course anticipating his denial of Jesus on Good Friday. Peter's theology is one of grace and glory, without the cross of obedient, suffering sacrifice. His words touch a nerve in Jesus.

If Peter's words were a potential cause of sin for Jesus, it means that Jesus was himself tempted to avoid his suffering and death. Why would he not be? What could be more human? Especially if, as I have argued, Jesus did not know what would happen to him after his death. In this situation, the last thing he needs is for his best friend to be telling him not to let it happen. Notice also that this exchange provides additional support to my argument that Jesus did not know he would never sin in the future (see the chapter on the baptism of the Lord).

We are faced again with the hindsight fallacy. Just as we know, or believe, he was raised from the dead, we who live now know that Jesus resisted this temptation, but that does not mean Jesus knew he would. We have to avoid reading our after-the-fact knowledge into the heads of people who were living the history we read about.

The passage from Jeremiah can then be read as a description of Jesus's inner struggle, a struggle that Jesus probably has to live with until it reaches its climax at Gethsemane when he sweats blood, says that his soul is in anguish to the point of death, and prays to the Father "to let this cup pass from me" (Matthew 26:38–39).

TWENTY-THIRD SUNDAY ORDINARY TIME

How to Be a Peacemaker

Ezekiel 33:7–9
Romans 13:8–10
Matthew 18:15–20

THIS WEEK WE jump ahead two chapters from last week's gospel to a passage found only in Matthew. Luke has a single verse (17:3) in which Jesus simply says, "If your brother sins, rebuke him, and if he repents, forgive him."

In Matthew we have a fuller program for how to resolve conflicts and make peace within the Christian community. Once again, we see why the Church placed Matthew as the first gospel, the very first book, in the New Testament. Jesus says in the beatitudes (Matthew 5:9), "Blessed are the peacemakers for they shall be called sons of God." This passage gives us a road map for how to be peacemakers. We should all be grateful to St. Matthew for the inspiration he received from the Holy Spirit to provide us with this guide for resolving conflicts. I wish we paid more attention to it because I think it could help resolve conflicts, both within and without the Church.

The evil suffered by so many in the Church and the sins of sexual abuse done to them can be seen as a direct result of our collective failure to follow Matthew 18:15–20. More on this later, but our passage is not, in the first instance, about anything so horrible.

Notice what Matthew does not say. He does not say that if a

brother sins against us, we must try to forget about it and maybe it will just go away. Now, sometimes this happens. Our first job is to discern whether the sin has hurt us deeply enough that it will not "go away." Sometimes we know right away and should not wait. Jesus in Matthew does not say this, but in my experience, waiting a little can sometimes be a good idea. Some hurts we need to let go of.

Even when the sin that has hurt us does not go away, I think most people are still tempted to do nothing about it. Most of us shrink from confrontation; we make up all sorts of reasons to avoid it. Such as "It won't do any good," or "It will only make things worse," or "The relationship isn't worth it." We tend to ignore the harm that comes from not doing anything about it: lingering resentment, depression, anger.

We may also fear that by confronting the one who hurt us, we will learn the story is more complicated. I wish Matthew's Jesus mentioned this scenario: perhaps the injured party is not without sin in this conflict. However, this could be implied by the second step in the process when we bring in two or three witnesses. Perhaps people uninvolved in the story can provide insights those involved have missed.

Yet instead of fearing that our story of sin and hurt is more complicated, we should welcome it. The truth is liberating; it will set us free (Jn 8:32)! Free from the lingering resentment and all the emotional, psychic, and spiritual harm it can do to ourselves and others.

Still, how can we be so certain our brother, or sister, has sinned against us? I would amend verse 15 to "If you *believe* your brother or sister sins against you, go and tell him or her, listen and *see if you can resolve the conflict*." The italics are my additions. This approach is in line with the humility Jesus insists upon elsewhere. I am thinking specifically of Matthew 7:5: "You hypocrite, first take the log out of your own eye, and then you will see clearly to take the speck out of your brother's eye."

We should not assume the sin or problem we have is all the doing of our neighbor. We may be partially, or even entirely, responsible for what we are experiencing. However, we may well discover this only if we have an honest conversation with our neighbor. Speaking of others, this is yet another reason to follow up on a real sin-hurt. We may not be the only one who has been hurt in this way, and if we do nothing, the sinner could continue to do more harm.

This thought takes us into the sexual abuse crisis in the Church. Think of all the harm done because so many remained silent! I am thinking here of those with the power to do something about it. This passage is not literally applicable to the sex abuse problem because it is wrong to expect children to confront their adult abusers directly. However, we can and should encourage them to confide in a parent or someone they trust, or the abuse will continue. It then becomes that person's duty to confront this kind of sin in the Church. We owe it to our more vulnerable brothers and sisters not to remain silent.

This takes us to the third step in resolving the sin-conflict: tell it to two or three other members of the community. This is another way to help us discern whether this is a genuine problem or one that we have blown out of proportion. It is important to listen to what the others have to say and trust the Holy Spirit will reveal the truth of what is to be done. As Jesus tells us in verse 20, "For where there are two or three who have gathered in my name, I am there in the midst of them."

The final step is to tell the story to the church. Does this mean the entire community, Church leadership, the priest, the bishop? It is not clear, partly because when Matthew wrote, the Church had no such structure. The point is to inform the appropriate members of the Church community.

One problem that arose during the sex abuse calamity was

that all too often "the Church" meant only the priest or the bishop. That experience and this passage tell me that if we do not receive a satisfactory resolution to the sin-conflict from Church authorities, we have to keep going. Perhaps we inform all parishioners. Perhaps we even need to go to the civil authorities or journalists. The failure to do so is almost as important a factor in the sex abuse crisis as the inaction of Church authorities and the actions of the abusers. The passage from Ezekiel confirms the gravity, and the potential consequences, of "remaining silent" when we need to speak out against evil. God may hold us accountable for what we did not do.

Why does Matthew's Jesus say that if the sinner refuses to listen to the Church, we should treat him as a Gentile or a tax collector? What does this even mean?

It does not mean to treat the sinner as an evil person who is forever beyond redemption. Jesus welcomed tax collectors into his community, but only when they showed faith and repented of their sins (Matthew 9:9–13). The point is that the Christian community does have to police itself to some extent. It means we will have to exclude people from full membership in the community, hopefully for a limited period of time, but in some cases indefinitely. If we do not, the civil police will end up doing this for us, and that is not a good outcome. This is another horrible potential result of the sexual abuse scandal.

Our passage ends with "For where two or three are gathered in my name, there am I in the midst of them." I take "there am I in the midst of them" to mean the Holy Spirit of Jesus. I do sense the Holy Spirit when I am talking about the faith with one or two or a few more people. Jesus here is telling us that our faith is a dialogue. Just as we have this conversation with God every time we pray, we need to do something analogous with our fellow believers. I always end up learning more about myself, others, and faith in God. It is a crucial way to strengthen our faith.

This form of community is different from the community of the Church, or *ekklesia*. Ancient Greek gives us another word to denote a more intimate form of communion: *koinonia*. A healthy faith requires we participate in both forms of community. *Koinonia* is often translated as "fellowship," but this word carries all sorts of stale connotations, at least for me. It reminds me of tiresome church dinners made up of tasteless casseroles and small talk.

We live in a time when many people struggle to find or hang on to their faith, to find Jesus. Verse 20 tells us if we want to find Jesus, seek out at least one or two other soul mates, and we will.

TWENTY-FOURTH SUNDAY ORDINARY TIME

Sirach 27:30–28:9
Romans 14:7–9
Matthew 18:21–35

THE CHRISTIAN DUTY to forgive everyone for everything, endlessly, whether they are sorry or not, is the toughest part of following Jesus, in my experience. But what does it mean to forgive? I believe this is a word we use unthinkingly; it has many shades of meaning. We need to explore them to put Jesus's message into practice.

Let's start, as usual, with the Greek word Matthew uses: *apheso*. It means to "let go; to cancel or pardon a loan." By extension it also means to forgive the guilt which is the "debt" of sin. The connection in *apheso* between the forgiveness of debt and forgiveness of sin makes the parable of the unforgiving servant apt. I think we should also keep in mind Matthew 6:12, 14, 15—the Lord's Prayer. Matthew is once again helping us to understand how to put Jesus's commandment into practice; we find this parable only in Matthew.

A few points about the parable are worth mentioning. The debt of the servant to his lord was ten thousand talents. One talent was a huge sum, between one and ten thousand dollars. The debt in question here is a fortune, many millions of dollars—far more money than any of the people listening to Jesus's parable would ever earn or see in their lifetimes.

Note that the servant only asks his lord for more time to

repay the debt, but the generous lord goes further and forgives him the entire debt. On the other hand, the hundred-denarii debt owed to this servant amounts to something like twenty bucks. The moral message of this parable is clear. If we never lose sight of our own sinfulness, our need for forgiveness, we will be motivated to forgive others who have wronged us.

This moral insight perhaps should be the foundation of the spiritual life. I do not get out of bed in the morning without calling to mind my own failures. Catholics, and Christians in general, are often accused of being obsessed with guilt and sin. The counter to that is straightforward.

Number one, there is a big difference between sins and the guilt we feel about those sins. If we repent and confess our sins, we are assured of forgiveness and the elimination of guilt. Number two, by remembering our sins but not our guilt, we can move on from the self-absorption a guilty conscience produces and feel genuine compassion for others who have wronged us and who are in need of our forgiveness. In fact, when I remember the worst things I have done, I am moved to a grateful joy that I have been forgiven.

Notice how the lord first feels pity or compassion for his servant, and then forgives the debt entirely. The servant does not feel this when he refuses to forgive what is owed to him. The ability to feel compassion for the debtor—sinner—appears to be the heart of the matter. This message is in line with what Jesus says elsewhere in the gospels. He attacks self-righteousness relentlessly because of the hardness of heart it leads to. As usual, I have questions.

My first question is, what does forgiveness mean? I propose there are several degrees of forgiveness. The sine qua non of forgiveness means we do not want to punish the one who has hurt us. A second step is to wish the other person well. In fact, we must pray for the one who has sinned against us and try to love him or her. Once we get the hang of it, it's liberating.

Initially, forgiveness is hard! I know I could not do it without help from the Holy Spirit. I have found this help by praying for those who have sinned against me.

That said, we can easily fool ourselves when it comes to forgiveness. When someone has really hurt us, the resentment and bitterness can hide in buried corners of our soul without our being fully aware of it. One way to keep ourselves honest is to contemplate whether we played a role in the sinful situation. Often we may need to seek forgiveness, from God or even the one who sinned against us, for something we did or failed to do.

Maybe this is only me, but I find myself far more likely to overlook sins of omission than sins of commission. I am not so sure God looks at things this way, however, so when I pray, I often ask God to help me discover what I am failing to do that I could or should do. We can confidently ask God to reveal our "secret sins" to us because we know God will forgive us and we need not remain in a guilty place. In fact, my experience is God will bless us many times over for opening ourselves up to this opportunity for greater humility. By becoming more aware of our need for forgiveness, we will be better able to forgive others.

Forgiving is good psychic hygiene as well. Why do we hang on to what hurts us? It's a heavy burden to carry around all the time; it slows us down. Letting go is another way to understand what Jesus means when he says, "Come to me all you who labor and are heavy laden. . . . For my yoke is easy and my burden light" (Matthew 11:28–30).

What if the one who sinned against us shows no sign of repentance? Must we forgive regardless? Yes! I think the message of Jesus here is clear. Otherwise, we would not be talking about forgiving someone seventy times seven.

Does forgiveness mean our relationship with the other must be restored to the status quo ante? Must we treat the other as if the wrong never happened? Forget as well as forgive? This is where it can get tricky. In some instances, I would say yes, in others no.

Here is where the repentance of the sinner is important. If the sinner asks for forgiveness, shows true sorrow, and offers to try to make up for the wrong done if it is not irreparable, then you may want to consider this. But this level of forgiveness is supererogatory; it cannot be what Jesus is talking about.

If we think about physical or sexual abusers, Jesus cannot possibly want us to continue to suffer in such abusive relationships, particularly if the abuser shows no sign of repenting. It will be difficult enough to forgive such a person if we get out of the situation.

If this is true, it may be that genuine forgiveness means accepting that the other person is one who may do this kind of thing again—therefore accepting that as a result, the relationship is going to be different from the way it was before. Truly accepting this change can be very hard. But I also think it is important to accept that the relationship has not ended. It may feel like it has. We might even want it to. Yet even if we never see this person again, the relationship continues. Just as our relationship with those who have physically died is not over.

Scripture scholars tell us that parables immediately following one of Jesus's sayings may not necessarily have been intended by Jesus to illustrate the teaching. The evangelists put together many parables with Jesus's teachings, but they did not always know which parables were intended to illustrate a specific teaching. The gospels were written decades after Jesus's death, and the specific context of the parables was not always clear. In any case, parables are often more complicated and challenging than the more straightforward teachings. I believe today's passage is no exception. Jesus has just finished telling Peter to forgive his brother seventy time seven. This passage is found in Luke as well. Matthew alone adds the parable of the unmerciful servant from material perhaps only he had.

My final question is whether Matthew's parable illustrates Jesus's teaching about forgiveness or undermines it. The parable appears to be a clear indictment of the unmerciful servant's failure to forgive. He looks especially bad for not forgiving a tiny debt when the king forgave him a debt worth a fortune.

The problem is that in the end, the king rescinds his forgiveness of the unmerciful servant and "deliver[s] him to the jailers, till he should pay all his debt." Lest we wonder whether the king represents God, Matthew's Jesus goes on to tell us, "So also my heavenly Father will do to every one of you, if you do not forgive your brother from your heart."

Finally, does not this parable set us up in a trap of contradiction that undermines the entire teaching on the importance of forgiveness? Jesus has told Peter he must forgive his brother seventy times seven, but God, it seems, gives us only one chance to forgive! I can push this line of thinking further. We are told by Jesus we are to imitate God. Does this mean that we are to forgive *almost* everything, but that like God we too are never to forgive another's failure to forgive?

One way we can make sense of this apparent contradiction is that Jesus, or Matthew, inspired by the Holy Spirit of Jesus, is warning us against the sin of presumption. We should be careful not to presume God will forgive us if we do not forgive others. In other words, this passage is a warning against presuming we know who God is and what God will do. God is loving and merciful but also remains mysterious to us. Next week's reading will make this point once again.

Another way to make sense of this parable is to consider that what the king is demanding here is true repentance. We are to forgive even the unrepentant. Yet the king here is only demanding the servant repay the debt, and once this is done, the relationship has been restored. In other words, the king is now insisting upon repentance before true forgiveness can occur. This sounds like what may happen to us in purgatory. Ultimate forgiveness and reconciliation are promised, even to the unforgiving. It's just that the process will take longer than if we had ourselves forgiven others.

TWENTY-FIFTH SUNDAY ORDINARY TIME

Isaiah 55:6–9
Philippians 1:20c–24, 27a
Matthew 20:1–16

THIS WEEK WE have one of the most memorable passages in the Old Testament, a warning against thinking we know who God is: "For my thoughts are not your thoughts, nor are your ways my ways, says the Lord." We can see this week's gospel as in line with last week's: God loves us, yet God remains a mystery, and we must be careful not to presume we can ever grasp completely who God is.

Our gospel reading this week, found only in Matthew, may resemble last week's in another way: according to John Dominic Crossan, at least, the landowner—who represents God—behaves problematically. In *The Power of Parables*, Crossan argues this parable would have provoked first-century Palestinian peasants into questioning the structural injustice of their system.[86]

Why does the landowner accuse the day laborers of being "idle"? Once he throws this accusation at them directly and even exaggerates it by accusing them of being idle "all day," something he cannot know, the word is used a second time in our passage. A third reference, in verse 6, refers to them as "standing around." The workers' reasonable response is that no one has hired them. Why then does the landowner keep accusing them of idleness? Does this not sound like some rich people in our own time, who censure all the unemployed for being lazy?

The word translated as "idle" is *argoi*. The Greek word is, if anything, more insulting than the English word used to translate it. Bauer lists three translations, each one worse than the one before: 1) unemployed; 2) idle, lazy; 3) useless, unproductive. If the story is really about the landowner's generosity, why does he need to use this accusatory word?

I believe a careful reading of this passage should caution us against identifying the landowner too closely with God. Blaming the victims and the poor for their plight seems out of character for the Father that Jesus reveals to us. We cannot be too sure we know the Father, as the Isaiah reading warns us.

A less debatable meaning of this parable is that God's justice differs from our sense of justice. One important conflict faced by the early Church was between those who had been Jews and remained observant Jews who followed the Law and the Gentiles newly converted to Christianity who did not feel bound by the Law's strict requirements, such as circumcision. We see this tension in Paul's letters, especially Galatians. God chose the Jews to be God's people thousands of years before Jesus arrived on the scene: who do these upstarts think they are?

Many Jewish Christians may have resented these newcomers who appeared to have it "too easy," just as the workers who had labored all day were indignant at being paid the same as those who had only worked an hour. Jesus says this parable is "like" the kingdom he is proclaiming. This kingdom is both already present and not yet fully realized until Jesus comes again. To the extent that the Kingdom is already present, especially in the Church, the parable seems designed to make the point that God's chosen people should accept the newcomers as their equals before God. Still, I am not entirely satisfied with this interpretation either.

The workers complain they "bore the day's burden and the heat." This would appear to make following Jesus and entering the Kingdom nothing but drudgery! Yet elsewhere in the gospels Jesus repeatedly presents the Kingdom as a gift that brings joy and eases our burdens, rather than as tedious toil: "Come to me, all who labor and are heavy laden, and I will give you rest" (Matthew 11:28).

It is true that Jesus also declares that he came not to abolish the Law but to fulfill it. Moreover, Jesus insists his commandments require more righteousness than is possessed by the observant scribes and Pharisees when he challenges his listeners, "Unless your righteousness exceeds that of the scribes and Pharisees you will never enter the kingdom."

What is going on here? Is the kingdom Jesus is proclaiming harder or easier than following the Jewish Law?

The way I square this circle of apparent contradictions is by concluding that following Jesus must be something that flows from our heart, from the depths of our soul. As I've mentioned before, so often in secular life we do x in order to get y. St. Thomas called this *a bonum utile*, or a useful good. There is nothing wrong with useful goods. Sometimes we have to do things we don't particularly like in order to gain something we really need. Most of us must work to care for ourselves and our families.

But life becomes absurd if it consists only of work we do in order to get something else. This is one reason God gave us a Sabbath day of rest. Our souls crave activities we do purely because we love doing them. Aquinas called this kind of good the *bonum honestum*. We like a friend because we like spending time with her; the reward is intrinsic to the relationship. If we like her because she is useful to us in some way, it's not a real friendship any longer. Once we love whatever it is we are doing, it is a joyful gift to do it. I love gardening, so working hard in the yard is not wearisome toil.

When we apply this way of thinking to today's parable, we come up with a different take on the mistake of the resentful workers. To enter the Kingdom, it is not enough to do the right thing; we also have to do the right thing for the right reasons. If we expect rewards outside of the gifts we receive for doing the work, we don't "get it." Sometimes the work we do to build the Kingdom will feel like drudgery, to be sure. Sometimes when praying we can feel like we are just going through the motions. Sometimes I grow weary of the work involved in feeding and clothing our many guests on Monday morning.

It is important to keep doing these things anyway, no matter what we happen to be feeling at the moment. Feelings are so unreliable and changeable! One of the gifts of the Holy Spirit (Isaiah 11:2) is "strength," or "fortitude." Fortitude is a virtue, a strength, a good habit, that enables us to endure hardship as well as stand up to danger. If we are doing the Lord's work, I think we will receive this gift when we need it.

In addition, as I have written before, we need to feel some discomfort at times when we are building the Kingdom. It is a sign that we are on the right path and strengthening our souls and the health of our faith, just as exercise is sometimes uncomfortable but necessary for our body's health. If we never suffer even a little bit, our faith can get flabby. It also means we are not really following Jesus, because that is not the way he lived.

TWENTY-SIXTH SUNDAY ORDINARY TIME

The Danger of Saying Yes!

Ezekiel 18:25–28
Philippians 2:1–11
Matthew 21:28–32

I HAVE ALWAYS liked this parable, found only in Matthew, because I am by nature a naysayer, just like the first son.

The context of this parable is important. Jesus is in the Temple and he has just fended off some entrapping questions from the chief priests and elders: "By what authority are you doing these things?" (Matthew 21:23). By "these things" they were probably referring primarily to Jesus throwing the money changers out of the Temple (Matthew 21:12–13, and not included in our Sunday readings at this point). They also might have been thinking of healing the blind and the lame in the Temple and children crying out to him, "Hosanna to the Son of David!" (Matthew 21:15).

As with last week's Matthew-only parable of the laborers in the vineyard, we seem to be dealing with a problem besetting his Jewish-Christian community. Why are Gentiles and sinners following Jesus and entering the Kingdom, whereas so many Jews and especially Jewish religious leaders were hostile to Jesus's mission? Why are the last first, the first last?

The parable answers this question in an uncharacteristically clear way. What matters is not lip service to God but rather what we do. Jesus says in Matthew 7:21: "Not everyone who says to me, 'Lord, Lord' shall enter the kingdom of heaven, but he who does the will of my Father who is in heaven."

Is there danger in saying "Yes!" to God? This question should be of great interest to us if we have said yes to Jesus and are trying to follow him. Jesus is telling us, however, that those who say no to God may actually be more responsive to doing God's will. Should we then reject Jesus? This parable reminds me of a friend who used to tell me that atheists are more likely to convert to Christianity than agnostics. By clearly rejecting God and Jesus's message, we may come to be more aware of the issues at stake than if we bumble along as lukewarm believers—or if we try to evade the entire problem of life's meaning with an unreflective, conformist agnosticism.

All this is helpful information when we encounter people who are hostile to Jesus's message. But the parable goes further. It suggests that saying yes may truly hinder us from doing God's will. How?

Given what we know of Matthew's problems with Jewish religious leadership, Jesus was probably speaking about the Jewish religious leaders, who regarded themselves as saying yes to God even though, arguably, they were blind to God's will because of their rejection of Jesus. Yet we should be cautious about assuming Christian leaders, or believers, are immune to this kind of know-it-all religious conservatism. What ought to save us from the pitfall is our belief in the Holy Spirit, which is always at work in the world, inside and outside the Church. That said, it can be difficult to discern which new teachers, movements, or ideas are genuinely of the Spirit and which are not.

To be a Christian is always a work in progress. Early on, our faith was called the Way. It is a road, a path. We are in need of continual conversion. That's why we have Lent, Advent, and confession. The danger of saying yes is that we may rest too assured that we are one and done with God. No more spiritual work is necessary. The parable is telling us that embedded in our yes to Jesus may lie a no, and we need to be aware of that and work on it. Even better: allow God to work on it. How?

In prayer, we can ask God to reveal our "secret sins" to us. If we do this and learn to cultivate an inner silence through regular, disciplined meditation, I believe we will be able to hear God's voice. It may sound painful to be told about our secret sins, but that's a misunderstanding of what sin is. Sins diminish our humanity, our "aliveness." Secret ones are especially dangerous, just as the illness we aren't aware of often ends up killing us. This is part of what Jesus means when he tells us to "keep watch."

My secret sins are usually sins of omission. They are easy to miss. I don't think I am unusual in this respect, so you may find the same to be true of yourself.

In addition to prayer, finding a spiritual advisor to see at least once a month can help. Over time, this person can help to "keep you honest" about your spiritual life.

Third, try to develop a true friend in the Spirit. This is someone courageous and insightful enough to tell you the truth about yourself, even if it is unpleasant.

Fourth, go to church regularly and get involved. If you do, I think you will quickly run into some challenges that will help you see where you may have been saying no to God without realizing it. This is one reason I believe it's no good trying to be a Christian in private.

The epistle is important to me this week because it contains biblical support for a key facet of my Christology (see appendix B). I also discussed these issues in the twenty-second Sunday of Ordinary Time. The key word here is in verse 7: *ekenosen*. It means "to empty," and more figuratively to abase, neutralize, or to make of no effect. In Philippians 2:6–7, St. Paul writes of Jesus, "Who, subsisting in God's form, did not deem being on equal terms with God a thing to be grasped. But instead emptied himself, taking a slave's form, coming to be in a likeness of human beings."

TWENTY-SEVENTH SUNDAY ORDINARY TIME

Isaiah 5:1–7
Philippians 4:6–9
Matthew 21:33–43

BEFORE LAUNCHING INTO what I think is the heart of today's reading, I want to make a few desultory observations.

First, note that the owner of the vineyard is a metaphor for God, who is presented as one who "owns" or created the world but is also absent from it. Are we being told God is an absentee landlord? Or is this how the wicked tenants perceive God, and is that the root of their bad behavior? I believe the answer is that God is, in fact, the "owner" of everything in our world; we are but the trustees of it, and we are too often tempted to see God as absent and to forget we, like the tenants, will have to give God "an account" of how we have lived.

Faithful Christians are now the new tenants of the Kingdom of God. This parable poses a challenge to us. Are we "producing the fruits of it"? We have less excuse than the religious establishment of Jesus's time for not understanding his message. We have the New Testament, the Church, and two thousand years of tradition.

What is the kingdom Jesus is talking about? Is it the present favor of God? Jesus has elsewhere told the people that "the Kingdom of God has come upon you" (Matthew 12:28). Or are we talking about the future, final fulfillment of the Kingdom, the promise of the full and final blessing of God? I think we should understand "kingdom" here in both senses.

We already know the context of this week's gospel: it follows immediately last week's. Jesus has overturned the money changers' tables and is directly confronting the Jewish religious establishment. The parable of the wicked tenants is found in all three synoptics, but Matthew makes some subtle and significant changes to it.

For example, only Matthew has the tenants stone the householder's servants. Stoning was a punishment the ancient Jews sometimes used against those who broke the religious law. It is possible Matthew is calling more attention to the parallels between the way prophets were often mistreated and what the tenants did to the servants in this parable. All three gospel writers tell us that because the chief priests "feared the people," they didn't arrest Jesus. But only Matthew adds that this was because the people held Jesus to be a prophet. Matthew's connection between Jesus and the prophets sharpens the parable's challenge to the Jewish religious leaders.

Matthew alone has the chief priests answer the question Jesus poses: what will the owner of the vineyard do to the wicked tenants? The "death sentence" answer is the same in all three gospels, but whereas Mark and Luke embed the answer in the parable, Matthew moves it out of the parable and into history. Matthew has the chief priests, in effect, condemn themselves!

Most important of all, Matthew has Jesus tell the chief priests and elders directly, "Therefore I tell you, the Kingdom of God will be taken away from you and given to a nation producing the fruits of it." The other synoptics keep this message inside the parable, making it an indirect warning to the Jewish leaders.

It is impossible to know precisely what the historical Jesus said to the chief priests and elders. In one sense it doesn't matter. They certainly got the message: Jesus was clearly challenging their authority and perhaps even threatening their safety.

Even more terrifying for these leaders: the people they supposedly led were on Jesus's side. All three synoptics note that after hearing this parable, the leaders immediately want to arrest Jesus; this is logical and can even be seen as a form of self-defense. But they had a problem: they feared the multitude even more than Jesus! They must have been very, very afraid.

In one important sense, however, Matthew's Jesus is milder on the chief priests than the other synoptics. While the Jewish leaders condemn the tenants (i.e., themselves) to a "miserable death," Jesus himself does not. He simply notes drily that the Kingdom of God will be taken from them and given to others.

Note also how in Matthew alone, by telling the chief priests the Kingdom of God will be taken from them, Jesus is also affirming they are currently in charge of this kingdom. This is why Jesus had to go to Jerusalem and the Temple and confront them directly: the religious revolution he wanted required it.

I read this parable to be an essential key to understanding the gospel message. Jesus's mission was to proclaim the arrival of the Kingdom of God. His message now requires him to destroy the existing Jewish religious establishment and replace it with something quite different. Matthew's Jesus has elsewhere told us (16:18) that the Church is the replacement. Jesus was not a political revolutionary, but he certainly was a nonviolent, religious revolutionary. He was surely aware this life-and-death struggle with the religious status quo would likely cost him his life, and he was prepared to die for his mission.

We have seen that when compared to Mark and Luke, Matthew sharpens the conflict between Jesus and the Temple leaders. We cannot know whether Matthew's version is closer to what happened than the other evangelists'. But all three include the "cleansing of the Temple" episode and other statements and actions that made Jesus's position clear. Turning over the money changers' tables is such a strange act that it is almost certainly historical. It is certain that Jesus attacked the religious authority of the Temple leaders, they were aware of this, they feared him, and this is why they wanted him dead.

This raises the following questions: Why did Jesus need to proclaim total spiritual war on the Jewish religious establishment? What was so terrible about this institution that made Jesus conclude it was not reformable but had to be destroyed and replaced? Jesus took an extreme position that ended his life, so he had to have very good reasons for doing so. I believe this question can, and should, guide our reading of the gospels. We are looking here at the dramatic climax of the gospel story; the conflict between Jesus and the chief priests leads to the Crucifixion. One good reason to read a story more than once is that after we know how it ends, we can better understand the events that led to it. The evangelists almost certainly constructed their gospels with this in mind, as we see throughout them repeated conflicts between Jesus and the religious leaders of his time.

I believe I have found more important clues to Jesus's radical rejection of the Jewish religious establishment by reading the Apocrypha, especially Sirach and Wisdom (see appendix E). These books were written only one to two hundred years before Jesus was born, so they give us a good sense of the reigning theology among Jewish religious thinkers. We sometimes know people better by what they feel compelled to reject than what they affirm; often we define ourselves most clearly by what we cannot accept. I am a child of the 1960s, and many in my generation defined themselves by the rejection of the Vietnam War and racism.

We can certainly point to many specific issues that divided Jesus from the religious establishment, such as his healing on the Sabbath and the establishment's more generally placing adherence to the letter of the law above love of God and neighbor. Perhaps a more important piece in this puzzle is that Matthew's

Jesus affirms that the chief priests possess the Kingdom of God. Part of the problem was the assumption that they, and only they, held the keys to this kingdom. They kept "sinners and tax collectors" out: Jesus came to bring them in.

Another dimension of this conflict is the failure of the Jewish mission to the Gentiles. The Old Testament is filled with prophecies about how ultimately "all the nations" will come to Jerusalem and worship the only god, the God of Israel. Missionaries were sent out and met with some success. The Jewish diaspora helped to spread the Word throughout the known civilized world. Many Roman citizens were "God-fearers"—that is, people who admired the moral teaching of the Jewish Bible and attended synagogue.

However, most Gentiles recoiled from full membership in the Jewish community, in many cases repulsed by the requirement of circumcision as the price of admission. This is an enormously complicated theological-historical topic, and I am oversimplifying it. But I think it is fair to say that continued rigid Jewish adherence to the letter of the law was an obstacle to the spread of God's Word, the fulfillment of the prophecies of the Gentile mission, and the role God's chosen people were to play in sharing God's Word with all the nations. This theme is certainly repeated often, in many different contexts, in our four gospels.

I have offered several possible answers to the question of why Jesus felt he had to challenge and destroy the Temple. There is no single answer to such an enormous question. I believe when confronting the death struggle between Jesus and the Temple leaders, we are in the presence of a mystery. Reading the gospels carefully, again and again, can help deepen our participation in this mystery, but I don't think it can fully dispel it.

As for the question we began with, whether we Christians are better tenants of God's kingdom than the Jewish leaders, I have no answer. I think our record is mixed. The Church has done, is doing, many wonderful *and* horrible things.

Yet I would argue our situation is now different from that of the Jerusalem Temple. Most Christians understand the Holy Spirit, God's presence in our world, is not "our possession." It does not exist in any one particular place. It works inside and outside the Church. God's Holy Spirit is at work in the world. We cannot pretend to stop it or control it. We can scarcely understand it!

TWENTY-EIGHTH SUNDAY ORDINARY TIME

Isaiah 25:6–10a
Philippians 4:12–14, 19–20
Matthew 22:1–14

TODAY'S GOSPEL IS found also in Luke, although in a different and shorter version. The parable we have in Matthew is something of a complicated morass. Why should invited guests called in from the streets be thrown out of the feast and punished for not wearing proper wedding garments? It is also odd that some of the other invited guests mistreated and murdered the king's servants, whose only crime was inviting them to the party! This enrages the king, who escalates the conflict into a war by killing the murderers and burning their city.

This is another parable that is telling us what the Kingdom of God is "like." But I thought Jesus's kingdom was a peaceful one, filled with love and forgiveness for sinners. We're looking at a bloody mess! I make sense of today's gospel by reading it as a parable that is primarily revealing what the gospels and especially gospel parables are "like," and secondarily revealing what the Kingdom is "like."

Let's begin with figuring out who Jesus's audience was for the original parable. Then we need to look at Matthew's audience; the reason this parable presents so many problems for us is because in order to meet the needs of his community, the Holy Spirit inspired St. Matthew to revise Jesus's original. The end result is difficult and complicated, true. But it also presents us with a fuller and richer understanding of both Jesus and the early Church.

Jesus's audience in Matthew consists of the chief priests and the elders of the people, the same audience he has had for the past three weeks of "the Kingdom is like" parables. The fact that he told so many similar parables to the same audience and that so many of them have been passed down to us tells me that this was a huge issue for him and that his audience struggled to deal with understanding the Kingdom. Why wouldn't they? We do.

Once again Jesus is revealing to these religious leaders that although they believe they "own" the Kingdom of God, in fact they do not. This parable suggests a random selection of people will be entering the Kingdom before the exalted chief priests and elders.

Before we turn to St. Matthew's audience, let's pause for a moment and savor the images Jesus uses for the Kingdom. He uses the wedding-celebration metaphor often. The Kingdom is like a huge feast. Not just any feast, but a wedding feast, the biggest kind that existed in Jesus's time. And not just any wedding feast, but the wedding feast of a king. It can't get any better than that! Wedding feasts then, as now, were a time when folks pulled out all the stops and spent extravagantly. Who can spend more than a king?

I love wine, so I really love the Isaiah reading's emphasis on "choice wines." One of the greatest pleasures in this life is the matching of excellent wine with good food, and Isaiah tells us we will have "juicy, rich food" along with "pure, choice wine." I can hardly wait!

The Isaiah reference to wine and the gospel story of a wedding feast recall Jesus's first miracle in the Gospel of St. John, the wedding at Cana. There Jesus turned water into hundreds of gallons of the best wine anyone had tasted. These stories of the Kingdom may be a good reason for us to occasionally have such feasts, allowing ourselves to experience them as an anticipation and a participation in the Kingdom, which is, after all, both already and not yet.

Nietzsche complained that Christians "do not look redeemed." Throwing a good feast every now and then is, in fact, a very Christian thing to do. It might help us look and feel a little more redeemed here and now.

St. Matthew wrote his gospel around the year 85, according to the biblical scholars. As we have seen, his community was composed of Jewish converts to Christianity who believed they were now the true Israel. Yet NJBC says they were likely placed outside of Judaism by the rabbis of Jamnia in the year 80. It was a bitter family feud, and this helps account for the many polemical parables and remarks against the Jewish leaders we find in St. Matthew's gospel.

While Matthew's community consisted largely of Jewish converts, it was also open to the Gentile mission. It seems, therefore, that he had at least two audiences: the Jewish converts of his community as well as the growing number of Gentiles who were entering his community.

Now we are in a better position to understand what is going on with the man without a wedding garment. Joachim Jeremias[87] believes this is a second, independent parable that Matthew has inserted into the parable of the wedding feast. For one thing, Luke and the Gospel of Thomas omit this episode entirely from their account of the wedding feast. Second, Matthew here abruptly shifts from using the word "servants" to "attendants."

Why would Matthew insert a second parable here? Jeremias argues, and I agree, that the answer lies with the Church's Gentile mission. By inviting everyone and anyone to the table, the original parable implies no conversion or repentance is necessary to enter the Kingdom, or the Church. Now, this is certainly not Jesus's vision of the Kingdom. He called sinners and tax collectors, but he also insisted they change their lives. Matthew wanted to avoid any misunderstanding that no change in life was necessary. So he added this independent parable in which the wedding garment symbolizes the new life in Christ expected of Christian converts.

Jesus was not concerned with this misunderstanding when he told the original parable because *his* audience was the chief priests and elders. While Jesus's vision of the Kingdom included Gentiles, the Gentile mission did not exist when he was speaking in the Temple.

St. Paul, just like St. Matthew, confronted the danger that the gospel of free grace can lead some to duck their moral responsibilities, as in Galatians 5–6 where Paul argues that Christian freedom from the Mosaic Law and the gift of the Holy Spirit should not be used as an "opportunity for the flesh." Instead, this freedom must lead us to loving service of one another. The fact that St. Paul needed to write about this reveals that it *was* a real problem in the early Church. It still seems to be a problem.

While Matthew's parable of the wedding feast is confusing if we take it at face value, once we understand that it is made up of at least two layers because of the two different audiences, we gain a deeper grasp of how St. Matthew's gospel was written. How *all* the gospels were written, in fact.

This parable also shows how history and parable interpenetrate one another. The gospel writers did not clearly separate history from parable. Nor should we. But we do need to distinguish them in order to understand what we are reading.

The Church needed to adapt Jesus's original parable to meet its own new historical situation. This is important not only in order to understand what we are reading but also to understand how the Holy Spirit inspired the creation of the gospel in history, in "real time."

Thinking about the liberties St. Matthew took with Jesus's parable started me down a path of thought. I don't think "Bible-olatry" (turning the Bible into an idol) is a big problem for Catholics; on the contrary, maybe we don't take the Bible seriously enough.

I love the Bible and I especially love the gospels. Otherwise, I wouldn't be spending all this time writing about them. Can we love the gospels too much? Or in the wrong way?

St. Matthew probably had in his hands something very close to the original parable of Jesus. Just think about that for a moment. Can you imagine being in his position? What would you do with such a treasure? As I stated in my chapter on the sixth Sunday of Ordinary Time, I cannot imagine taking any liberties with something so sublime; but St. Matthew did. Matthew felt free to make big editorial changes to this precious possession, going so far as to insert a quite different parable into it. He did this in order to make his gospel better suited to the pressing demands of the Gentile mission. As a Gentile, let me say I am very glad Matthew realized how important this mission was. I might not have come to know Jesus had it not succeeded.

There is a kind of biblical piety that treats the text as if every word were the unalterable, perfect expression of God's will. However, it is liberating to understand that history, and its urgent demands, shaped the writers and the writing of the sacred text. For one thing, it helps us to understand how the Holy Spirit works in real time. It also helps to unravel some passages that seem incoherent, as in today's problem with the guest who was thrown out of the banquet for improper attire.

Taking the Bible seriously means not always reading it literally.

Knowing how freely the gospel writers handled the material they had to work with ought to free us up in the way we read what they wrote. We also are living in a historical moment with pressing demands upon us. We need to keep this in mind when we read and interpret the gospels. The gospels were made for us; we were not made for the gospels!

Does it make any sense to read the gospels in a more rigid way than they were written?

TWENTY-NINTH SUNDAY ORDINARY TIME

Isaiah 45:1, 4–6
1 Thessalonians 1:1–5b
Matthew 22:15–21

WE CONTINUE THIS week with yet another episode in the conflict between Jesus and the Jewish religious-political establishment. The focus now shifts from the chief priests and the elders to the Pharisees, revealing Jesus's irreconcilable differences with all members of the Jewish leadership, the entire status quo of the Temple, chief priests, scribes, elders, and even the money changers. In Matthew, a conflict with the final group, the Sadducees, follows immediately after today's passage (although unfortunately our lectionary skips this encounter). Matthew wants to be sure to touch all the bases!

Before we try to figure out what Jesus meant by the famous "Render to Caesar" line, I want to explore verse 16 because the RSV translation bothers me here. I refer to when the Pharisees say to Jesus, "Teacher, we know that you are true, and teach the way of God truthfully, and care for no man; for you do not regard the position of men."

No, no, no, Pharisees; Jesus cares for everyone! Even more perplexing is that the Pharisees here are trying, albeit duplicitously, to flatter Jesus. What is going on?

I believe the RSV has botched the translation in verse 16. Hart is closer to the original when he renders it this way: "Teacher, we know that you are truthful and that you teach the way of God in truth, and you harbor no anxiety toward anyone, for you are not a respecter of men's persons."

Many readers might be confused by Hart's "men's persons." The word he translates as "persons" *is prosopon*. This is the Greek root of a word that made its way into Latin, medieval French, and eventually into English as "person." In Greek the word had a different original sense, however. It referred to a person's face, external circumstances, or outward, surface appearance. In Latin and medieval French it could mean the mask an actor wore during a performance. I think Hart would have done better to translate the phrase "You are not a respecter of men's status."

The Greek text has even stronger language than comes through in most translations. Double negatives are common and acceptable grammatically in other languages, unlike English. When we drop the double negative, something gets lost in translation. For this and other reasons I will explain, I think a literal translation of 16b is a good idea here: "You don't court no one's favor anywhere-anytime, because you don't care about a person's status."

Not courting people's favor because of their status is far different from "caring for no man." I found "you court no man's favor" in Bauer.

I am spending so much time on this verse because I think it is a crucial and often overlooked dimension of Jesus's gospel message. Jesus is utterly indifferent to social status. He cares nothing about his own social position, nor about that of those with whom he is interacting. Many of his disciples were uneducated fishers. We see this again and again, in the way he welcomes into his kingdom sinners, lepers, the poor, the sick, and rich, high-status people as well. If Jesus rejected the privileged, he would still be "caring" about social status, but in the opposite way. Let's not forget that Joseph of Arimathea was a rich man and a disciple of Jesus (Matthew 27:57).

Status anxiety is a common feature of modern life. It starts in middle school, or at least it did for me. For some, it may be difficult to imitate Jesus's indifference to status. We may be worried about our own social position and therefore tempted to judge others by how associating with them will help or hurt our status climb. A price must be paid if we ignore our social status.

On the other hand, status anxiety can mess up important life decisions, such as the choice of a career, a spouse, how we spend our money, time, and talents. We may betray our inner, authentic self and life for a false self and life that is tied to external rewards. Jesus warns of this particular danger in status chasing when he says in Matthew 16:26, "For what will it profit a man, if he should gain the whole cosmos but lose his soul?"

I believe the way to transcend status anxiety is to allow ourselves to experience God's love for us. That is what Jesus did. Knowing God loves us does not abolish the oppressiveness of the social order but rather puts it in its proper place. Once we let this happen, it is liberating! It requires so much hard, soul-draining work to worry about social status.

The problem for most of us, I believe, is that we don't experience deeply enough the love God has for us. At least, not the way Jesus did. We experience the world through our senses, but God cannot ordinarily be sensed directly. Without this experience, it is hard not to remain chained to our status in this world. Is there anything we can do to really feel God's love and presence in our life?

I am convinced the answer is yes; there are things we can do and other things we can avoid in order to increase our experience of God's loving presence. True, there is a consensus that we are chosen by God and that God ultimately takes the initiative here. Yet it is, I believe, a two-way street. We have a role to play. We can experience God through our senses via the sacraments; in community with others; in nature; and in prayer (see appendix C).

Following Jesus is tough: loving our enemy, forgiving everyone, doing justice to the poor. But his invitation to transcend soul-wearying status anxiety and experience the joyful liberation of letting it go can explain this otherwise baffling statement: "Take my yoke upon you, and learn from me; for I am gentle and lowly in heart, and you will find rest for your souls. For my yoke is easy and my burden is light" (Matthew 11:29–30).

Once we shrug off the drudgery of status chasing, we will have far more energy to do what matters than we dreamed possible!

Note also that in praising Jesus for his indifference to social status, the Pharisees are (unconsciously?) criticizing themselves. They directly connect Jesus's not courting the favor of anyone with the fact that he "teaches the way of God truthfully." The corollary of their statement is that if he did court the favor of people, he would not teach the way of God truthfully. Do they realize this may apply to themselves? The history of the official "court prophets" versus the mistreatment of so many genuine Jewish prophets provides examples of this phenomenon; see, for example, Amos 7:10–17. The problem persists in our own day, when certain religious leaders or thinkers tell political leaders what they want to hear.

The famous line of today's passage is, of course, "Render therefore to Caesar the things that are Caesar's and to God the things that are God's." What does this mean?

Jesus seems to be giving permission for devout Jews to pay taxes to Rome. Whether to pay these taxes was a true question of conscience Pharisees struggled with, according to NJBC. Although their question to Jesus was duplicitous and malicious, it was also a real question for them as it meant acknowledging a foreign, pagan sovereignty over Israel. Does this not belie God's sovereignty over the Chosen People?

The inscription on the coin in the passage reads *Tiberius Caesar son of the divine Augustus, great high priest*. By adding that we are to render to God the things that are God's, Jesus clearly rejects the claim that Augustus, or the state, is divine. His statement encourages his followers to resist going along with anything that would violate faith in God's ultimate supremacy over the Roman Empire. And of course, many of his followers did just that, dying as martyrs rather than renouncing their faith in Jesus as Lord.

If Jesus had called on people not to pay taxes, it could have led to violent rebellion and repressive countermeasures; he was committed to nonviolent change. He also may have believed God would soon usher in the Kingdom.

All of these explanations reflect the current scholarly consensus. I am now going to speculate a bit beyond this consensus. Jesus was even more hostile to the Jewish authorities than he was to the Romans. Like so many prophets before him, Jesus did not equate God's rule with all-too-human Jewish theocratic rule over Israel. He may have reasoned that Roman rule over Israel was no worse from God's perspective than Jewish rule, so why not pay Roman taxes?

I am not sure the historical Jesus saw things this way, but I would argue that evil though it often was, the Roman Empire turned out to be very good for the spread and ultimate success of Christianity. Through its roads, security, and common language, the empire made travel and communication throughout the Mediterranean world far easier than it ever had been. St. Paul writes in Galatians 4:4 that God sent Jesus "when the time had fully come." This refers to salvation history, of course, but I think it also has to do with the ways in which the Roman Empire made the expansion of Christianity possible.

Roman persecution of Christians was sporadic and not systematic, depending largely on local conditions, according to Church historian Henry Chadwick.[88] The state did not take Christianity seriously before the third century, giving the

Church breathing space to expand and consolidate its position. The occasional martyrdom of heroic Christians actually increased the Church's prestige. "*Sanguis marcurum ascsenen christianorum,*" as Tertullian famously wrote: "The blood of martyrs is the seed of the Church."

The Church is pointing us in a similar direction with this week's passage from Isaiah. The prophet tells us that it is God who arms Cyrus, "though [he] knew [God] not." The Persian king Cyrus defeated the Babylonians, allowing the Jews exiled there to return to Israel. When we apply Isaiah's insight to this week's gospel, we could say that God used the Roman emperors to achieve God's purpose, even though "they knew [God] not."

Today's reading offers us a final liberating and consoling message. I write this just before the November election of 2020, a time when the country is frenzied with political anxiety. Politics are important. Christians need to take the duties of citizenship seriously. But there is something far more important than politics.

As Jesus's nonchalance about taxes reveals, our relationship with God is what matters most.

THIRTIETH SUNDAY ORDINARY TIME

Exodus 22:20–26
I Thessalonians 1:5c–10
Matthew 22:34–40

THIS WEEK'S GOSPEL reading is Jesus at his best and one of his most famous sayings; yet I have never heard anyone else so much as mention my favorite element, an innovation Jesus subtly inserts into his creative use of Scripture.

Our reading begins with, "But when the Pharisees heard that he had silenced the Sadducees..."

The Church's Year A lectionary skipped over the Sadducees episode recounted in Matthew 22:23–33, so we won't spend much time on it. But we should be aware that Matthew's Jesus has now had conflicts and challenging dialogues with all the major groups of the Jewish Temple's religious establishment: chief priests, elders, scribes, Pharisees, Sadducees, even the money changers and Herodians. Jesus rejected everything they stood for, and the people were with him, not with the big shots. No wonder the leaders wanted him killed.

This question posed here appears to be an honest one rather than an attempt at the game of "gotcha" as were so many of the other questions Jesus faced. The NJBC tells us that the Pharisees were committed to popular education; summarizing the Torah was indispensable to that end. Moreover, the Pharisees' devotion to the Law led them to elaborate it with many minor rules, threatening one's grasp of what was most essential. It would seem that this lawyer, or *nomikos*, which refers to a scribe or one learned in the Torah, is asking Jesus for help in resolving a genuine dilemma for him and his colleagues.

The lawyer asks him which is the great commandment in the Law. Jesus answers the question in his own way, by putting two separate commandments together into one. This was one of his greatest innovations, displaying his mastery of Torah tradition. The first commandment had a central place in Jewish liturgy and piety; it is found in Deuteronomy 6:5: "You shall love the Lord your God with all your heart, and with all your soul, and with all your might." But that is not what Matthew's Jesus says! Nor does Mark and Luke's Jesus say this either.

Matthew's Jesus drops "might" and replaces it with "mind." The other evangelists keep "might," but they both include "mind," just as Matthew does—and as Deuteronomy does not. The odds are good the historical Jesus used "mind" because this word does not appear in the Deuteronomy text Jesus quotes and yet all three synoptic gospels have it.

Jesus, not the Torah, commands us to love God with all our mind. Let's just pause and think about that for a moment. The word translated as "mind" is *dianoia* in Greek. This word carries a more active connotation. Bauer translates it as "mind as a kind of thinking." I have also seen translations of it as "understanding" or "deep thought." The Greek word connects "mind" with its exercise in thinking and understanding.

Now, you may think you know what thinking is, but Jesus (and *dianoia*) is asking us to dig a little deeper. The great twentieth-century German philosopher Martin Heidegger wrote an entire book entitled *What Is Called Thinking?* For him, true thinking is always tied to our participation in being. Jesus thought so, too, because loving God is analogous to participation in being.

Jesus, however, unlike Heidegger, didn't stop with thinking. Today's reading is an invitation to think about thinking, and to become more deeply aware of how thinking can lead us to loving God and neighbor.

"Love" is another word, like "thinking," that we can easily misconstrue. The NJBC informs us that "love" here does not refer primarily to an emotion but to a covenant fidelity based on willing and doing. It is difficult to command love-as-feeling, but not so hard to imagine commanding this other form of love. The Christian tradition is replete with examples of the tensions between faith and reason. But Jesus is telling us here that ultimately, in loving God, we are to harmonize our heart (will or desire) with our understanding and with our soul (or life).

The call to bring heart, soul, and mind together in loving God reminds me that God does not need our love; we are the ones who need to do it because loving God is the best way to integrate the various dimensions of our fragmented selves.

"Love God with all your mind," Jesus tells us. He then demonstrates in two ways what he commands. First, by adding *dianoia* to the familiar Deuteronomy commandment (6:5). Second, by connecting that commandment to one buried in Leviticus: "You shall love your neighbor as yourself" (19:18). This commandment was not as central to Jewish life as the first. Jesus is loving God with his mind as he refashions the tradition by making a creative connection.

This is the foundation of Christian humanism. It calls to mind Jesus saying, "The sabbath was made for man, not man for the sabbath" (Mark 2:27). Jesus's innovative answer here also recalls something said of him early on in Matthew 7:28–9: "And it happened that, when Jesus completed these sayings, the crowds were astounded at his teaching; for he was teaching them like one possessing authority, and not like their scribes."

The piety of the Pharisees may have prevented them from loving God with the creative mind of Jesus. Jesus invites us to follow him, and he even here commands us to love God with all our thinking.

Still, the sign of the highest use of the intellect is to grasp and accept the limits of reason. When it comes to loving and knowing God, those with an intellectual conscience are going to realize their mind can only take them so far. Paradoxically, my experience is that while using my mind to understand God does deepen my knowledge of God, it also makes me more aware that God is unfathomable mystery.

One specific example of this is when I try to understand creation by reading about quantum mechanics and the mysteries of cosmology. More theologically, the most obvious example would be the mystery of the Incarnation, that Jesus is both fully human and completely God.

Maybe a better example is the way creation reveals God to be the Author of Beauty—for example, the way the moon right now is lightly veiled by high clouds yet still shines through them with a mystical light.

Is this one great commandment, or two? Is there a tension between the two? In my experience, there can be a tension, and much in the spiritual life depends upon keeping the two together in harmony. In the gospels Jesus fought repeatedly against subordinating human beings to what was thought to be divine law: *Yes, heal people on the Sabbath even if it is work and technically a violation of God's law!*

In our time, it seems to me we are more prone to subordinate the love of God to the love of neighbor. There is a kind of humanism that is embarrassed or indifferent to God. What is the harm in that? Some such humanists seem to do a better job of working for justice and loving their neighbor than many Christians. God bless them! I don't know how (or why) they do it. I can only speak for myself.

Loving our neighbor means, in part, working for justice for the least privileged members of our community. This is hard work at times, and for Christians it is not optional. It can drain us. Resting in God through prayer, liturgy, retreats, pilgrimages, reading, contemplation, or, yes, even on the Sabbath, can "restore your soul" (Psalms 23:3). Of course, so can mindless entertainment or a secular vacation, and they are good, too. But what I call resting in God is more directly connected with restoring the soul-energy I need to love my neighbor.

A second way the two commandments are connected can be found in 1 John 4:10–11: "In this is love, not that we loved God, but that he loved us and sent his Son to be the expiation for our sins. Beloved, if God so loved us, we also ought to love one another." Once we truly experience the love God has for us, we have some love we can—that in fact we must—give away to others.

Once someone is converted, these two moments of receiving God's love and giving love can get mixed up and confounded. But I remember what I was like before I felt and believed God loved me just as I was. I didn't have much inside me to give away to others, especially to people who made me uncomfortable.

My experience working for justice has taught me a third reason why love of God is essential if we want to love our neighbor. No matter how hard we work, it may seem at times as though we are failing to make much of a difference. I have been working to end chronic homelessness in Washington, DC, for many years now. We have made some progress; fewer people are living on the streets. But we still have a long way to go.

God calls us to be faithful, not successful. God wants us to do our part, and we must continue to do it no matter what. Of course, we must be smart about using our time and talents effectively and "be wise as serpents and innocent as doves" (Matthew 10:16). But God offers us the peace of trusting that ultimate success does not depend solely on our efforts. Our trust in God can give us the energy and confidence to keep going even when the cause seems hopeless. We are not crude utilitarians, doing the work only to achieve a result; nor need we be too discouraged when that result does not happen.

Rather, we are invited to see the work as intrinsically rewarding, as a participation in God's ongoing, creative life-loving for all creation. Quite often I do have this sense; it makes it easier to keep going.

We are doing the work to build the kingdom Jesus proclaimed, to deepen our relationship with God and with our neighbor. That calls to mind another reason why loving God is integral to loving our neighbor. How far we need to go in loving our neighbor is a tough question any honest person must face. This much I know: God does want us to push beyond our comfort zone. To keep our God-given bodies healthy, we need to exercise to the point where it hurts a little. Why should our souls be any different?

What I have found again and again is that when I do this, God finds a way to reward me. Here's one example. Going to St. Matthew's Monday-morning program means getting up at 5:30, among other things. It's not always comfortable. But getting to know our guests well over a long period of time has all but cured me of a problem I have had off and on my entire life: self-pity. I don't think I need to explain why. This connects loving God and love of neighbor with self-love: a trifecta!

Let's say you know an alcoholic. Loving him will require you to challenge him about this. It could lead to conflict, or even the end of the relationship. If you love him too much, to the exclusion of all else, if nothing transcends this love, you may shrink from this confrontation. Loving God can empower you to challenge the addiction and truly fulfill your love for this person.

These are all practical reasons why the love of God and the love of neighbor and self are really two sides of the same coin. Now I want to go one step further and venture onto a more theoretical plane. Jesus's central mission was the paradoxical proclamation that the Kingdom of God is already present and that its ultimate fulfillment lies in the future. This is the perfect message to achieve lasting social change.

The proclamation of the Kingdom provides a radical, utopian critique of the status quo that leads us, requires us, to work for change. We are to love all our neighbors as God does. This means an end to all violence, injustice, hunger, and oppression. Now!

Since the time of Jesus, we have made progress in some ways toward an imperfect moral consensus. We no longer pay money to watch our neighbors get torn to bits by wild beasts in a colosseum. We have, for the most part, ended slavery, although sex trafficking is an exception. We know torture is wrong, even if it does still happen sometimes. Many of us try to end hunger for people we do not even know by giving to global charitable organizations. For most people in the ancient world, these achievements would have been unthinkable.

Yet we also know we are far from achieving the kingdom on earth Jesus proclaimed. More work needs to be done. The radical demands of Jesus's kingdom require immediate action in our world yet transcend what seems to be possible now, precisely because of the "already, not yet" truth of Jesus's kingdom. The demands have one foot in heaven and another here on earth. That twofold tension prevents us from complacency on the one hand and despair on the other. The job seems so far from over, yet at the same time we need not despair because ultimately God is on our side and the victory of the Kingdom is assured, even if it takes divine intervention in the end.

Without a radical utopian critique of the status quo, we will passively accept the horrors of our current situation because we cannot conceive of the alternative. And nothing will change. But if the utopia is only about this world, it can be ignored as too, well, utopian! Or it can lead us to despair that we will ever get there. This is why faith in God is necessary for us to love our neighbor and to work tirelessly for justice here and now.

The final reason the two are connected is that they were for Jesus. If you believe, as I do, Jesus was unmatched in his love for other human beings, and if you believe, as I do, he was better at it than we are, then maybe that is because he also loved God more than we do. After all, again and again, Jesus told us how crucial faith in the Father is.

We walk with two legs, we breathe in and breathe out. To me, loving God and loving neighbor are just as interdependent. Together they form a whole life.

ALL SAINTS

Revelations 7:2–4, 9–14
1 John 3:1–3
Matthew 5:1–12a

I WROTE ABOUT the beatitudes way back in week four of Ordinary Time. There is no need to repeat here what I wrote there as you can read that again if you want to.

Why are we reading the beatitudes again on All Saints' Day? If we are going to repeat any portion of Matthew's gospel, the beatitudes would be it! A second reason is that these verses from Matthew are good road signs on the way toward sainthood.

Thomas Merton observed that all Christians are called to be saints. St. Paul takes this for granted in his epistles. In fact, sainthood should be our purpose in life if we are following Jesus. Is it possible? Yes, of course it is! Many people have been declared saints, and many more are saints even though unrecognized by the Church.

But is it possible to say to ourselves, "I want to be a saint" without feeling ridiculous? Is it false humility which makes us shrink from this? And if we have trouble saying this even to ourselves, imagine saying it to someone else!

We are far more comfortable saying, "I'm not a saint." And then fill in the blank. The next time you hear someone saying, "I'm not a saint," try countering it with "How do you know?"

THIRTY-SECOND SUNDAY ORDINARY TIME

Wisdom of Solomon 6:12–16
1 Thessalonians 4:13–18
Matthew 25:1–13

I HAVE A Lutheran friend who struggles with what he sees as his church's overemphasis on faith in Jesus at the expense of good works; he also fears that this approach risks excluding everyone who lacks faith. Today's gospel reading is perfect for him.

This parable is right up my alley as well. I confess to being too proud of planning ahead. It has something to do with hating unpleasant surprises that could have been avoided. This allegorical story is unique to Matthew, although it may be connected to hints in Luke 12:35–38: "Let your loins be girded and your lamps burning, and be like men who are waiting for their master to come home from the marriage feast, so that they may open to him at once when he comes and knocks."

The parable of the wise and foolish maidens comes in the chapter just before the beginning of Jesus's passion. This part of Matthew is filled with eschatological sayings from Jesus—that is, death, judgment, heaven, his second coming, and the end of time.

What does it mean to be wise, or *phrónimoi*? The word occurs in 1 Corinthians 10:15 where the RSV translates it as "sensible"; Hart uses "sagacious." These are helpful clues about how we should think about *phrónimoi*, viz. people who are wise in a practical sense. The word is used this way by Matthew in the masculine "twin" to this allegory, which comes just before it at Matthew

24:45–51. Strong believes it implies a "cautious" character, while Bauer adds "prudent and thoughtful" to the connotations.

The story has some apparent contradictions, and these suggest that the early Church, or Matthew's community, adapted the story Jesus taught to help them deal with a real problem they faced: the delay of the Parousia, or Jesus's return. We have often seen the Kingdom of God likened to a marriage feast. But does the bridegroom represent Jesus? Jeremias says envisioning the Messiah as a bridegroom is "quite foreign to the Old Testament and to Late Judaism."[89]

The main point seems to come in verse 13: "Watch therefore, for you know neither the day nor the hour." The original audience of the parable would have understood the point to be the unexpected suddenness of the bridegroom's return. This is a point Jesus made repeatedly. The parable of the rich fool in Luke 12:16–21 comes to mind. After the rich fool has made all his plans for a life of ease, God says to him, "Fool! This night your soul is required of you."

Because we do not know when we will face God's judgment, we need to be prepared right now. Jesus is comparing the kingdom of the heavens to the situation faced by the ten maidens. Part of the ambiguity in this story is the "already, not yet" character of the Kingdom. Jesus calls on everyone to make a decision immediately because the Kingdom has already arrived with his proclamation of the Good News. But an additional reason, after his death, is that he could return at any moment.

The early Church was troubled because Jesus did not return as quickly as they had hoped and expected. The danger was that the early fervor would cool, and for some it did. This probably led Matthew to see this parable as more about the "not yet" aspect of the Kingdom, so he included it with other stories about the Parousia, wanted us to see the bridegroom as Christ, and added the confusing bit about staying awake while we wait—which no one did—rather than sagaciously planning ahead for the unknown, which is what the five wise maidens did.

Why did not the wise girls share their oil with the foolish ones? Uncharitable of them, no? The oil the wise virgins took with them stands for good works in this allegory. St. Augustine believed the oil signifies charity.[90] If we know we are subject to God's judgment at some unknown time, we will be certain to perform some good works. On judgment day, I cannot share my good works with you: this is a matter of personal responsibility we each have to face on our own. That is the point of the story.

I take another helpful message from this week's gospel. It sometimes seems as though the spiritual life is so abstract that it is beyond the practical, everyday tasks we all have to do. This story is telling us the opposite. What could be more mundane than bringing some extra oil to a wedding party? Yet the failure to do so was decisive. This tells me that many of the seemingly humdrum, boring tasks I often don't feel like doing are precisely what I should be doing—such as buying extra eggs at the supermarket and then cooking them so I can bring hard-boiled eggs to our unhoused guests at St. Matthew's.

The story shows that faith alone is not enough. It seems to me faith and works are on a continuum, and the one will naturally lead to the other. All the virgins showed faith; they all showed up. But showing up, heedlessly going through the motions, is not enough. We have to take spiritual and moral preparation as seriously as we do planning for retirement, for a trip, all the practical aspects of life. If we do not, the bridegroom will tell us, "I do not know you," and we will not be able to join the party that is the Kingdom.

Notice the bridegroom does not condemn the foolish virgins but rather tells them, "I do not know you." This suggests the situation of those who, say, show up for Mass or go to church but who do not develop a relationship with Jesus, the Holy Spirit, or God. To me it suggests that we "get to know" God through faithfully performing many of the mundane tasks God calls upon us to do. This is so encouraging!

This week's gospel passage reminds me of another one in Matthew 7:21–23 that I think is worth quoting in full. Jesus is here talking to "the crowds": "Not everyone who says to me, 'Lord, Lord' shall enter the kingdom of heaven, but he who does the will of my Father who is in heaven. On that day many will say to me, 'Lord, Lord, did we not prophesy in your name, and cast out demons in your name, and do many mighty works in your name?' And then will I declare to them, 'I never knew you; depart from me, you evildoers.'"

Some discernment is essential: what is "the will of my Father who is in heaven"? Jesus is here warning us that even "religious" things like prophesying, casting out demons, and mighty works (miracles) may not cut it. God has to "know" us. What does this mean?

One analogy from human relationships is helpful here. I cannot get to know you unless you sometimes tell me what you are struggling with. This is the difference between small talk among acquaintances and the real talk that happens among friends. The same holds true with God. We have to be honest with God about our problems, ask for God's guidance and support, and be receptive to the answers (see appendix C).

We get to know God through prayer, reading the Bible, the sacraments, and regularly doing things we think the Spirit is telling us to do, even when—especially when—it makes us uncomfortable. It's a long journey, and trial and error are part of it. But I know from my own experience that if we spend time in silent prayer, we will receive messages about what to do, and if we do those things, we will come to know the Lord, and the Lord will come to know us.

This is where our first reading comes into play. It's a paean to Wisdom. Now, Israel had a long, rich Wisdom tradition and, as I mentioned back in week twenty-seven, Jesus's relationship to this tradition is ambivalent at best (see appendix E). However, the Christian tradition developed a connection between Wisdom and the Holy Spirit—Hagia Sophia in Greek, Sancta Sophia in Latin. Both mean "Holy Wisdom." The idea is that the Holy Spirit, the Spirit of Jesus, will lead us toward true wisdom.

I like the term and tradition of Holy Wisdom to distinguish it from worldly wisdom. They are related but definitely not the same. One of Jesus's problems with the Wisdom tradition of Israel was it had become too worldly.

What does this week's first reading add to our understanding of the wisdom of the "wise maidens"? The main point here is a practical one: to obtain Wisdom, we need to seek her. That seems obvious, but how do we do this? If we really love Wisdom, we will find ourselves staying up all night sometimes, or arising very early. That's what "watches for her at dawn . . . for her sake keeps vigil" means. Do we lose sleep over our pursuit of Wisdom? If we love and desire her, we will.

Staying up all night seeking wisdom—in other words, seeking guidance on what to do when we are faced with a difficult decision so we are worthy to enter the Kingdom—is sometimes important. For one thing, it shows we really are willing to make sacrifices to seek wisdom. But also, when I do it, I sometimes receive insights I would not receive if I stayed stuck to my daily routine. I write them down and check on them in the sober light of day. Roughly half the time, I believe I've got something, but many of the insights don't hold up.

Disrupting normal sleep patterns, i.e. a vigil, is akin to fasting, a disruption of normal eating patterns. Vigils, like fasts, have been traditional practices in many of the world's religions for thousands of years. These are methods people have used to hear God's voice. Why should we think our practice of Christianity today would be any different?

THIRTY-THIRD SUNDAY ORDINARY TIME

Proverbs 31:10–13, 19–20, 30–31
I Thessalonians 5:1–6
Matthew 25:14–30

I'VE ALWAYS LIKED today's gospel reading. But it is a mess! And a head scratcher. Let's start with the things that don't make sense.

Is the master supposed to be God? It seems so, because he punishes the "bad" servant materially and in an apparently supernatural way, condemning him to the "outer darkness" where people will "weep and gnash their teeth." And he rewards the good servants not only materially but perhaps transcendentally by saying, "Enter into the joy of your master."

The entire twenty-fourth and twenty-fifth chapters of Matthew are about the Parousia, Jesus's second coming, so the context of this parable tells us that Matthew identifies the return of the long-delayed master with Jesus. The departure of the master is Jesus's ascension, and Jesus's second coming is the master's return "after a long time," as Matthew's community struggled with the delay of the Parousia.

But the master CANNOT be Jesus! Because as the worthless servant says, the master is "a hard man, reaping where [he] did not sow, and gathering where [he] did not winnow." And the master himself repeats this insult! Jesus's entire message about the Father and the witness of his life contradicts the image of a greedy and merciless master. The Greek word we translate as "hard," *sklēròs*, has several other, harsher connotations. When applied to things, it can mean "rough" or "violent"; Bauer tells us that when applied to people, it means "hard, strict, harsh, cruel, merciless." In other words, the master is a rich, greedy bastard!

Does God, or Jesus, really want the rich to become richer and the poor poorer? Absolutely not! God would never say, "But from him who has not, even what he has will be taken away." Turning God into an anti-Robin Hood violates everything we know about the Law and the Prophets, and Jesus's own ministry.

The amount of money is another problem. Five talents was a lot of money, probably at least five thousand dollars in today's money. So why does the master tell his servant, "You have been faithful over a little, I will set you over much"? The rapacious master also demands his servant violate the Torah's prohibition on charging interest (cf. Exodus 22:25; Deuteronomy 23:19; Leviticus 25:36–7). Nowhere else is interest mentioned in the New Testament. It is inconceivable that Jesus would identify himself with anyone who punishes a servant for *not* charging interest.

What is going on here is essentially the same phenomenon we saw last week with the ten-maidens parable: Jesus's original challenge parable has been turned into a Parousia parable because by the time Matthew wrote his gospel, the delay of Jesus's return had become a big problem for the Christian community. Let's follow the same approach we used before and begin by rediscovering the original challenge parable.

The "bad guy" in this parable is still the servant who buried the talent. But his mistake is above all theological, and only as a result of this is it moral. The master is not the true God of Israel but rather a false conception of God stultifying God's people. The lazy servant's fear-filled vision of a merciless God is all wrong, and it squashes his spirit so that he buries what he has been given. What has he been given?

Despite the later exaggeration to five talents, the original amount of money is "little," as Matthew tells us twice in verses 21 and 23 and as Luke confirms in his version of this parable, where the amount of money is "very little" (cf. Luke 19:17). Along with NJBC, I suggest the money stands for religious tradition, as the word *parédōken* used in the command to "hand over" his possessions in verses 14, 20, 22 is a technical term for tradition.

Tradition is something that is "handed over" from generation to generation. Our word "tradition" is also based on the Latin *tradere*, to "hand on" or "betray"! The word "traitor" has the same Latin root. Fascinating that the root for handing on a tradition also means to betray it, because of course that ambivalence about the process is always accurate. Jesus's parable is, among other things, an illustration of the very perilous dangers involved in "handing on" tradition.

The failure of the "lazy" servant is not that he didn't make any money. His failure is that his fear of God's mercilessness led him to bury and hide from others the glory of God's Word. Sins of omission are likely to be our "secret sins" (Psalms 19:12), ones we are unaware of and hence the most dangerous of all. Burying the money meant the servant did absolutely nothing with it. He went on with his life as if nothing had happened. This behavior makes me conclude that he never really had anything at all. Because if God's Word truly lives inside us, doing nothing with it is simply impossible. I think of Matthew 5:14–16:

> YOU ARE THE light of the world. A city set upon a hill cannot be hidden. Neither do they light a lamp and place it under a dry-goods basket, but rather they place it upon lampstand, and it illumines all who are in the house. So let your light shine out before humanity, so that they may see your good works and may glorify your Father in the heavens.

The challenge Jesus is throwing at his audience of Jewish religious leaders is urgent: *It's later than you think! Act now before it is too late.* He made this point repeatedly throughout his ministry to those he met.

The richness of this parable is further revealed when we remember that "fear of the Lord" is always a good thing in the Old Testament, as in "Be not wise in your own eyes; fear the Lord and turn away from evil" (Prov 3:7). This is a typical example found throughout the Wisdom tradition. You can find it in the Torah as well: in Leviticus 25:17 and Deuteronomy 31:12–13. But, the parable seems to be warning us, too much of a good thing is a bad thing. While fear of the Lord is recommended often, far more often we can find what is perhaps the most common command in the whole Bible, Old and New Testaments: "Do not be afraid." The references here are too numerous to list, but Genesis 15:1 and Luke 1:30 are typical.

The parable might well have been a challenge especially to the archconservative Sadducees who blocked the kind of creative development of Jewish tradition that Jesus stood for. But the Pharisees also were strict interpreters of Torah.

Given Jesus's hostility to Jewish religious leaders, it is not surprising that the original parable would be a challenge to religious leaders. What is somewhat surprising is that two of the servants come off very well in the parable. Perhaps we are to see them as contrasts to the "lazy" servant, as examples of what one should do with religious tradition—namely, to take some risks with it. Jesus certainly did.

Seeing the money as a symbol for religious tradition makes sense of the punishment given to the fearful (a more accurate label than "lazy," I believe) servant. God is not stealing money from the poor to give to the rich; the parable is about spiritual, not material, life. Jesus is warning us, "If your faith-action is so hamstrung by fear that you bury it, you will lose it. On the other hand, if your faith empowers you to take risks, it will grow."

This parable is like last's week story of the ten maidens in two ways. First, both see faith as intrinsically linked to what we do with it. (Maybe "faith-action," as I wrote above.) Second, both suggest that weak faith-action is perilous. We can count on our faith-action being tested. Failure to act can weaken our faith, just as weak faith can paralyze action.

The delay of the master in the original parable was not the main point; it was necessary in order to give the servants time to show what they would do with their money, with the trust they had received from the master. Matthew has seized on the delay of the master as key to the story. As with the ten maidens, he has again turned an original challenge parable into a Parousia parable. We have seen this phenomenon so often now that I begin to think the early Church was almost traumatized by the delay in Jesus's return. Let's think about this.

At first, I was critical of Matthew and the other gospel writers for playing so fast and loose with the parables of Jesus. But now I sympathize with these writers and even think they have something to teach us. It seems as if anytime anyone is delayed in a parable, they thought, "That must be Jesus!" They looked for help with their powerful disappointment anywhere they could find it. It makes me feel how intensely they longed for his return, and this makes me love them. Do we long for Jesus's return as much as they did?

A second lesson we could learn from them is not to be too afraid to adapt Jesus's sayings to our own situation and our own needs. That's what Matthew and his community did. And is that not precisely the message of today's parable anyway? Be creative, take risks, don't bury the tradition out of fear.

Many commentators believe that when, in verse 30, the master calls for the worthless servant to be punished a second time and cast into the outer darkness where there will be weeping and gnashing of teeth, it refers to eternal damnation. I doubt this additional punishment was part of the original parable. The master has already punished the worthless servant by taking away his money, symbolic of trust, faith-action, and tradition. I believe this punishment is original.

The punishment of verse 30 was probably added when the parable was interpreted eschatologically by the early Church. In any case, I see nothing in verse 30 that leads me to think it has anything at all to do with *eternal* damnation. I think we are reading that into the story. It is more plausible to see exile to the outer darkness as a temporary measure, akin to purgatory.

After all, if eternal punishment is really a possibility should we make a mistake with the tradition handed on to us, would not burying it to avoid this risk be a reasonable response? You cannot tell people not to be afraid and at the same time threaten them with eternal torture. In fact, the message of this parable is itself another powerful argument *against* belief in a hell of eternal punishment.

CHRIST THE KING

Ezekiel 34:11–12, 15–17
1 Corinthians 15:20–26, 28
Matthew 25:31–46

THIS BEAUTIFUL PASSAGE from St. Matthew is our unofficial motto at my parish's Monday-morning program serving unhoused people and others who need help. The reading is concerned with a concrete, practical question, and in order to understand it aright, we need to begin with two questions. First, who is Jesus talking to, and second, who is Jesus talking about?

Jesus is here talking to his disciples privately in the culmination of his eschatological discourse that began back in 24:1. Matthew places this just before the beginning of Jesus's passion, so his death is imminent. After Jesus predicts the destruction of the Temple, the disciples ask him in 24:3, "Tell us, when will this be, and what will be the sign of your coming and of the close of the age?"

Jesus is talking about what will happen to all the Gentiles of the world at the last judgment. We know this because of the words in verse 32: "all the nations" will be gathered before the Son of Man. The plural "nations" means Gentiles, as distinct from Israel.

Jesus, his disciples, and the early Church were seemingly convinced that Jesus's second coming and the last judgment would happen very soon, before the gospel had time to spread very far. That means the question boils down to this: "What will happen in the last judgment to all the people who have never heard of you, Jesus? Will they be punished for lack of faith in their savior?" Jeremias tells us this was the common view in Jesus's time.[91] Our passage exists only in Matthew, but Jeremias also believes the answer Jesus gave here is of such startling originality that it must have been from the Master himself.

The question of what will happen to people who have not heard of him is, if anything, even more important today than it was in Jesus's time, despite the global spread of Christianity. We know throughout history there have been many people who never heard the gospel. Moreover, we may well ask what it means to be unaware of the gospel message. Many people today may have heard such distorted versions of Jesus that they might as well be as unaware of him as the Incas were when the Spanish arrived.

Jesus distinguished between justification of sinners in his lifetime and eschatological justification. He welcomed sinners, mediating God's forgiveness to the "lost children of Israel," and invited them into the kingdom whose arrival he proclaimed. On the other hand, he promised God's justification at the last judgment to those of his disciples who were found worthy of him, and the demands here are severe: open confession of him, even at the risk of martyrdom (Matthew 10:32ff, par.), obedience (Matthew 7:21ff, par.), readiness to forgive (Matthew 6:14ff), merciful love (Matthew 5:7), and endurance to the end (Matthew 13:13, par.).

That is a demanding list of requirements! Obviously, some of them, such as open confession of him, would be impossible for those who had never even heard of him. As I argue in appendix A and below, there are many good reasons to believe those found wanting at the last judgment are not condemned to a hell of eternal torment. Instead, they may need to be purified by a temporary form of punishment in preparation for eternal life with God.

Our passage this week reveals that Matthew 7:21–27 appears to shape Jesus's vision of the final judgment. In the Matthew 7 passage, it is clear that what matters is not lip service, saying "Lord, Lord," but rather doing the will "of [his] Father who is in heaven." Jesus here spells out six of the seven traditional corporal works of mercy as an illustrative, but probably not exhaustive, list of what he means by doing his Father's will. (Burying the dead is the seventh corporal work of mercy not included here.)

The NJBC points out that "visit" the sick weakens the force of the word it translates, *episkeptomai*, because this word means to "care for" or "nurse." The assumption would be the sick person is alone and without anyone to care for him or her. Aside from this, these acts of loving of service, of a faith that is lived, speak so powerfully and clearly that we need say no more about them.

This passage is another reminder of the often-concealed dangers posed by sins of omission. If you are like me, you are more worried about being judged for the bad things you have done. Yet those on the left hand of Jesus have apparently done nothing wrong. Rather, they failed to do what was good, and for that they are condemned.

Still, the reason to perform these acts of loving service to those in need is not to ward off punishment. That's too negative and fear soaked. Doing the right thing for the wrong reason is not what Jesus is talking about. Notice the humility and proper motivation of the blessed ones. They are astonished at their benediction! They did not act out of a selfish desire for salvation, nor are they especially proud of their good works. They didn't see Jesus in the poor folk they served, because they have never even heard of him. They were moved by compassion and found reward enough in simply serving those in need.

The reward for serving others is intrinsic to the behavior; it is not some external reward. The people we are serving will notice and care whether we are doing it because we care for them or because we really care about something else.

This beautiful passage is about those who don't know Jesus,

but it applies to those of us who do as well because it associates service to the needy with love of Christ. It means we all need to find some kind of corporate work of mercy and do it regularly. This list is probably not exhaustive; there may well be other ways to serve those in need, but this is a good place to start. We need to use some discernment about what we can do and what gives us joy. Because if what we are doing does not give us joy, it's not right for us, and we will not be able to sustain it. This is where our relationship with the Spirit of Jesus and prayer are so important.

For years now I have found joy in bringing a dozen or two hard-boiled eggs and grapes every Monday to our homeless guests and buying winter coats and clothes for them when it gets cold. I like the home-based ritual of boiling the eggs for them on Sunday, and then putting them into my bike's panniers Monday morning. It's not all that hard to do, really, but that's what makes it possible, joyful, for me to do it every week. I also enjoy watching my friends take an egg or two as they go through the line. Eggs are nutritious, and they can keep an extra to eat later. I believe it is an act perched between the symbolic and . . . whatever the opposite of symbolic is!

Winter is an especially hard time for the homeless. They have no way to store winter clothes during the summer, and no home to shelter them from the cold. I have found a kind merchant who sells me winter hats, gloves, thermal underwear, and coats at cost because I buy large quantities and he knows they are for the unhoused. It is simply unacceptable that in a nation and city as rich as ours, as many as one hundred people without a home die each year in Washington, DC, many due to hypothermia. Until we execute a solution to that, I will keep buying winter clothing.

These are relatively small acts; that is not the point for me. What I find important is to start with something I can manage and which gives me joy. Once we start down this path, the Spirit will likely guide us to additional ways to serve that bring joy.

After years of jobs where the results of my work were sometimes hard to see, I needed to find something different, where I can directly experience the consequence of what I do and be certain it is good. There can never be anything wrong with giving healthy food to someone in need.

When the Son of Man speaks of serving "the least of these my brethren," is he referring only to Christians? No, he means everyone. First, notice that the word "brethren" is dropped in verse 45. More important, as we noted above, the Son of Man is talking about the Gentiles throughout the entire world, most of whom presumably have never heard of Jesus. Where are they going to find Christians to serve?

A thornier problem is posed by the final verse, which speaks of the ultimate destiny for those who did, and did not, serve the needy: "And they will go away into eternal punishment, but the righteous into eternal life."

This verse is taken as the strongest scriptural support for the notion that hell is a place of never-ending torture for the damned. I believe the universalist position is more in line with the biblical witness, which means I believe that ultimately all people will be saved and no one will be consigned to eternal torment. (That said, because God is mystery and we are talking about the end of time, I cannot claim to *know* what will happen.) I discuss this important issue in more detail in appendix A.

Here I will limit myself to exploring the meaning of this final verse, as well as the first reading from Ezekiel. We translate *kólasin* as "punishment," but what kind of punishment? It turns out the Greek word can have the sense of corrective or disciplinary punishment. This would imply that, yes, these people will be punished, but in order to be purified and made worthy for eternal life with God. In other words, as I've suggested, something akin to purgatory. However, *kólasin* is ambiguous in its meaning, and according to Abbott-Smith, it can simply mean punishment without any connotation of its being corrective at all.

Then there is *aiōnion*, which is usually translated as "eternal," and which we've discussed previously. But this word is even more ambiguous in its meaning than *kólasin*. The English word "eon" best captures the full range of meanings in *aiōnion*. And this is no accident, because "eon" comes from the Greek *aiōnion*. The English word refers to a very long time, an indefinite period. It can also mean eternity.

I believe the ambiguity inherent in both these Greek words has been lost in translation. When we read Matthew 25:46, in most English translations it sounds like a perfect "proof text" for the notion that there is a hell where the damned are punished forever. When we look at the Greek text, the issue is far from clear, however.

I am not suggesting that this argument by itself settles the question of universal salvation. I am suggesting that when advocates for hell cite this verse as the strongest support in the Bible for their position, they are "leaning on a broken reed." There are far more biblical passages that speak of an ultimate universal salvation after death, judgment, and punishment.

The first reading from Ezekiel sounds like a perfect description of Jesus's mission. He sought out the lost children of Israel, and he often uses pastoral imagery. All is going well until we run into verse 16, translated by the NAB this way: "But the sleek and the strong I will destroy, shepherding them rightly."

Alas, that I do not know Hebrew! But it seems as though once again we are caught up in a translation problem, this time one based on textual differences. The RSV translates the passage this way: "And the fat and the strong I will watch over; I will feed them justice." A footnote tells us that "destroy" is found in the Septuagint, the Greek version of the Old Testament.

I think we can safely conclude that our first reading confirms the shepherding image of the gospel, as well as its ambiguity about the eternal destiny of those condemned at the last judgment.

ABBREVIATIONS

ACCS=Manlio Simonetti (ed.), *Ancient Christian Commentary on Scripture* (vols. 1a and 1b, Downers Grove, 2001)

AS=G. Abbot-Smith, *A Manual Lexicon of the New Testament* (New York, 1922) Used online at: https://gntreader.com

NAB=New American Bible text from the revised Sunday Lectionary. Used in Vatican II Sunday Missal (Boston, 1998)

NDoT=Joseph A. Komanchak; Mary Collins; Dermot A. Lane (eds.), *The New Dictionary of Theology* (Wilmington, 1988)

NJBC=Raymond E. Brown, S.S.; Joseph A. Fitzmyer, S.J.; Roland E. Murphy, O. Carm. (eds.), *The New Jerome Bible Commentary* (Englewood Cliffs, 1990)

Par.=parallel passages found in all three synoptic gospels. If the parallel passage is found in only one other gospel, I indicate the gospel where it is found, e.g. par. Luke indicates the parallel passage can be found only in Luke.

RSV=Revised Standard Version, a translation of the Bible. Used in *The Oxford Annotated Bible With the Apocrypha* (New York, 1965)

TNT=David Bentley Hart, *The New Testament: A Translation*, by David Bentley Hart (New Haven, 2017)

TASBS=David Bentley Hart, *That All Shall be Saved* (New Haven, 2019)

APPENDIX A

Universalism

DOES JESUS THREATEN to punish those who reject him and his message with eternal torture in hell?

This is a question that has bothered me ever since I began to take the Good News—the gospel—seriously. Because how is that good news? The traditional Old Testament view was that those who died went to a mysterious, shadowy place called Sheol: not a great place, but not a place of eternal torment either. The ancient Israelites did not believe in life after death; their views on this subject did not differ from their Mesopotamian neighbors, according to the NJBC.[92] Sheol, described vividly in Isaiah 14, "is not a form of survival but a denial of survival." It is no more than "a vast tomb where the bodies of the dead lie inert."

The view that life ends with the death of our physical body was the standard view in the ancient world, and it is the default belief of the modern secular world as well. From this point of departure, Jesus's promise of eternal life is certainly good news.

The catch would be that if you do not have faith in Jesus and do not lead a righteous life, you may be condemned to a hell of everlasting punishment. This is what "infernalists" believe. But if this is the case, I do not see how Jesus's message is good news. We cannot conceive of anything worse than spending eternity in the agony of hellfire. Even to present this as a possibility we need to worry about seems cruel. I felt tempted to say to God, "You can keep your so-called 'good news,' your conditional promise of eternal life, if the price is the risk of eternal punishment." Is it not better, as so many contemporary secular people have decided, to live our lives as best we can and accept death as final?

Moreover, Jesus's message is one of healing, love, and peace. How can his vision of a loving, merciful God be reconciled with a God who would condemn me and others to eternal damnation?

Yet I accepted the possibility of hell for many years. I assumed it was biblical, and that Jesus had indeed threatened the wicked and the unbelievers with this kind of punishment. In addition, I had too many suspicions that rejecting hell was part of a larger theological trend in contemporary liberal Christianity I wanted no part of.

The trend I refer to is watering down the Christian message to make it more appealing to more people. American Christianity is often tempted to equate the gospel with success, our sacred "pursuit of happiness," and prosperity. Do not mega-churches, and their well-paid pastors, depend upon giving large numbers of people (or consumers of religion) what they want?

America likes to see itself as a Christian country. But how can Jesus's message of nonviolence be reconciled with American militarism? How can his ethic of humble service to the poor and the outcast be squared with our capitalist consumer economy that is destroying the planet and creating vast income inequality? How often do we hear from the pulpit of our need to forgive and love our enemies?

I saw the rejection of hell as part of this broader effort to ignore Jesus's hard teachings to make his message more popular. Still, I was troubled by the apparent contradiction of Jesus's Good News with the threat of hellfire. Then I read David Bentley Hart's *That All Shall Be Saved*. This book helped convince me of the merits of the universalist position.

Universalists believe we are all going to be judged by God. They also believe in hell, but not in its eternity. They believe that every human person will *eventually* be saved and live eternally with God. David Bentley Hart has no doubt this is the case. My reflections on the gospels here are informed by this conviction.

However, I part company with David Bentley Hart to some extent. I believe the universalist position has greater scriptural support and far stronger theological arguments in its favor than the infernalist view. On the other hand, God is mystery, and when it comes to what will happen at the end of time, I believe it is appropriate for human reason to maintain its humility.

While biblical support for a hell of eternal punishment is weak, the record is somewhat ambiguous, as we will see below. This is a second reason I shrink from absolute certainty about universalism.

A third concern raised by universalism is ethical. When it comes to our final judgment, I want to avoid two perilous extremes. On the one hand lies the sin of despair: we are convinced our sins can never be forgiven, we are lost and damned forever, so there is no point in trying to live or live well. On the other hand lies the sin of presumption: we are certain we will be saved no matter what we do, so we do not try to avoid sins. Of course, if I am a universalist, I can believe people can be condemned to the punishment of hell for a very long time, just not forever. This greatly mitigates, in my mind, the fear of presumption. Still, there are moral reasons, in addition to theological ones, for us to shrink from the absolute certainty David Bentley Hart seems to have that universalism is true.

Nevertheless, I believe the arguments in favor of universalism are far more persuasive than the ones put forward by infernalists. If you are troubled by this position, I recommend you read Hart's book. Because the infernalist position has been so dominant for so long, at least in Western Christianity, I am going to try to summarize his book in what follows.

The first blow struck against my former belief in hell was the discovery that universalism is actually an ancient and traditional, not a modern, position.[93] In fact, the universalist position was at its most widespread in the Church's first half millennium, according to the historical evidence Hart relies upon. Universalists were not in the minority, either, at least in many places, particularly in the East. Universalists did believe in hell, though they saw it as we envision purgatory: a place where those who need it must go to be purified, as described by St. Paul in 1 Corinthians 3.

This changed everything for me! The argument that abandoning belief in an eternal hell was tied up with the great modern watering down of Christianity no longer had any merit. I agree with G. K. Chesterton that tradition is the democracy of the dead. The notion that universalism is a traditional view held by many ancient Christians who lived closer to our savior in time and place than I leveled the playing field.

But what about the Bible? It seemed to me the New Testament was filled with references to a hell of eternal punishment for those who rejected Jesus and broke his commandments. Reading Hart's book was a reminder of how our theological preconceptions can color our reading of Scripture, especially when we rely on translations.

We can begin by pointing out that the whole idea of an eternal hell of punishment is entirely absent from St. Paul's letters. On the contrary, as I indicate in the first Sunday of Lent, St. Paul writes that all are saved because of Jesus Christ (cf. Rom 5:18). We need to remember that although St. Paul did not know the historical Jesus, his letters were written well before the gospels and therefore are closer in time to the historical Jesus.

Most "damning" (pun intended) of all for the eternal-hell-of-ingenious-tortures position is that there is no single Greek word for such a hell in the New Testament!

There is frequent mention of the realm of the dead, Hades, which is generally understood as being located under the earth—

and which in Hebrew is called Sheol. This is where, according to venerable belief, practically all the dead await the end of time.[94]

For example, in Luke 16:19–31 both the rich man and Lazarus are placed in Hades, although they occupy very different regions in that place. Hart does not point out that the rich man says in verse 25, "I am in agony in this flame," although Hart does translate the verse this way in his translation of the New Testament. This suggests Luke's Hades, unlike Sheol, may have been seen as a place of punishment, at least for some of the departed. But there is no reason to assume this punishment is eternal. Furthermore, Lazarus and the patriarch Abraham are also in Hades, and they are both seen as blessed men who are not being punished at all. We will return to this point below.

Finally, we come across "the Gehenna," the Greek form of Ge-Hinnom, "Valley of Hinnom." This term appears eleven times in the synoptic gospels, and only once more in the New Testament, in the Letter of James. Hart asserts that if there is any word in the New Testament that comes close to what we understand to be hell today, this would be it. The RSV translates Gehenna as "hell" but with a footnote indicating the Greek work.

But does Gehenna really correspond to what we understand hell to be? The first reason to doubt that it does is that unlike hell, Gehenna is an actual place on earth that can be seen with one's own eyes. It is southwest of Jerusalem, and Hart points out its terrain "is not particularly inviting, but neither is it particularly infernal." It is not clear why by Christ's time it had become a metaphor for a place of divine judgment, punishment, and purification, usually after death.

A crucial point is that Gehenna is a place on earth used *as a metaphor* for a range of possible meanings tied to divine judgment and different kinds of punishment, whereas the English word "hell" is not a metaphor; it is not a physical place on earth but rather denotes a (supposed) metaphysical reality of eternal damnation and torment. "Gehenna" and "hell" have different meanings.

We do not even know with any certainty what connotations Gehenna may have had for Jesus or his listeners in first-century Palestine. Hart writes,

> CLEARLY IT WAS understood sometimes as a place of final destruction, sometimes simply as a place of punishment, and sometimes as a place of purgatorial regeneration. Certainly no one now can say with any confidence precisely what Jesus's understanding of the Gehenna's fire was (no matter how adamant the infernalist party may wax in their assertions to the contrary), or what duration he might have assigned to those subjected to it, or even how metaphorically he intended such imagery to be taken.[95]

Jesus spoke in parables; he used prophetic and apocalyptic language all the time, so it would be rash to assume that any time he spoke about Gehenna, we must interpret him literally. Hart concludes it is impossible to know whether the metaphor of Gehenna should be interpreted as one of annihilation or purification: Jesus's metaphors can be interpreted either way.

Sometimes Jesus uses metaphors that seem to imply annihilation (cf. Mattjew 10:28 and, it is thought, most conclusively Matthew 25:46). The latter verse is translated by the RSV, "And they will go away into eternal punishment, but the righteous into eternal life." This is the favorite proof text used by infernalists to support their view that Jesus threatens us all with a hell of eternal punishment.

One problem with this translation, as Hart points out in his own translation of the New Testament, is that the word translated as "punishment," *kolasis*, originally meant "pruning," and then came to mean "punishment" but with the connotation of "correction." This form of punishment of limited duration is what we normally associate with purgatory. It is true that by the time of the New Testament, the word could mean any kind of legal punishment, "but the word's special connotation of corrective rather than retributive punishment was still appreciated and observed by educated writers for centuries after the time of Christ."[96] Rather than slam-dunk support for a hell of eternal punishment, we have something far more ambiguous.

A second problem with the RSV translation is that the word translated to mean "eternal" is *aionion*. As Hart points out in the postscript to his translation, the root of this word is *aion* or *aeon*. I think it is helpful to think of the word as akin to the English word "eon," because, after all, this English word comes from the Greek! In English, "eon" can mean a really long time, an indefinite period of time, or eternity. And that ambiguity, that range of meanings, corresponds to the Greek word's meaning.

Therefore, to translate the words of Matthew 25:46 simply as "eternal punishment" obscures the ambiguity of both words! Moreover, this simplistic equation of *aion* with "eternity" is repeated throughout most English translations of the New Testament.

We now have three words that are far more ambiguous in Greek than in the English used to translate them: *Gehenna* (hell), *aion* (eternal), and *kolasis* (punishment). If you thought that a hell of eternal punishment was clearly supported by the Bible, you need to stop relying on English translations and go back to the original Greek! It begins to look to me as though the folks doing the translating read their own theological presuppositions into the translations.

I know this problem well. Until I was convinced by universalism, I read the Bible the same way, bringing my own theology into my interpretation of the text. Hart does a good job in his book of putting before us the many texts that support universalism—there are far more of these than there are passages that point toward eternal hellfire.[97]

One example of this is Matthew 18:34–35, the story of the unjust steward whose huge debt was forgiven but who in his turn threw his debtors into prison. Jesus tells us that his master then put his steward into prison "until he should repay everything owing to him." Jesus concludes by saying his heavenly Father will do the same to us unless we forgive one another. This is punishment that is corrective, not eternal. Luke 12:47–48 and 59 expresses a similar idea of punishment that is suited to the crime and of limited duration. Hart concludes, "Nowhere [in the Bible] is there any description of a kingdom of perpetual cruelty presided over by Satan, as though he were a kind of chthonian god."[98]

St. Paul's letters are full of universalist references, while the doctrine of a hell of eternal torment is totally absent. For example, 1 Corinthians 15:22 states, "For just as in Adam all die, so also in Christ all will be given life." Other such verses abound (viz. 2 Corinthians 5:14; Ephesians 1:9–10; Romans 11:32).

We can find plenty of support for universalism in the non-Pauline epistles as well. First John 2:2: "And he is atonement for our sins, and not only for ours, but for the whole cosmos." Or 2 Peter 3:9. Then there is 1 Timothy 4:10: "we have hoped in a living God who is the savior of all human beings, especially those who have faith." As Hart asks, what is the meaning of that word, "especially"? Are the faithful "especially" saved? Or is it rather that those who have faith are those who especially hope in a living God who is the savior of all human beings?

God's universal salvific will is established Catholic doctrine (see the *Catechism of the Catholic Church*, 1037), and it has support in 1 Timothy 2:3–6: "our savior God, who intends all human beings to be saved and to come to a full knowledge of truth. For there is one God, and also one mediator of God and human beings: a human being, the Anointed One Jesus, who gave himself as liberation fee for all."

Can God will something so important to be the case but then be defeated by mere human will? According to the catechism, the Church teaches that hell exists and that it is eternal. However, the Church has never held that anyone actually is in hell. In fact, we may pray and hope that it is empty, along with the famous twentieth-century Catholic theologian Hans Urs von Balthasar.

John's gospel also has quite a few passages supporting universalism: 12:32; 12:47; 17:2. My favorite is 12:32, which Hart translates, "And I, when I am lifted up from the earth, will drag everyone to me." I like the verb "drag" here, as it suggests that some people are coming to Jesus unwillingly. An important assumption of the infernalist position is that the dignity of our free will means we may be subject to eternal hellfire if we choose badly and reject Christ's salvation. John 12:32 confronts this assumption head-on and tells us, "No! Christ's power is greater than your so-called free will."

Luke 16:16 expresses a similar idea: "Until John, there were the Law and the Prophets; since then the good tidings of God's kingdom are being proclaimed, and everyone is being forced into it."

Christians believe in free will, and so do I. But especially in modern times, we are aware of the limits to our freedom. We are conditioned by our culture, society, economy, family upbringing, education, and psychological maladies. And then there is the vast realm of the unconscious. Finally, as Jesus pointed out from the cross when he asked God to forgive the greatest sin in history, ignorance—lack of full knowledge of what we are doing—can so reduce our freedom that forgiveness is what is appropriate.

When I look back on many decisions I made years ago, I certainly see how I fall into the category of not knowing what I was doing. These decisions were freely made, but because I lacked both self-knowledge and knowledge of what I was doing and the context, the decisions seem distant from the person I am today. This makes it easier to forgive the bad decisions. I am certain we all see our past this way. Now imagine how God, with perfect knowledge of everything, will look at our decisions.

Therefore, as Hart argues, it is incommensurate with the limitations imposed on human freedom to punish us eternally because of our bad decisions.[99] Our decisions are made in time; for the punishment to fit the crime, the penalty for them should as well.

What then does Jesus say about eschatology (the last things)—that is, death, judgment, heaven, hell, and his second coming? My point of departure for answering this question is that Jesus did not know precisely what happens to us after death nor when he will come again in glory. In his full humanity, Jesus would have imperfect knowledge of what happened in historical time, in the immanent frame. On the other hand, the universalist position maintains that all will be saved *at the end of time*. This means that for universalists, it is possible some people might be punished in hell until the end of time. As God, Jesus would have known about eternal realities, as they transcend historical time. Why did he not tell us clearly what would happen to us? We cannot know. It is another reason I part company with David Bentley Hart's certainty about universalism.

Some infernalists might believe that based on Jesus's words in the gospel, some people are condemned to eternal punishment as soon as they die. I used to believe this. Now I will argue that Jesus did not know what will happen to us when we die, nor the precise details of heaven, hell, or when time will end. I base this on my reading of Scripture and on the Christological doctrine that Jesus is both true God and true man. One of the most important scriptural passages is the kenosis St. Paul discusses in Philippians 2:5–8, where the apostle tells us that the second person of the Trinity "emptied himself" to take on human form. For a full explanation of the kenosis and my Christology, please see appendix B.

Another important text supporting the idea that Jesus did not have precise information about the last things is Matthew 24:36 (par. Mark 13:32). After Jesus has described his second coming, he says, "But about that day and hour no one knows—neither the angels of the heavens nor the Son—except the Father only."

Jesus does appear to hazard a guess about the timing of the Second Coming in Matthew 24:34 and par. when he declares, "Amen, I tell you that this generation most definitely does not pass away until all these things happen." But the problem here is that he is wrong! As NJBC drily observes, "This is a troublesome verse."[100] While Jesus's resurrection and the fall of Jerusalem in 70 AD partially fulfill the Parousia, neither fulfills "all these things," viz. "the Son of Man coming upon the clouds of the sky with power and great glory" (Matthew 24:30). Moreover, does not Jesus's prediction in verse 34 contradict his confession in verse 36 that only the Father knows when Jesus will come again?

A likely explanation for this difficulty, offered by NJBC, is that Mark and Matthew are attempting to answer the difficulty of Jesus's erroneous prediction that "all these things" will happen within a generation. These evangelists recognize that "only God knows" when Jesus will come again—because by the time they wrote, Jesus's prediction had turned out wrong.

I recognize I have been discussing the mixed messages the evangelists have given us about when the Parousia will take place rather than what happens to us after we die. Yet the Parousia, heaven, hell, and judgement are all related; all are eschatological realities. And just as the New Testament gives us ambiguous information about the Parousia, the same holds true for what it tells us about life after death.

This is a final reason to believe Jesus did not know definitively what happens to us after death within time: the New Testament is filled with texts, including the ones I have cited but many more, that are contradictory. As Hart points out, we can cite verses that seem to promise salvation to all and place beside them others that speak of a future judgment between the righteous and the wicked and an eschatological exclusion or destruction of evildoers.[101] The fact that Jesus speaks of eschatological reality with poetic metaphors that seem contradictory tells me he did not know for certain what was going to happen.

If Jesus did not impart precise information about heaven, hell, death, judgment, and the Second Coming, how do we make sense of the eschatology we read about in the gospels?

I concur with Hart's formulation. His way of understanding the Bible is important as it not only makes sense of the apparent contradictions we have noted but also lays out the framework for how and when "all shall be saved."

According to this view, based on an older approach elaborated by Origen and Gregory of Nyssa,

> THE TWO SIDES of the New Testament's eschatological language represent not two antithetical possibilities tantalizingly or menacingly dangled before us, but rather two different moments within a seamless narrative, two distinct eschatological horizons, one enclosed within the other. In this way of seeing the matter, one set of images marks the furthest limit of the immanent course of history, and the division therein—right at the threshold between this age and the "Age to come" (*'olam ha-ba*, in Hebrew)—between those who have surrendered to God's love and those who have not; and the other set refers to that final horizon of all horizons, "beyond all ages," where even those who have traveled as far from God as it is possible to go, through every possible self-imposed hell, will at the last find themselves in the home to which they are called from

everlasting, their hearts purged of every last residue of hatred and pride.[102]

Hart believes this framework makes sense of 1 Corinthians 15:23–28. We read there of three stages, the first two in the immanent frame of history; the final stage is beyond the end of time and history. Christ is the "first fruits," and I take this to mean Christ's resurrection, which has already happened in history. The second moment in history is when Christ comes again in glory, and at this point all who belong to Christ are exalted (15:23). This period is when Christ reigns, and it ends only when Christ has destroyed every rule, authority, and power (15:24).

The third moment is beyond the end of time and history when the Kingdom is given over to the Father, and only then is when "all shall be saved," as explained in the final verse, 28: "And when all things have been subordinated to him, then will the Son himself also be subordinated to the one who has subordinated all things to him, so that God may be all in all."

One final reason to affirm universalism has nothing to do with Scripture but instead with interfaith dialogue. Or dialogue with those of no faith. If I believe everyone who rejects Jesus will burn in hell forever, it is going to color the way I relate to those outside the faith—and not in a good way. It will make it more difficult for us to have a dialogue based on mutual respect. Conversely, if my dialogue partners know I think they are going to hell because of our differences, it is likely to antagonize them.

Confident that all will ultimately be saved no matter what we believe or do not believe in this life, universalism allows believers to have peaceful, respectful dialogues with everyone who is not a believer in Jesus as the Son of God.

APPENDIX B

Christology

THROUGHOUT THESE MEDITATIONS, I emphasize Jesus's full humanity, and especially his lack of precise and certain knowledge of the historical future. In what follows I want to explain why.

The big picture answer is that I am assuming most of you reading this book are regular churchgoers, as otherwise you would not be so interested in reading about the Scripture you hear every Sunday. Assuming this to be true, I agree with Karl Rahner, the great twentieth-century century Catholic theologian, who wrote the typical mistake of the faithful is to believe in Jesus's divinity at the expense of his full humanity. My experience confirms this judgment, along with the inverse: the difficulty of those outside the Church is to believe in Jesus's divinity.

I recall a conversation I had years ago with a devout young Catholic woman about the controversial movie *The Temptations of Christ*. I am not certain it is a good movie, but I argued it is not problematic to affirm that Jesus experienced sexual temptation. I referred to Hebrews 4:15: "For we have not a high priest who is unable to sympathize with our weaknesses, but one who in every respect has been tempted as we are, yet without sinning."

When confronted with this Scripture passage, she replied, "I don't care what the Bible says! Jesus was never tempted in that way."

One reason to emphasize Jesus's humanity is simply to

restore some balance to the equation. A second reason has to do with my background as a moral theologian. If we deny that Jesus was a human being just like us, it lets us off the hook: "You can't expect me to forgive my tormentors, as Jesus did. I'm not the Son of God, but just a human being."

Jesus is God's Word to us. God the Father created us, and Jesus is God's way of telling us, "This is how to live: I created you to live this way. If you follow Jesus's pattern, you will be in harmony with the human nature I have given you." If we allow ourselves to think Jesus was not just like us in every way except for never sinning, he can no longer function as a model on how to live a truly human life in accord with our God-given human nature.

The Christian belief in the Incarnation, the doctrine that Jesus is both true God and true man, is, for most of us, the most difficult of all dogmas to believe. I am convinced, however, that if we hold fast to Jesus's full humanity, it is far easier to believe in his divinity than vice versa.

Take, for example, the question of whether Jesus had full and precise knowledge of the future. For God, there is no before or after; time is not linear, proceeding in one direction from present to future, as it is for us. God lives in eternity, and of course God is omniscient. God not only "knows" the future but is actually present in the future, as if it were now.

I maintain that the historical Jesus had no such knowledge of the future. One scriptural warrant for this position is Philippians 2:7, the kenosis. St. Paul writes that although Jesus subsisted in God's form, when he was incarnated as the son of Mary, he "emptied himself" of divine attributes and took on the shape of a human being.

I would add to this scriptural support one borne by my own lived experience. It is essential to our humanity that we do not know what will happen in the future. Or perhaps it is better to say that it would be inhuman for anyone to know the future. I cannot imagine having a truly human relationship with such a creature. Can you?

Several gospel passages suggest Jesus did know what would happen in the future. We are concerned primarily here with Jesus's predictions of his death and resurrection. Several considerations ought to make us cautious about reading these texts as clear, precise prophecies of what would befall Jesus in Jerusalem.

First, we all have some sense of what is likely to happen, and Jesus is no exception.

In view of the mounting opposition against him, especially among the aristocratic priests and laity in Jerusalem, Jesus would have had to be a simpleton not to have foreseen the possibility of a violent death when visiting the capital at Passover.[103] Jesus was no simpleton! I would amend the NJBC and argue Jesus could well have seen his death as not merely possible but likely.

Second, Scripture scholars generally warn us to beware of "prophecies after the fact" retrojected into the life of Jesus"[104] by the evangelists, who wrote many years after Jesus lived and thus knew what would happen. For example, on the twenty-second Sunday of Ordinary Time we encounter this passage: "From then on, Jesus the Anointed began to explain to his disciples that it was necessary for him to go forth into Jerusalem and to suffer many things from the elders and ruling priests and scribes, and to be put to death and to be raised on the third day" (Matthew 16:21, par.).

Jesus's mission required him to go up to Jerusalem. He knew the Jewish religious establishment feared and hated him. He also knew he was not going to back away from his criticism of them. Therefore, any person in his position would surely know he was heading for trouble. Nothing in this passage requires divine or extraordinary prophetic insight, except for the "raised on the third day" part. For theological and scriptural reasons I will develop below, I think these words are an example of a prophecy after the fact.

A more trivial example of Jesus's supposed prediction of the future is when he says Peter will deny him three times before the cock crows (Matthew 26:34). This is rather an example of Jesus's penetrating knowledge of others. Peter and Jesus were very close; it does not strain credulity to suppose Jesus knew Peter would not be able to run away as the other disciples did but when pressed would lack the courage to stand up for Jesus. Peter's faltering effort to walk on the water (Matthew 14:28–33) illustrates in a similar way both his courage and its limits. We can easily make too much of the "cock crows" element in this story. This was simply a way of saying "before the sun rises."

Jesus is often called a prophet in the gospels. His words and deeds confirm he was one in the Jewish prophetic tradition. However, the role of the prophet is not primarily to predict the future but rather to be God's voice to the people of Israel.[105]

A similar problem we have as readers, because we know what happened to Jesus, is to read into these predictions more than is there. Whenever we are reading of events that have happened, we must continually remind ourselves of a chasm separating us from the people who lived before us: we know how things turned out, while they did not.

For example, did you notice that Jesus's prediction above at Matthew 16:21 makes no mention of being crucified by the Romans? Many readers are tempted to read this into the prediction or not notice its absence. In any event, this omission suggests Jesus's quite human, incomplete knowledge of the future.

We can find more powerful passages in Scripture that suggest Jesus lacked divine omniscience. For example, in Luke 2:52, "Jesus progressed in wisdom and age and favor before God and men." This verse indicates that, like us, Jesus was born not knowing everything but instead gradually figured things out.

Jesus's encounter with the Syrophoenician woman illustrates Jesus's human capacity to grow in wisdom, even to change his mind when presented with new information (see my discussion of this passage, Matthew 15:21–28, for week twenty). Jesus appears out of character here, mistreating a suffering mother who, as a Gentile woman, is also doubly marginalized. He refers to her as a "dog," and at first refuses to heal her daughter tormented by a demon. Jesus appears to share some of the same negative views his countrymen had of foreigners. And why wouldn't he?

The woman's faith changes Jesus's mind—as so often happens in the gospels. Jesus also appears to change his mind here and elsewhere in the gospels regarding his statement at verse 24, "I was sent only to the lost sheep of the house of Israel."

The three synoptic gospels tell us Jesus made an important eschatological prediction that turned out to be incorrect. Starting at Matthew 24:4, par., Jesus tells his disciples about the signs of the Parousia, the future return of Christ in glory (the Second Coming) to judge the living and the dead, and to terminate the present world order. After describing various "afflictions" that will occur, Jesus continues:

> AND IMMEDIATELY AFTER the affliction of those days the sun will be darkened, and the moon will not give her light, and the stars will fall from the sky, and the powers of the heavens will be shaken. And then the sign of the Son of Man will appear in the sky, and then all the tribes of the earth will beat their breasts and will see the Son of Man coming upon the clouds of the sky with power and great glory; And he will send forth his angels with a great trumpeting, and they will gather together the chosen from the four winds, from end to end of the heavens. But learn the lesson of the fig tree: Now, when its branch softens and produces leaves, you know that the summer is near; So too, when you see all these things you know that he is near, at the door. *Amen, I tell you*

> *that this generation most definitely does not pass away until all these things happen.* (Matthew 24:29–34, par.; emphasis added)

Jesus's generation did pass away without all these things happening.

Incoherently, Matthew and Mark add a verse almost immediately after Jesus's erroneous prediction: "But about that day and hour no one knows—neither the angels of the heavens nor the Son—except the Father only" (Matthew 24:36, par. Mark).

Jesus was wrong about his Parousia prediction, but he was quite right in saying that only God the Father knows when it will occur. It is possible that the evangelists added this verse as a cleanup operation when they wrote their gospels because by the time they were writing, they knew the embarrassing truth: Jesus's prediction was wrong. It is to their credit that they included Jesus's erroneous prediction (Luke did not do so), and the fact that it was by then an embarrassment is strong evidence that Jesus's prediction is historical—that is, he did say it. But it is inaccurate as a prediction of history.

The clearest, most powerful scriptural support for Jesus's lack of divine foreknowledge is his prayer and agony in Gethsemane, Matthew 26:36–46 (par.): "My Father, if it is possible, let this cup pass from me; yet not as I will, but as you will." Obviously, this prayer to avoid death on the cross makes no sense if Jesus knows the Father will not spare him crucifixion. The fact that Jesus's will can differ from the Father's will is precisely what is at issue here. Because the "Father's will" is what will happen.

Thanks to Jesus's lack of divine foreknowledge, this prayer is a model for us: a model for prayer and for faith. It reveals there is nothing at all wrong with being clear about telling God what we want when we pray. Then comes the second crucial and decisive step: "yet not as I will, but as you will." Faith means we trust that if God does not answer our prayer as we want, it is because God has a better idea.

When our most heartfelt prayers appear to be unanswered, we can be comforted and strengthened to know God did not give even his own beloved Son what he most wanted when he prayed. Jesus was sweating blood, after all! He asked not to be crucified, yet he was.

The Resurrection is, for me, perhaps the most powerful argument against Jesus's having divine foreknowledge. Suppose Jesus knew he would be raised on the third day, as Matthew 16:21 suggests? Does not that make a sham of his "agony" in the garden, his fervent prayer to be spared crucifixion? Not to mention his quotation on the cross of Psalm 22, "My God, my God, why have you forsaken me?"

I know that crucifixion is a horrible, long, painful way to die. But if I knew I would a couple days later be raised from the dead to live in glory at God's right hand eternally, I think I just might be able to handle it.

Abandoned by all his friends, betrayed by one of them, denied by another, Jesus had only his trust in God to support him through the torture and agony of his passion. He, like us, did not have the assurance of divine omniscience. All he had was his faith in God. Jesus's total surrender in faith to God is one reason to believe he is the divine Son of God. And it is one reason why this book is named *The Faith of Jesus*.

APPENDIX C

How to Experience God's Love through Centering Prayer

KARL RAHNER, THE great twentieth-century Roman Catholic theologian, wrote that the Christian of the future will have to be a mystic to be a Christian at all. I agree with him—and his "future" is now! The secular forces arrayed against transcendent experience, especially religious transcendence, have grown so powerful that a believer needs strong weapons to resist the pull toward the flat trap of the purely immanent order.

This is a departure from the Church's tradition, as it was thought one needed a special calling to be a mystic. Based on my experience, I believe all who are called to follow Jesus are called to pursue some kind of "mystical experience," by which I mean, primarily, to feel loved by God, to experience God's loving presence.

Jesus's Great Commandment (Matthew 22:34–40) is that we are to love God with all our heart, soul, and mind; and our neighbor as ourselves. My experience is that to fulfill this commandment, we must first feel loved by God. Otherwise, what love do we have to give? This is especially true when it comes to loving our enemies, or even our neighbor. Because a neighbor, as opposed to a friend, is someone we may not have much in common with or may not even like very much.

Loving a neighbor and loving an enemy is not natural! To fulfill these commandments, we are going to need supernatural help. We are going to have to experience God's love for us.

This idea seems to be confirmed by 1 John 4:10–11, 19: "In this is love, not that we loved God but that he loved us and sent his Son to be the expiation for our sins. Beloved, if God so loved us, we also ought to love one another. . . . We love because he first loved us."

The question then becomes, how do we experience God's love for us? We can read about it in the Bible, as we have been doing in this book, and we might hear about it in homilies at Mass. But for many, these are only words. For Catholics, the sacraments, especially communion and reconciliation, can be powerful ways to experience God's love for us. We can also feel it from other human beings. I recommend all these ways—and whatever else works for you!

The most powerful and certain way I have experienced God's love for me is through prayer, but not just any kind of prayer—centering prayer. This kind of prayer is wordless. It resembles meditation but is centered in the God of the Christian tradition. I want in this appendix to offer some advice about it for those who want to pursue this form of prayer.

I have a second motive for closing this book with some words on contemplative prayer. Everything I have written so far has been in the positive way (via positiva) or cataphatic approach to God, through positive statements: God is love, God is eternal, omniscient, forgiving, merciful, and so forth. I have used my mind, the thoughts of others, and the words of Scripture to try to learn of and love God. In doing so I believe we also learn of God's love for us. This is well and good. After all, Jesus commands us to love God with all our mind.

Yet God is also unknowable mystery. We are spiritual beings with physical bodies. We live in a material world, and what we know we perceive through our senses. But God is Spirit. Through our senses, we can only know about "things," and God is not a "thing." An exclusive reliance on the cataphatic way can fool us into thinking we know God better than we do. The negative way, or the apophatic approach, affirms that God lies beyond the horizon of our comprehension.

We can never truly know God with our intellect, but we can truly love God with our will. Doing so leads us to experience God's love for us in a deeper and more intimate way than is possible with any other approach I know of. This brings to light another connection between centering prayer and the love of others. We can reach God through love by means of our will—and the same holds true for love of our neighbor and enemy, as this too comes from a love rooted in a firm will.

This appendix, then, is a kind of corrective, or apology, for all the cataphatic, propositional reasoning that has come before it. Perhaps it should be read first.

What follows is based first on my reading of that famous mystical classic, *The Cloud of Unknowing*, written by an anonymous English priest of the fourteenth century. The second source is the experience of following the teaching of that book through many years.

***

According to St. Augustine, "Because God has made us for Himself, our hearts are restless until they rest in Him." We have a built-in longing that transcends anything this world has to offer. That's how I understand St. Augustine's words. This insight must be the point of departure for anyone searching for God.

Even though the author of *The Cloud of Unknowing* never cites these words of St. Augustine, they could be the motto for the book, because by reading it we learn how to "rest in Him." What does the author mean by "the cloud of unknowing"?

> DO NOT THINK that because I call it a "darkness" or a "cloud" it is the sort of cloud you see in the sky, or

the kind of darkness you know at home when the light is out. . . . By "darkness" I mean "a lack of knowing"—just as anything that you do not know or may have forgotten may be said to be "dark" to you, for you cannot see it with your inward eye. For this reason it is called "a cloud," not of the sky, of course, but "of unknowing," a cloud of unknowing between you and your God. (*The Cloud of Unknowing*, 1961)

The author, greatly influenced by Dionysius the Areopagite, is a firm believer in the via negativa; we must put a "cloud of forgetting" beneath us and all creation in order to grow close to God (p 66). We cannot know God with our intellect because our intellect is designed to know created matter, and this is not God.

THEREFORE, I WILL leave on one side everything I can think, and choose for my love that thing which I cannot think! Why? Because he may well be loved, but not thought. By love he can be caught and held, but by thinking never. . . . Strike that thick cloud of unknowing with the sharp dart of longing love, and on no account whatever think of giving up. (Ch. 6)

Love, which rests in the will, is the way to reach God. We will never get there with the thoughts of our mind. "Love may reach up to God himself even in this life—but not knowledge," says the unknown author. In fact, for us to reach God in this way, the thoughts of the mind are the enemy!

How can one empty one's mind of all thought and be filled only with "a longing love for God"? The author recommends finding one word of a single syllable, such as "God" or "love," and holding fast to this, while resolutely letting go of all discursive thought. Even holy thoughts of the Lord's passion and God's goodness must be put away "deep down in the cloud of forgetting" if we are ever to penetrate the cloud of unknowing between ourselves and God. "A naked intention directed to God, and himself alone, is wholly sufficient" (p 69).

The author advises us to be single-minded in our pursuit of God in this way. He claims that we will avoid sin and gain virtue only through this method of contemplative prayer. Therefore, he tells us, "Never give up your firm intention: beat away at this cloud of unknowing between you and God with that sharp dart of longing love. Hate to think about anything less than God, and let nothing whatever distract you from this purpose. It is only thus that you can destroy the ground and root of sin" (p 77).

He emphasizes that although we need God's grace to be called to this "work," it is very hard work and we must keep at it. What makes the work so difficult is "the stamping out all remembrance of God's creation, and in keeping them covered by that cloud of forgetting" (p 94). I can vouch for how tough this is!

I have been doing this kind of centering prayer for at least fifteen minutes every morning for more than twenty years; before that I did it less regularly. Even now there are days when I find it difficult to empty my mind of all thought for more than a few moments. Yet it does get easier over time. More importantly, the rewards grow and become inexpressible! It often feels as though my "true life" is lived in those fifteen minutes spent in the cloud of unknowing.

I am going to offer one analogy to explain how centering prayer has become easier for me; maybe it will help you also. When I am cycling and reach a hill, I usually like to stand up in my pedals and sprint up the hill as fast as I can. I gather up all the frustrations of the day and "take them out" on that hill and my legs! It is a catharsis.

Now, think of how nothing in this world is ultimately satisfying. We finally get the job we always wanted, and it is good, but ... not quite as good as we thought it would be. People may try to define us by our job, but that is only a role we are playing—we are more than our career. We fall in love and it is wonderful, especially at first. But then over time we realize that it takes work to maintain the relationship; that suffering and loss are also part of love; that we are alone after all, as no one can ever truly understand us—we are a mystery even to ourselves. Great achievements and recognition are wonderful; we all need them. But they are not enough. Creation is filled with wonders and it is truly good. But nothing is ever enough for us!

It can seem as though all our "work" in this life is nothing but shadow boxing, and this is where centering prayer comes to the rescue. We can take the "longing love" that piles up inside as we accumulate all the unsatisfying trinkets this world offers us, and use it to power "the sharp dart of longing love" to pierce the cloud of unknowing.

In my experience, it also works the other way around. I have found such peace and fulfillment doing this "work" of prayer that at times I see everything else I do with my time as a kind of play-acting. I have realized that often I took things too seriously, and this can help when confronted with a frustrating situation. True, many of the tasks we do can be rewarding. But not always. Centering prayer helps cultivate a detachment from everything, which leads to a deep sense of peace.

Because I know that in a sense I am closer to my true purpose in life when I am in centering prayer, I am more at peace with the inevitable letdowns life's activities serve up so regularly. But this "work" can be difficult, especially at first. Many people may feel discouraged and tempted to give up.

In chapter 35, the author offers two "spiritual dodges" to help make the "hard work much easier": "Try to look, as it were, over their shoulders, seeking something else—which is God, shrouded in the cloud of unknowing." This is good advice! When these thoughts come to mind, in other words, we must not allow ourselves to become frustrated and upset. The thoughts may well be "of God" to some extent. It would serve us well to gently let them go and look beyond them.

The second "dodge" is recommended when our mind is filled with thoughts we feel powerless to stop. In this case, the author suggests, "Cower down before them like some cringing captive overcome in battle, and reckon that it is ridiculous to fight against them any longer. In this way you surrender yourself to God while you are in the hands of your enemies, and feeling that you have been overcome forever."

I have tried this too, and I feel as though God smiles on my human weakness. True humility is nothing more nor less than accepting the truth about oneself—the truth in this moment, at least.

I part company a bit with the author here because I have found at times that God is trying to tell me something about the thoughts that keep bubbling up when I'm trying to do contemplative prayer. Sometimes God is telling me that these thoughts are my real problem, and that for me to try to get close to God, I first need to deal with them. This is true, for example, when the thoughts are about how others have wounded me. Forgive! A related point made by our author is that if we are in mortal sin, we must go to confession and stop this kind of sin if we hope to make any progress through the cloud.

I will go still further: I believe God actually speaks to me during centering prayer. It makes sense, does it not? We must create an inner silence so that we can hear when God speaks. Sometimes, the messages convey relatively simple acts for me to undertake. Other times, God seems to be telling me to do something that entails real sacrifice. I know it is God speaking because a) I would not have thought of these things myself, and b) the orders I receive involve loving God or others more fully and are always good for my soul.

In other cases, God is not telling me to "do" anything at all but is rather answering a prayer. It might be an insight about a problem, greater awareness of sin, or the sweet consolation that I am loved.

Now I want to make a point the author does not when saying, "Strike that thick cloud of unknowing with the sharp dart of longing love, and on no account whatever think of giving up." I agree with this, but I want to add that doing so resolutely every day, no matter what, is the best way I know of experiencing God's love for me.

As I stated at the beginning of these reflections, it will be very difficult, if not impossible, to fulfill Jesus's Great Commandment unless we experience God's love for us. Many Christians I know, even the devout, say they do not feel God's love for them. Very well, then; here is one way that has worked wonders for me.

To this end, I part company with the author of *The Cloud of Unknowing* once more in that I believe we can repeat the phrase "God loves me" rather than a one-syllable word, such as "love" or "God," as he recommends. When I was hurting, I would sometimes repeat, "God help me." I do agree that the fewer words, the better. But I found that I can make these words "rhyme" with my breathing, and then these words, like my breathing, become a second nature that I can easily "forget" consciously. Turning off our conscious thoughts is what matters most. But repeating a short phrase endlessly as we wait for God can have an enormous impact over time.

I do agree with our author that we must be persistent with our centering prayer and never give up, as Jesus also tells us (Luke 18:1–8; 11:5–8; 9–13, par. Matthew). It took years of praying "God loves me" before I finally felt God's love for me deep inside. But here is something that will make me sound stupid. It took a few more years after that before I felt the equally powerful conviction that God loves everybody else just as much as me! Neither more nor less. What a lesson in humility.

I agree with our author that this kind of centering prayer is "hard work." Many days it feels like a total waste of time. Keep at it! Find at least fifteen minutes to do it, and do it every day. I found that if I did not do it before rising in the morning, I would end up not doing it. It is too easy for me to get consumed by all the things I must do each day. I don't think it matters when you do it: whatever works. If you can do it for more than fifteen minutes, that's better. I suggest starting with that amount of time because virtually no one can argue he or she is so busy that fifteen minutes is too much.

God will give us consolations along the way to keep us at it. I have already mentioned that I feel God speaks to me at times during this work. This has been enormously helpful to me, as it has given me needed direction at times, and it has also strengthened my faith in God. It is a way to make real Jesus's offer of a genuine friendship with God (John 15:14–15).

Yet there is still more God has given me, and here words fail me! They cannot describe how doing this work has altered forever the way I see my place in God's creation and my relationship to God. We are eventually carried up and away into the wordless mystery that is God.

Early on in this work, I often had the feeling that it was "my real" job—that whatever else I was doing with my life was secondary, possibly distracting, or even phony evasions of what my "real" life was about. This was true when I taught theology at the Catholic University of America as well as when I covered workplace health and safety for the magazine that had hired me. Our fourteenth-century author has had precisely the same experience! "But I am doing what I am because I want to tell you and to let you see how much more worth-while this spiritual exercise is than any other physical or spiritual work, even when this is done under the inspiration of grace" (p 79).

My final thought: I agree with the anonymous English mystic about the value of this spiritual exercise. That is why I recommend all readers begin with this final appendix and follow its advice as you read the book that is before you. God bless you!

BIBLIOGRAPHY

Abbott-Smith, George. *Abbott-Smith's Manual Greek Lexicon of the New Testament.* https://gntreader.com/?b=EPH&c=1&v=1

Alter, Robert, trans. *The Five Books of Moses.* New York: W. W. Norton & Company, 2007.

Anonymous. *The Cloud of Unknowing.* New York: Penguin Press, 1978

Aquinas, Thomas. *Summa Theologica.* Westminster, Maryland: Christian Classics, 1981.

Bauer, Walter. *A Greek-English Lexicon of the New Testament.* Chicago: University of Chicago Press, 1979.

Brown, Raymond E., Fitzmyer, Joseph A., Murphy, Roland E., eds. *The New Jerome Bible Commentary.* Englewood Cliffs, NJ: Prentice Hall, 1990.

Brown, Raymond E. *The Community of the Beloved Disciple.* New York: Paulist Press, 1979.

Chadwick, Henry. *The Early Church.* New York: Penguin Books, 1976.

Cross, F. L., Livingstone, E. A., eds. *The Oxford Dictionary of the Christian Church.* London: Oxford University Press, 1974.

Crossan, John Dominic. *The Power of Parable.* New York: Harper One, 2012.

Girard, Rene. *The Scapegoat.* Baltimore: Johns Hopkins University Press, 1986.

Girard, Rene. *Things Hidden Since the Foundation of the World: Research Undertaken win Collaboration with Jean-Michel Oughourlian and Guy Lefort.* Stanford: Stanford University Press, 1987.

Hart, David Bentley. *That All Shall Be Saved*. New Haven: Yale University Press, 2019.

Hart, David Bentley, trans. *The New Testament*. New Haven: Yale University Press, 2017.

Jeremias, Joachim. *Rediscovering the Parables*. New York: Charles Scribner's Sons, 1966.

Julian of Norwich. *Revelations of Divine Love*. Hammondsworth, England: Penguin Books, 1986.

Komonchak, Joseph; Collins, Mary; Lane, Dermot A., eds. *The New Dictionary of Theology*. Wilmington, Delaware: Michael Glazier, Inc., 1988.

Marcel, Gabriel. *The Mystery of Being*, Vol. II. South Bend Indiana: Regnery/Gateway, Inc., 1979.

Meeks, Wayne, ed. *From the Writings of St. Paul*. New York: W. W. Norton & Company, 1972

Merton, Thomas. *Advent and Christmas with Thomas Merton*. Liguori, Missouri: Liguori, 1989.

The Oxford Annotated Bible with the Apocrypha. New York: Oxford University Press, 1965.

Rad, Gerhard von. *Wisdom in Israel*. Nashville: Abingdon Press, 1978.

Simonetti, Manlio, ed. *Ancient Christian Commentary on Scripture: New Testament,* Vols. 1a, 1b. Downer's Grove, Ill: InterVarsity Press, 2001.

Taylor, Charles. *A Secular Age*. Cambridge, Massachusetts: The Belknap Press of Harvard University, 2007.

Vatican II Sunday Missal: Millennium Edition. Boston: Pauline Press, 1998.

ENDNOTES

1. Anonymous, *The Cloud of Unknowing* (New York: Penguin Press, 1978), No. 6, page 68.
2. In translating Greek I have used Walter Bauer, *A Greek-English Lexicon of the New Testament* (Chicago: University of Chicago Press, 1979) and Abbott-Smith's Manual Greek Lexicon of the New Testament found at https://gntreader.com/?b=EPH&c=1&v=1 Abbott-Smith is abbreviated as AS; Bauer as B. I have also relied on David Bentley Hart's fine translation of The New Testament, see note iii.
3. *The New Testament, trans. David Bentley Hart* (New Haven: Yale University Press, 2017), 50..
4. Raymond E. Brown, S.S., Joseph A. Fitzmyer, S.J., Roland E. Murphy, O. Carm., eds. *The New Jerome Bible Commentary* (Englewood Cliffs, N.J.: Prentice Hall, 1990) 668. Abbreviated as NJBC.
5. Thomas Merton, *Advent and Christmas with Thomas Merton* (Liguori, Missouri: Liguori, 1989).
6. Wayne A. Meeks, ed., *From the Writings of St. Paul (New York: W.W. Norton & Company, 1972) 365-374.*
7. Ibid., 371, emphasis in the original.
8. NJBC, 1310.
9. Manlio Simonetti, ed., *Ancient Christian Commentary on Scripture: New Testament*, Vols. 1a and 1b, (Downer's Grove, Ill: InterVarsity Press, 2001) Abbreviated as ACCS.
10. Ibid., 1b, 217.
11. Ibid., 1a, 4.
12. NJBC, 235.
13. ACCS, 18-19.
14. NJBC, 636.
15. ACCS, 1a, 33.
16. NJBC, 1304.
17. ACCS, 1a, 31.
18. AS.

19 *Vatican II Sunday Missal: Millennium Edition* (Boston: Pauline Books & Media, 1998) Abbreviated as NAB.
20 *The Oxford Annotated Bible with the Apocrypha,* (New York: Oxford University Press, 1965) Abbreviated as RSV.
21 AS.
22 ACCS, 1a, 22.
23 Ibid., 26.
24 Ibid., 22
25 ACCS, 1a, 30.
26 F.L. Cross and E.A. Livingstone, eds., *The Oxford Dictionary of the Christian Church,* (London: Oxford University Press, 1974), 127. Abbreviated as ODCC.
27 NJBC, 639.
28 Ibid., 640.
29 Ibid., 640.
30 Hart, *The New Testament,* 7.
31 NJBC, 640.
32 ACCS, 92.
33 St. Thomas Aquinas, *Summa Theologica,* (Westminster, Maryland: Christian Classics, 1981), I,II, Q18, a4.
34 NJBC, 641.
35 Ibid., 631.
36 Ibid., 641.
37 ACCS, 1a, 97. Emphasis added.
38 NJBC, 642.
39 Ibid., 641.
40 Ibid.,643.
41 Ibid., 644,
42 *New York Times* Feb. 7, 2021 Article by Harold Isaac, Andre Paualtre and Maria Abi-Haabib. https://www.nytimes.com/2021/02/07/world/americas/haiti-protests-President-Jovenel-Mois.html?searchResultPosition=1
43 AS.
44 Poll by Yakult UK found at: https://www.christianheadlines.com/contributors/michael-foust/89-percent-of-british-young-adults-say-life-has-no-meaning-poll-finds.html
45 Julian of Norwich, *Revelations of Divine Love,* (Hammondsworth, England: Penguin Books, 1986), 103-104.

46 David Bentley Hart, *That All Shall Be Saved*, (New Haven: Yale University Press, 2019), 185.
47 Hart, *The New Testament, 296.* Emphasis added.
48 NJBC, 845-846.
49 Hart, *The New Testament, 296.*
50 Ibid., 297.
51 Hart, *That All Shall Be Saved, 201.*
52 ACCS, 1b, 57.
53 Ibid.
54 Raymond E. Brown, S.S., *The Community of the Beloved Disciple*, (New York: Paulist Press, 1979), 187.
55 *The Five Books of Moses*, trans. Robert Alter (New York: W. W. Norton & Company, 2007), 153.
56 Rene Girard, *The Scapegoat*, (Baltimore: Johns Hopkins University Press, 1986), 112-124.
57 NJBC, 664.
58 Ibid., 673.
59 ACCS, 1b, 304.
60 Ibid.
61 Hart, *The New Testament, 7.*
62 NJBC, 733.
63 NJBC, 300.
64 Rene Girard, *Things Hidden since the Foundation of the Word: Research Undertaken in Collaboration with Jean-Michel Oughourlian and Guy Lefort*, (Stanford, Calif.: Stanford University Press, 1987).
65 Brown, *Beloved Disciple, 139.*
66 Ibid., 35-40.
67 NJBC, 674.
68 https://abcnews.go.com/US/charleston-victims-mother-tells-dylann-roof-forgive/story?id=44704096
69 ACCS, 1b, 313.
70 Aquinas *Summa, I, II, Q68, a1, 2.*
71 https://www.pewresearch.org/fact-tank/2019/08/05/transubstantiation-eucharist-u-s-catholics/
72 Joseph Komonchak, Mary Collins, Dermot A. Lane, eds., *The New Dictionary of Theology*, (Wilmington, Delaware: Michael Glazier, Inc., 1988), 342-355.

73 Hart, *That All Shall. Be Saved, 112.*
74 ACCS, 1a, 207-8.
75 Gabriel Marcel, *The Mystery of Being,* Vol. ii (South Bend, Indiana: Regnery/Gateway, Inc., 1979), 146ff.
76 See Raymond E. Brown, S.S., *The Death of the Messiah, Vol. 1,* (New York: Doubleday, 1993), 28ff.
77 ACCS, 1a, 205.
78 https://earlychurchhistory.org/martyrs/christian-martyrs-now/
79 NJBC, 652.
80 Charles Taylor, *A Secular Age,* (Cambridge, Massachusetts: The Belknap Press of Harvard University Press, 2007), see especially Chapter 15, 539ff.
81 Gerhard von Rad, *Wisdom in Israel,* (Nashville: Abingdon Press, 1978), 240ff.
82 ACCS, 1a, 264.
83 Ibid., 270.
84 NJBC, 657.
85 ACCS, 1b, 13.
86 John Dominic Crossan, *The Power of Parable,* (New York: Harper One, 2012), 95ff.
87 Joachim Jeremias, *Rediscovering the Parables,* (New York: Charles Scribner's Sons, 1966), 52.
88 Henry Chadwick, *The Early Church,* (New York: Penguin Books, 1976), 31.
89 Jeremias, *Rediscovering the Parables, 40.*
90 ACCS, 1b, 216.
91 Jeremias, *Rediscovering the Parables,*
92 NJBC, 1313.
93 Hart, *That All Shall Be Saved, 1-3.*
94 Ibid., 112
95 Ibid., 114-5
96 Ibid., 117
97 Ibid., 95ff.
98 Ibid., 94.
99 Ibid., 159.
100 NJBC, 667-668.
101 Hart, Ibid., 102

102 Ibid., 103-4
103 NJBC, 1326.
104 NJBC, p. 660
105 Ibid., 187.

www.ingramcontent.com/pod-product-compliance
Lightning Source LLC
Chambersburg PA
CBHW020516080526
44583CB00013B/622